The Excel Statistics Companion 2.0

Kenneth M. Rosenberg
SUNY – Oswego

Australia • Brazil • Canada • Mexico • Singapore • Spain • United Kingdom • United States

© 2007 Thomson Wadsworth, a part of The Thomson Corporation. Thomson, the Star logo, and Wadsworth are trademarks used herein under license.

ALL RIGHTS RESERVED. No part of this work covered by the copyright hereon may be reproduced or used in any form or by any means—graphic, electronic, or mechanical, including photocopying, recording, taping, Web distribution, information storage and retrieval systems, or in any other manner—without the written permission of the publisher.

Printed in Canada

2 3 4 5 6 7 10 09 08 07

Printer: Webcom

ISBN-13: 978-0-495-18695-3
ISBN-10: 0-495-18695-3

Cover image: © Imtek Imagineering/ Masterfile
www.masterfile.com

Thomson Higher Education
10 Davis Drive
Belmont, CA 94002-3098
USA

For more information about our products, contact us at:
Thomson Learning Academic Resource Center
1-800-423-0563

For permission to use material from this text or product, submit a request online at
http://www.thomsonrights.com.
Any additional questions about permissions can be submitted by email to
thomsonrights@thomson.com.

For Carol

Ken Rosenberg was born and raised in Boston, Massachusetts, where he attended Boston Latin School by day and, a short walk away, Fenway Park on many a spring afternoon. After earning his undergraduate B.S. degree in psychology at Tufts University (1963), he left Red Sox Nation to attend Purdue University as an NIMH Neurobiology Fellow and graduate research assistant to V. H. Denenberg. Rosenberg graduated from Purdue in 1969 and, with M.S. and Ph.D. degrees in experimental psychology in hand, left W. Lafayette, Indiana, with his wife Carol to join the Department of Psychology at the State University of New York/Oswego. Having taken graduate coursework from two prominent teachers of statistics, Ben Winer and his former student Don Brown – not to mention the ongoing data analysis responsibilities of a research assistant in Vic Denenberg's laboratory – teaching a course in statistics for SUNY/Oswego's Department of Psychology was a logical assignment. Fall 2005 marks the beginning of Rosenberg's 36th year at SUNY/Oswego. Such a long residence in Oswego may have something to do with beautiful Lake Ontario and the wonderful weather in Upstate New York. But the decision to stay in Oswego was, and still is, driven principally by the opportunity to work together with bright, dedicated, and productive faculty in a wonderfully collegial atmosphere.

In addition to numerous journal articles and presentations in the area of developmental psychobiology, Rosenberg is the author of *Statistics for Behavioral Sciences* (Wm. C. Brown, 1990), a collection of PC-based tutorials published as *Stat/Tutor* (Wm. C. Brown, 1990), coauthor (with Helen Daly) of *Foundations of Behavioral Research* (Harcourt, Brace, Jovanovich, 1993), and author of version 1.0 of *The Excel Statistics Companion* (Wadsworth, 2004). Ken and Carol Rosenberg have two grown sons, two wonderful daughters-in-law, and two delicious grandsons, and now live in an empty nest with their calico kitty, Shmoo.

Brief Contents of the Excel Statistics Companion 2.0 CD-ROM and Manual

Contents of the CD-ROM

Contents of the Manual

Detailed Contents of the *ESC* Workbooks

i. *Basic Skills* is a tutorial for the novice Windows/Excel user. The file reviews and permits practice of the limited set of Excel and Windows skills needed to have a successful experience with *The Excel Statistics Companion*.

ii. *Function List* names and explains the Excel paste functions that are the most relevant to introductory statistics. The explanations avoid the often technical language of Excel's *Help* materials.

Folder 01. Descriptive Statistics
1-1. The *Describing Data* workbook covers measures of central tendency and variability followed by two automated sampling experiments that illustrate how the statistics of central tendency and variability are or are not affected by systematic changes to the data.

1-2. The *Functions and Tools* workbook introduces the Descriptive Statistics and Rank and Percentile tools as well as the PERCENTILE and PERCENTRANK paste functions.

1-3. The *Frequency Distributions* workbook uses the output of Excel's Histogram tool to create ungrouped and grouped frequency distribution tables.

1-4. *Making Charts* teaches the use of Excel's chart wizard to plot the grouped frequency distribution previously created in the *Frequency Distributions* workbook. The chart wizard has an exceptional array of editing capabilities, and these are demonstrated followed by ample opportunity to practice.

1-5. *Practice Describing* presents an opportunity to rehearse any and all of the data description skills covered in the Folder 1 workbooks. The task is to do a thorough statistical analysis of a data set along with the preparation of a suitable chart.

Folder 02. The *z* Statistic
2-1. *Standardizing* presents two sampling experiments to illustrate the concept of *z* as the "standard normal" distribution – a common "language" into which any normal distribution may be converted.

2-2. *Comparing Distributions* is a combination demonstration and exercise program that builds on the concept of *z* as the standard normal statistic, which was introduced in workbook 2-1.

2-3. *Applying z* presents the opportunity to practice solving four types of problems using Excel's *z*-related paste functions.

Folder 03. Correlation and Regression
3-1. *Patterns of Association* uses automated sampling experiments, paste functions, and charts to convey the concept of association and its measurement.

3-2. *Type 1 Error* demonstrates empirically the vulnerability of the Pearson ***r*** statistic to Type 1 error, the appearance of a significant association between variables when none truly exists.

3-3. *Pearson **r*** leads the user through three different methods (definitional, computational, and *z* formula) that simulate "hand" computation of the Pearson ***r*** statistic. Next, the "new data" worksheet invites the user to change any current data values. The statistics and chart update instantly with each change.

3-4. *Spearman rho* presents the Spearman rho computation as a Pearson ***r*** analysis that is performed on ranked data. The mechanics of ranking are covered along with procedures for quick conversion of the table of raw data to a table of ranked data.

3-5. *Point Biserial* quantifies the association between two variables when one is dichotomous and mutually exclusive (yes/no, true/false, male/female, etc.).

3-6. *Linear Regression* shows how we can take advantage of an association between variables to make predictions of one to the other. The dynamic calculations allow for extensive experimentation and discovery.

Folder 04. Sampling Distributions
4-1. *The Binomial* simulates two different binomial (coin flipping) sampling experiments and compares the empirical (obtained) results to theoretically expected results.

4-2. *Central Limit Theorem* is an empirical test of the central limit theorem, including an examination of the impact of changing sample sizes.

Folder 05. Probability
5-1. *Computing Probability* demonstrates the process of computing probability within both the binomial and standard normal sampling distribution environments. The demonstration is followed by worksheets that provide opportunities for practice.

5-2 Solving Problems allows the user to practice applying the addition and multiplication rules for computing the probability of various samples that have been randomly drawn from a hypothetical basket of red, white, and blue balls.

Folder 06. The ***t*** Statistic – 1 Sample
6-1. *Estimating Error* examines the process of estimating the population standard deviation using sample data. User-run sampling experiments drive home the points raised in the demonstration.

6-2. *Rationale of the* **t** *Test* allows the user to manipulate effect size and sample size to assess the influence of these features of data on retention/rejection of the null hypothesis.

6-3. *Confidence Intervals* demonstrates two different methods for computing confidence intervals – one using paste functions and the other using Excel's Descriptive Statistics tool. Next, a sampling experiment tests the theoretical prediction that, in the long run, 5 out of the 100 confidence intervals will fail to include m , the mean of the population from which the samples were drawn.

6-4. *Testing the Pearson* ***r*** shows how to use the ***t*** statistic to evaluate the significance of the ***r*** statistic along with a demonstration of the sensitivity of the ***t*** test results to new data entries that degrade or enhance the degree of association between the X and Y variables.

Folder 07. The ***t*** Statistic – 2 Samples
7-1. *Inside the* **t** *Test* invites the user to manipulate effect size and within-sample variability to observe how these features of data affect the determination of statistical significance.

7-2. *Estimating Error* is a sampling experiment that generates and instantly analyzes the distribution of difference scores between 100 pairs of sample means.

7-3. *Paired-Samples* **t** *Test* demonstrates how correlation, the difference between sample means, and within-sample variability affect the value of the ***t*** statistic.

7-4. *Statistical Power* presents a series of experiments that show how sample size, effect size, and within-sample variability relate to correct and incorrect (Type 1 error and Type 2 error) statistical decisions.

7-5. *Independent vs Related* demonstrates why we need different statistical approaches for comparing the means of independent and related samples.

Folder 08. Single-Factor ANOVA
8-1. *The ANOVA Model* uses demonstrations and charts to explain the underlying logic of the analysis of variance (ANOVA). The sampling experiments allow the user to manipulate the size of treatment effects and within-sample variability and instantly see the impact of the inputs on the ANOVA results.

8-2. *Independent vs Related*, like workbook 7-4, demonstrates the importance of using the correct statistical approach when applying the analysis of variance to the data of within- and between-subject designs. The user can change effect size, within-sample variability, and individual differences among participants and instantly discover the impact of those changes on the ANOVA results.

8-3. *Unplanned Comparisons* demonstrates why we must have a special approach when making unplanned comparisons. The computation of the Tukey HSD test is dynamically linked to both independent and correlated data sets.

Folder 09. Two-Factor ANOVA
9-1. *Interpreting Results* displays data collected under the condition of H_0 true and then simulates main effects and interactions with systematic modifications to the data. Results of the simulations are displayed in charts and tables, which may then be interpreted in the context of the research problem.

9-2. *Creating Patterns*. With a single keystroke the user can generate data under the condition H_0 true followed by the systematic imposition of main effects and interactions. The statistics and charts, which update instantly following any change to the data, show how specific features of data are identified by the factorial ANOVA and reflected in its output.

9-3. *Computational Method* demonstrates the application of Excel's Data Analysis tool: Anova: Two-Factor With Replication. The latter tool performs a factorial analysis when independent groups are assigned to the cells of a between-subjects two-factor experimental design.

9-4. *Mixed Two-Way ANOVA*. When one factor of an experiment involves repeated measures of the same participants (within-subjects) and the second factor does not, we have a mixed design. This workbook demonstrates how one may combine the output of two Excel tools, Anova: Two-Factor **Without** Replication and Anova: Two-Factor **With** Replication, to perform the ANOVA for a mixed two-factor design.

Folder 10. Nonparametric Statistics

10-1. *Chi-Sq Goodness-of-Fit* demonstrates the computation of the chi-square (χ^2) goodness-of-fit test. Dynamic calculations allow the user to alter the fit of the data and explore the risk of Type 1 error.

10-2. *Chi-Sq Independence* demonstrates the computational steps for the chi-square (χ^2) test of independence, including the derivation of expected frequencies and the application of the CHITEST and CHIINV paste functions. A special exercise allows to user to explore patterns of contingency and independence.

10-3. *Mann-Whitney* demonstrates the rationale behind the Mann-Whitney ***U*** test, a test for comparing two independent groups when the data have ordinal scaling, along with the computation of the ***U*** statistic.

10-4. *Wilcoxon*. The relationship of the Wilcoxon test to its less powerful companion, the sign test, is demonstrated. The aim is to show how taking the magnitude of the difference between pairs (ordinal information) in addition to the sign of the difference (categorical information) enhances the power of the test.

Folder 11. Capstone

11-1. *Test selection* presents descriptions of 10 research problems along with data that are dynamically linked to the solutions. The task is to draw from the material covered in the first 10 folders and perform the analysis that is capable of answering the research question.

Preface

The Excel Statistics Companion 2.0 ("ESC") CD-ROM and User's Manual includes the traditional content one would expect to find in a college-level course in basic statistics – but with a modern twist. Unlike a textbook, the presentation is built around demonstrations, sampling experiments, and interactive problem-solving exercises that draw on Excel's tools, functions, and charting capabilities for pedagogical punch. *ESC* was *not* written to teach students how to do data analyses using Microsoft Excel – although gaining such skill from exposure to *ESC* is almost inevitable. Rather, *ESC* engages students in a process in which mastering abstract statistical concepts and their relationships to each other becomes less of a chore.

The Excel Advantage

Microsoft Excel's built-in statistical functions recalculate solutions instantly following any modification to the resident data – a process called "dynamic calculation." Within the textbook-like feel of *ESC's* carefully designed worksheets, dynamic calculations enable unlimited exploration of "What would happen if ..." scenarios. Change the data or underlying assumptions and key elements of the display – the empirical results of sampling experiments, numerical entries in formulae, and the contents of tables and charts – update instantly.

Like a textbook, *ESC* does include some displays of statistical calculations and examples that are fixed and do not respond to user inputs. But these are followed by the opportunities for exploration and discovery one would expect to find in a comprehensive learning resource. In the topic of hypothesis testing, for example, interactive displays show how within-sample variability and effect size influence the determination of statistical significance and that statistically significant results are possible even when only chance is operating. The topic of sampling distributions includes simulated coin-flipping experiments and an empirical test of the central limit theorem. In the topics of correlation and regression the hands-on experiments offer a fun way to learn about the statistical expression of association and prediction. Students have described the experience as "visual."

A Brief History of an Idea

Although greatly enhanced by today's modern and powerful spreadsheet technology, communicating abstract statistical concepts by means of hands-on sampling experiments is not a new idea. I first encountered it as a young graduate student in 1963 when I read *Introduction to Statistical Inference* (Li, 1957). Jerome Li did not want to burden his students with sophisticated mathematical proofs. Nor did he ask his students to accept the accuracy of key statistical principles on faith. When possible (and practical) he assigned sampling experiments to foster understanding of statistical basics.

Li constructed a normally distributed population of 500 values ($\mu = 50$, $\sigma = 10$) and wrote each individual value on a small metal-rimmed cardboard tag. Students sampled from the "tag" population as needed to demonstrate empirically many of the theoretically predicted properties of sampling distributions and the basic principles of hypothesis testing. The active learning aspect of Li's approach appealed to me, but the sampling experiments and subsequent statistical calculations were very time consuming and too impractical to do on a large scale. The bulky analog calculators of the time did little to ease the workload, and the personal computer had not yet been invented.

In the intervening years I created some computerized sampling experiments for classroom use, but those DOS-based programs quickly became obsolete with the arrival of Microsoft Windows in the early 1990s. More recently, in 2001, I was granted a sabbatical leave to create a new version of the kinds of computer-based sampling experiments, demonstrations, and opportunities for practice that had been so helpful in my earlier teaching of undergraduate statistics. With the ever-increasing availability of well-equipped PC and Macintosh laboratories on college campuses, data projectors for classroom use, and rising personal-computer ownership in the student population, the time seemed right. The result was *The Excel Statistics Companion*, version 1.0 (Rosenberg, 2004).

What's New in Version 2.0?

ESC 2.0 is an expanded and improved version of its predecessor. The displays include more sampling experiments and opportunities for problem-solving practice, incorporate more dynamic calculations, and cover more topics with screens that are less busy and instructions that are even easier to follow. The *Paired Samples **t** Test* is now in a separate workbook (7-3). Other new workbooks include *Solving Problems* (workbook 5-2), *Unplanned Comparisons* (workbook 8-3), and *Test Selection* ("capstone" workbook 11-1). The practice problems in most workbooks are dynamically linked to the answer keys, which means that any changes to the resident data will change both the problems and the solutions. This feature is especially powerful in the coverage of probability and in capstone workbook 11-1, *Test Selection*.

Layout of the Excel Workbooks

In general, the initial worksheets of most *ESC* workbooks do not rely on dynamic calculations; they introduce the topic at hand and set the stage for the later worksheets, in which the coverage transitions to hands-on sampling experiments, demonstrations, and exercises that dynamically link the statistical solutions to user inputs. It is in such worksheets where Excel's functions and tools present statistical content and connect the learner to the data in a way not possible with conventional print media.

Getting Started

No prior experience with Excel is necessary to have a successful experience with *ESC*. The *Basic Skills* workbook in the root directory of the self-loading CD-ROM guides the user through and permits the practice of all the fundamental Windows and Excel skills needed to run the *ESC* workbooks. The on-screen instructions are clear, detailed, and complete. But it is, nevertheless, well worth the time and effort to go through the entire *Basic Skills* workbook in a conscientious manner – even for students who have had some prior experience with Excel. Learning even one skill with which you were not previously familiar could make the difference between uncertainty and breezing through the *ESC* workbooks. Also, the images of various *ESC* screens that are reproduced in this book ("screen captures") show how your display should look when engaged with the interactive worksheets.

Users quickly become confident and comfortable using *The Excel Statistics Companion*. For that reason, it makes little sense to present screen captures for every menu and dialog box in the later workbooks that show skills already applied many times in the earlier workbooks. So, the practice of providing numerous screen captures for the earlier workbooks is gradually phased out for the later workbooks without sacrificing clarity and ease of use. Some screen captures of dialog boxes also appear in the Excel workbooks themselves for easy reference.

Another very useful resource on the CD-ROM is the *Function List* workbook. This Excel file lists the subset of Excel functions used by *ESC* and explains what they do in simple terms – avoiding the sometimes technical language of Excel's "help" descriptions.

Microsoft Excel: A Work in Progress

It is possible, maybe even likely, that the screen images and dialog boxes of the version of Excel you are running will not exactly match the screen-capture images shown in the User's Manual. The screens were captured from a PC running Excel 2000, so if you are running Windows XP or the CD-ROM's Macintosh version of *ESC*, expect to see some minor differences.

As with all major computer applications, Microsoft Excel is revised from time to time. Just as we get used to one version, a new and improved version is released. Running a new version of an application is rather like getting behind the wheel of a brand new luxury automobile when you are used to your 10-year old jalopy. Despite the unfamiliar feel of the new vehicle, you can find the controls, you can drive it, and eventually you get used to the new expansive arrangement of dashboard controls and gauges.

There is an Appendix at the end of *Basic Skills* with images of some Windows XP screens. If you are an XP user, these images should help orient you to XP's Excel environment. Otherwise, the Office Assistant (type the "?" on the standard toolbar) is a great source of information when transitioning between older and newer versions of Excel. Just type your question to the Office Assistant, and help will arrive.

Exercise Packet

The Exercise packet is a valuable component of the ESC learning package. Sets of problems, questions, and supplementary explanatory materials complement the ESC workbooks, and like-numbered materials (e.g., Excel Workbook 8-1 and Exercise 8-1) are coordinated. The exercises help students check their mastery of the material in the ESC workbooks. Some workbooks are exercises in themselves – namely, ESC workbook 1-5 - *Practice Describing*, workbook 2-3 - *Applying z*, and workbook 5-2 - *Solving Problems*. No hard-copy exercises accompany these Excel-based exercise workbooks.

Acknowledgements for the first (2004) edition

Writing ESC in its present incarnation would not have been possible without the valuable and insightful contributions of my peer reviewers. For the first edition the reviewers were Chris Chase, Claremont McKenna College, Beverly Dretzke, University of Wisconsin-Eau Claire, Chip Ettinger, Eastern Oregon University, Jon Grahe, Monmouth College, Frederick Gravetter, SUNY College at Brockport, Stephen Hall, Embry-Riddle Aeronautical University, Richard Hudiburg, University of North Alabama, Russell Hurlbut, University of Nevada, Las Vegas, Le Xuan Hy, Seattle University, Sheri Jackson, Jacksonville University, John Johnson, The Pennsylvania State University, Christopher Kello, George Mason University, William Langston, Middle Tennessee State University, G. William Lucker, University of Texas, El Paso, Mark Saviano, Brandeis University, Chris Spatz, Hendrix College, Eva Szeli, Mental Disability Rights International, Jim Zacks, Michigan State University. I am also indebted to the project manager of the first edition, J. Darin Derstine, who added his technical wizardry and eye for detail in the pre-production phase, Editorial Assistant Monica Sarmiento for her work on the *ESC User's Manual* and coordinating the peer review process, and my students, who endured three semesters of class testing and made many wonderful suggestions for revision. Special thanks go to my colleagues at State University of New York/Oswego for supporting the sabbatical leave I needed to get *ESC* off the ground, Thomson Learning representative Deborah VanPatten for her personal support, and a huge thank you to Wadsworth Psychology Publisher, Vicki Knight, who gave me the encouragement and material support that I needed to complete this project.

Acknowledgements for Version 2.0

Five peer reviewers evaluated the initial draft of *ESC* version 2.0. The product benefited substantially from their insightful suggestions. They are: T. Weathersby, Eastern University, William Sharp, The University of Mississippi, Warren Lacefield, Western Michigan University, Lynda Livingston, University of Puget Sound, and Mark Runco, California State University – Fullerton.

Thank you also to Erik Fortier, who managed the production phase of *ESC* version 2.0 and the development of the user interface, and Editorial Assistant Juliet Case, who coordinated the peer-review process. The last thank you is reserved for Vicki Knight, Wadsworth Psychology Publisher, who personally supervised the *ESC* project. I am truly grateful for the direct access I had to Vicki and the opportunity to exchange ideas with her on an ongoing basis.

The *ESC* User's Manual: Part I
Exercise Packet

Exercise 1-1: Describing Data

The first ESC workbook dealt with computing the statistics of **central tendency** using

a. Excel paste functions, and

b. manually entered Excel formulae.

Then came the computation of **variability** using:

a. the tabular method (This method, although not practical as a routine computational approach, will help you understand the underlying nature of the statistics of variability.),

b. Excel paste functions, and

c. manually entered Excel formulae.

The last two worksheets in workbook 1-1 allowed you to discover the answers to the following questions:

a. What happens to the statistics of central tendency when we add a constant to or subtract a constant from every value in the original distribution?

b. What happens to the statistics of variability when we increase or decrease the range of the data without changing central tendency?

Here is a review for evaluating your mastery of workbook 1-1. It will be helpful to write the "your data" array in the space below.

your data: ____

1. I used the _______ Excel paste function (f_x) to find the mean of the data set.

The output of the paste function equals __________.

2. I wrote the Excel formula =__________________________ to find the mean of the data set.

The output of my Excel formula equals____________.

3. I used the _______ Excel paste function to find the median of the data set. The output of the Excel paste function equals _________.

4. After sorting the data, I found that the value in the very middle of the array of 11 data values ($^1/_2$ the values above the middle and $^1/_2$ below) equals _________.

5. The smallest value in the data set equals _____, and the largest value equals _______.

6. The range of the data set equals ________.

7. The mode of the data set equals ________.

8. On the "tabular SS" worksheet, the sum of the deviation scores (column D) equals ____.

9. On the "tabular SS" worksheet, the sum of the squared deviations (column E) equals ____.

10. On the "paste SS" worksheet, I used the __________ paste function to find the Sum of Squares of the data set. According to that output, the SS value for "your data" equals ___________.

11. I used the ___________ Excel paste function to find the variance of the data set.

(Assume the data represent a population.) The variance for "your data" equals ______.

12. One may also find the variance by applying the following Excel formula to the SS value: =__________.

Using this method, the variance equals _________.

13. I can find the standard deviation (SD) by applying the following formula to the variance: =___________. Using this method, the SD = ________.

14. I can also find the standard deviation (of a population) using the _______ paste function. The standard deviation paste function outputs the value ______.

15. Using the tabular method (see tabular SS worksheet), the SS equals ____________.

16. On the "+ - constant" worksheet, what effect did adding a constant to or subtracting a constant from each original data value have on

   a. the measures of central tendency?

   b. the measures of variability?

17. On the "< > range" worksheet, what effect did increasing or decreasing the range of the data have on

   a. the measures of central tendency?

   b. the measures of variability?

18. Here is an additional practice problem. Analyze the data below and fill in the values for the statistics of central tendency and variability.

72	63	77	86	82	86
55	72	81	63	68	72
58	66	68	55	69	71
76	59	87	74	73	

Mean = __________

Median = __________

Mode = __________

Sum of Squares = __________

Variance = __________

Standard Deviation = __________

Exercise 1-2: Functions and Tools

ESC CD-ROM Workbook 1-2 expands coverage of Excel's statistical paste functions and tools. After you feel comfortable with the content of workbook 1-2, use the appropriate tools and paste functions to compute the answers to the questions below. The following data represent student test grades on a 40-point quiz.

40	31	32	32	28	24	33	27	29	32
38	23	17	37	30	30	26	30	29	31
26	25	34	23	31					

1. Use the A-Z (ascending sort) button to sort the data, and report the minimum and the maximum values in the array of quiz scores.
minimum = ____________ maximum = ______________

2. Now use the MIN and MAX paste functions to output the same information. MIN = ______ MAX = _______. Do your answers match your responses to question 1?

3. Using the AVERAGE paste function, the mean of the distribution of quiz scores is _______.

4. Run the Rank and Percentile tool on the array of quiz scores. Examine the output and fill in the blanks below.

   a. the rank of the quiz score **27** is ____________.

   b. the score **27** is on the _______ percentile.

   c. According to the PERCENTILE paste function, what quiz score is on the 70th percentile? ___________

   d. According to the PERCENTRANK paste function, the quiz score **32** is on the ________ percentile.

5. Using the STDEVP paste function, determine the standard deviation of the array of quiz scores. ___________

6. Run the Descriptive Statistics tool on the array of quiz scores. STDEVP uses the formula $\sqrt{SS/n}$ but the Descriptive Statistics tool and STDEV use the formula $\sqrt{SS/(n-1)}$ so the tool output will differ from your answer to #5.

The tool uses the formula that is appropriate for *estimating* the value of the population parameter σ, whereas the STDEV**P** paste function outputs a statistic for *describing* the variability in a population. The output of the STDEV paste function will match the value of the standard deviation reported by the Descriptive Statistics tool.

Exercise 1-3: Frequency Distributions

The key section of workbook 1-3 is presented on the "make grouped" worksheet. This worksheet lists the steps for making a grouped frequency distribution from an array of raw data using Excel's Histogram tool. Begin by opening workbook 1-3 and clicking the "make grouped" worksheet. Replace the data in column A of the "make grouped" worksheet with the data below.

61	59	62	61	55	75	72	73	65	81
68	82	63	76	75	57	68	57	64	68
57	64	57	59	70	68	63	61	65	62
67	74	68	62	70	62	65	71	67	61
63	56	66	76	76	67	59	62	64	67
74	65	61	57	56	83	64	63	45	71
57	53	71	72	63	60	52	73	55	69
62	57	85	54	61	66	59	70	66	46
65	72	65	52	58	67	66	61	50	76
64	58	59	75	68	71	66	65	74	64

The next step is to find the size of the class interval. The key values that you will need to determine the size of the class interval, and ultimately the column of *BIN* values, are listed below.

MIN = _______

MAX = _______

Range = _______

Range/15 = _______

Class Interval: typically the nearest odd number to the range/15 answer, but this is only a starting point that may be adjusted as necessary to ensure a desirable chart appearance.

Type the MIN in cell B3 of the "make grouped" worksheet, and count up by class-interval increments until you exceed the MAX value in the distribution.

With the data and adjacent *BIN* values in place, you are now ready to run the Histogram tool. See the detailed steps in workbook 1-3 if you get stuck

Exercise 1-4: Making Charts

Column A in the "new data" worksheet (the last worksheet in workbook 1-4), contains a distribution of 200 data values. Use the steps below to create a histogram (or line chart) of those data.

1. Divide the range by 15 and determine the nearest whole odd number for the size of the class interval. (In practice, this approach to determining the class interval width is just a starting point. Width may be adjusted up or down as necessary to improve the appearance of the chart.)

2. Starting with and including the minimum data value, count up to the top of your first class interval. For example, if the MIN of a distribution = 25 and the class interval = 5, the solution would be **29** for the first URL (*upper real limit*) value – as in the sequence 25, 26, 27, 28, **29**. Continue to add in class-interval increments – as in **29**, **34**, **39** ... – until the URL value exceeds the maximum value in the distribution. You can find the maximum value in the distribution with the MAX function.

3. The last step is to apply the Histogram data analysis tool to the raw data and URL arrays. Click Tools – Data Analysis – Histogram – **OK** and fill the dialog box fields as appropriate. Check New Worksheet Ply, click the New Worksheet Ply field, and type "quiz 1 chart" as the name for your new worksheet.

4. Go to the Histogram output table and overtype the *BIN* values with class-interval midpoints. In the example cited above, the first midpoint is 27 (25, 26, **27**, 28, 29), and so on in increments of 5 (**27**, **32**, **37**...).

5. Then run the Chart Wizard to make a line chart as covered in *ESC* workbook 1-4:

- **a.** Select the frequencies and click the Chart Wizard.
- **b.** Click Line and click Next.
- **c.** Click the Series tab at the top of the new box that appears, click the field next to Category (X) axis labels and select the array of midpoints for the X-axis labels. Click Next.
- **d.** Finish the rest of the Chart Wizard dialog and edit the resulting chart.

Exercise 2-1: Standardizing Distributions

1. Of two dieters, an Englishman lost 15 kilograms and an American lost 25 pounds. Apply the concept of a "common metric" to explain which of the dieters was more successful. (There are 2.2 pounds in a kilogram.)

2. Display the "experiment 1" worksheet in workbook 2-1 (Standardizing Distributions). In the table below, fill in the output of cells F12 and F13 as well as **I**12 and **I**13 and repeat for five experiments (i.e., 5 presses of the <**delete**> key).

	The Paramaters of the Distribution of Raw Data	The Paramaters of the Distribution of the *z* Statistic
1.	μ_x=_________________	μ_z=_________________
	σ_x=_________________	σ_z=_________________
2.	μ_x=_________________	μ_z=_________________
	σ_x=_________________	σ_z=_________________
3.	μ_x=_________________	μ_z=_________________
	σ_x=_________________	σ_z=_________________
4.	μ_x=_________________	μ_z=_________________
	σ_x=_________________	σ_z=_________________
5.	μ_x=_________________	μ_z=_________________
	σ_x=_________________	σ_z=_________________

What characteristics of the above output convince you that the *z* statistic represents a common metric?

Now, from the same Excel worksheet, type a percentile value into the highlighted cell (G20), do 5 experiments (i.e., type the <**delete**> key 5 times), and fill in the table below with the raw score and percentile results from each experiment.

	EXPERIMENTS				
	1	2	3	4	5
Raw X at the percentile entered in cell G20 equals:					
The z score at that same percentile equals:					

What feature of the above output demonstrates that the z statistic can serve as a common metric?

In experiment 2, no matter what values you set for the mean and standard deviation of the raw score distribution, the distribution of the z transformations had a mean of ______ and a standard deviation of ______.

Exercise 2-2: Comparing Distributions

Part I. Prof. Jones gave her students a midterm and a final examination and needs to compute a final grade in the course from the two scores. Briefly explain what problem(s) would complicate the task of averaging the scores of a very easy midterm exam (50 questions) with the scores of a very difficult final exam (100 questions)?

Part II. In workbook 2-2, two distributions of scores are converted to *z* scores. Consult the workbook as necessary to help you to transform the two distributions below to *z* scores. Before doing the transformation you will need to enter the data onto an Excel spreadsheet and compute (using the appropriate Excel paste functions) the means and standard deviations.

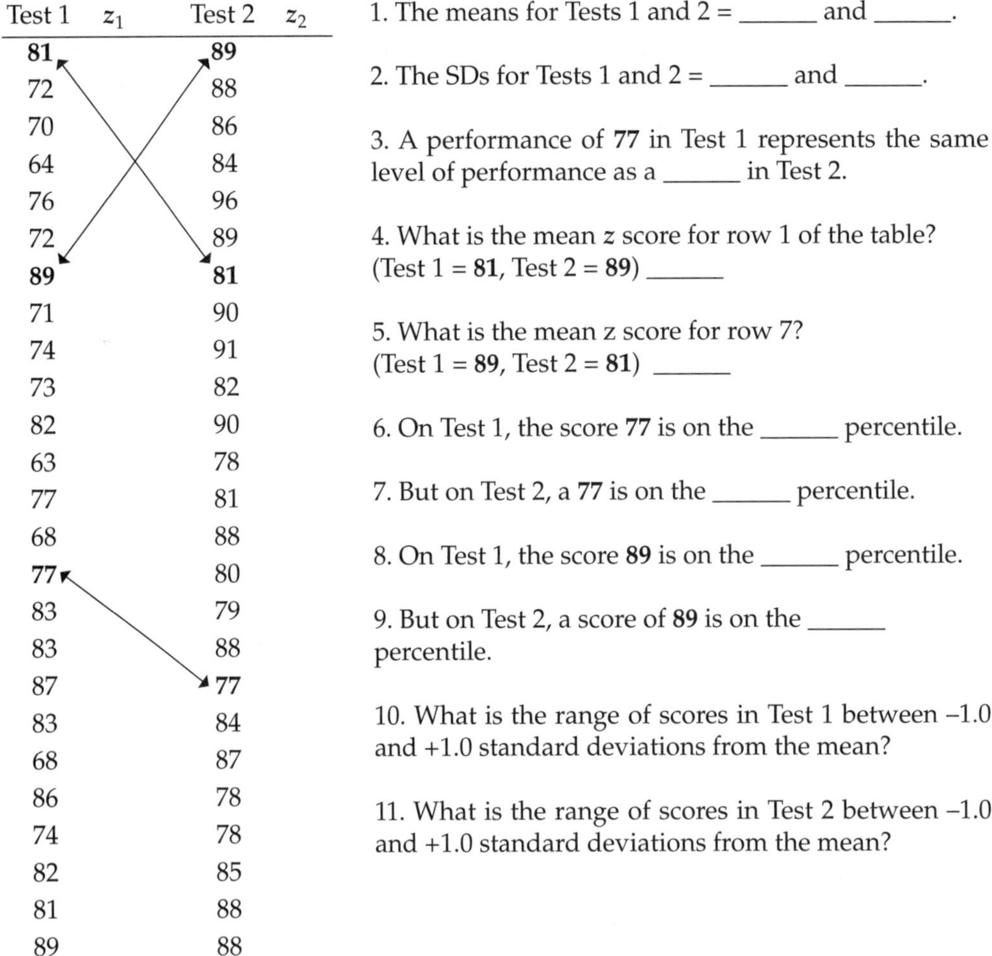

Test 1	z_1	Test 2	z_2
81		**89**	
72		88	
70		86	
64		84	
76		96	
72		89	
89		**81**	
71		90	
74		91	
73		82	
82		90	
63		78	
77		81	
68		88	
77		80	
83		79	
83		88	
87		**77**	
83		84	
68		87	
86		78	
74		78	
82		85	
81		88	
89		88	

1. The means for Tests 1 and 2 = ______ and ______.

2. The SDs for Tests 1 and 2 = ______ and ______.

3. A performance of **77** in Test 1 represents the same level of performance as a ______ in Test 2.

4. What is the mean *z* score for row 1 of the table? (Test 1 = **81**, Test 2 = **89**) ______

5. What is the mean z score for row 7? (Test 1 = **89**, Test 2 = **81**) ______

6. On Test 1, the score **77** is on the ______ percentile.

7. But on Test 2, a **77** is on the ______ percentile.

8. On Test 1, the score **89** is on the ______ percentile.

9. But on Test 2, a score of **89** is on the ______ percentile.

10. What is the range of scores in Test 1 between –1.0 and +1.0 standard deviations from the mean?

11. What is the range of scores in Test 2 between –1.0 and +1.0 standard deviations from the mean?

Exercise 3-1: Patterns of Association

1. A pattern of positive association will exist between two variables, X and Y, when low X scores tend to be paired with low Y scores and high X scores tend to be paired with high Y scores. Sometimes the Pearson ***r*** statistic, which quantifies the magnitude of X-Y association on a scale of zero to 1.00, shows a significant positive association between variables when none truly exists (see the "r zero" worksheet in workbook 3-1). This chance phenomenon is called a Type ___ error.

2. If there is a failure to find a significant association between two variables when one *does* truly exist, such an event is called a Type ___ error. (See the "positive" and "negative" worksheets in workbook 3-1.)

3. Name two measures of behavior that

   a. one could reasonably assume are <u>*negatively*</u> correlated.

   ____

   b. one could reasonably assume are <u>*positively*</u> correlated.

   ____

<u>**Circle the correct selection and/or fill in the blank.**</u>

4. The <u>critical value</u> of the Pearson ***r*** statistic is the value against which we must compare the computed value of the Pearson ***r*** . If the computed value of ***r*** exactly equals the critical value of ***r***, then the computed ***r*** is (significant / not significant) and the probability of a Type 1 error equals _____.

5. If one or both variables of a set of bivariate data have a <u>restricted range</u>, the computed ***r*** value for the data is likely to (overstate / understate) the degree of association between X and Y.

6. The presence of one or more "outliers" on an otherwise trendless scatterplot tends to (inflate / deflate) the magnitude of the Pearson ***r*** and thus (under-represent / over-represent) the true extent of the association between the variables.

7. What feature of a scatterplot tells you that the data are likely to have met the assumption of homoscedasticity?

8. What feature of a scatterplot tells you that the data are likely to have met the assumption of linearity?

9. What problem arises when the assumption of linearity is violated, as when the Pearson ***r*** is computed on variables with <u>curvi</u>linear association?

Exercise 3-2: An Empirical Demonstration of Type 1 Error

1. Nine columns of randomly generated data appear on the "random data" worksheet of workbook 3-2. If you select a specific array and compute a Pearson r between all possible pairs of columns, the expected value of any of the 36 possible Pearson r statistics should, theoretically, equal ______.

2. Five percent of the time, statistical analysis will reveal a significant positive or negative association between two variables even when only chance is governing the data-selection process. Therefore, when Excel computed the Pearson r statistic for all possible pairs among 9 columns of random values, we expected that, just by chance, approximately ______ would be significant.

3. When you ran the experiment (see the worksheet labeled "exercise"), how many of the 36 Pearson r values were significant? (With 21 pairs, the computed r statistic must be greater than or equal to .43 or less than or equal to –.43 to be considered significant.) ______

4. Identify the two columns of data for which the Pearson r was closest to zero. Similarly, identify the two columns for which r was the most positive and the two columns for which r was the most negative. (See the "my scatterplots" worksheet for examples.) As shown on the "my scatterplots" worksheet, use the Chart Wizard to prepare a neatly proportioned scatterplot for your zero, positively, and negatively associated data sets.

Exercise 3-3: Pearson *r*

1. Using the data below, calculate the Pearson *r* with each of the three methods presented in workbook 3-3. Simply overtype the data entries on the "Definitional 2" worksheet with the new data. Then copy and paste the new data onto cell B2 on the "Computational 2" and "z-score 2" worksheets (i.e., Paste right over the original data. Click **OK** if a warning appears about overwriting data.) This step will save you from re-typing the new data. Follow the directions on the latter worksheets to compute the Pearson *r*.

X	Y
89	84
71	96
47	33
45	55
78	54
60	69
45	69
25	42
58	82
57	49
40	76
40	64
68	72
80	68
28	17
86	76
10	30
70	80
21	30
35	20

a. For these data the Pearson *r* = ______. (Use either the CORREL paste function or Excel's Correlation tool.)

b. For these data, write the Pearson *r* formula for each of the three methods (as shown on the worksheets) and then rewrite the formula by filling in the correct statistical values.

<u>Circle the correct selection and/or fill in the blank.</u>

c. On a scale from zero to 1.00, the strength of association between X and Y equals _______. The direction of association is (positive / negative). So, (high / low) X values tend to be paired with (high / low) Y values.

d. Is *r* significant? Explain how you arrived at the determination of significance – or the lack thereof.

e. Do you remember the feature of data that defines negative association? On the "new data" worksheet, see if you can enter new data that will show a negative pattern of association between variables X and Y.

f. After you complete the practice problem on the "practice" worksheet, including all charts and computations, write a brief interpretation of the results. What do the statistics mean?

Exercise 3-4: Spearman *rho* (r_s)

These data represent the ratings that two independent judges recorded after observing and inspecting entrants to the National Dog Show. The scale runs between zero (no merit) to 100 (exquisite appearance and behavior). The task is to determine if there is a significant association (agreement) between the ratings of the two judges. Follow the procedures in workbook 3-4 to convert the data to ranks. Then do the correlation analysis.

Judge X	Judge Y
89	84
61	96
51	33
45	80
78	54
60	70
48	69
25	42
18	82
57	49
43	78
40	64
30	72
80	68
28	17
86	76
10	50
70	82
21	30
35	20

Circle the correct selection and/or fill in the blank.

a. For these data the Spearman *rho* = ______.

b. On a scale from zero to 1.00, the strength of association between X and Y equals _______. The direction of association is (positive / negative). So, (high / low) X values tend to be paired with (high / low) Y values.

c. Is *rho* significant? Explain how you arrived at the determination of significance – or the lack thereof. What do you conclude about the consistency of the ratings for the two judges? Do they tend to agree or disagree in how they are rating the show dogs?

Exercise 3-5: Point Biserial Correlation

As you have seen in the earlier workbooks, the Pearson ***r*** statistic allows us to assess association between variables that have interval or ratio scaling, and the Spearman ***rho*** statistic allows us to assess association between variables that have ordinal scaling. Sometimes, however, a situation arises in which only one variable of a pair has interval or ratio scaling and the other is dichotomous. To say that the variable is dichotomous means that it can take only one of two mutually exclusive values, such as yes/no, success/failure, single/married, and so forth. An example of such data appears in workbook 3-5 along with two methods for computing the appropriate statistic for correlation: r_{pbi} – the Point Biserial ***r***.

After reading through the r_{pbi} example and working through the practice problem, apply what you have learned to the following question.

For one week, parents kept a diary of how many hours their third-grade children watched TV or played video games. With the parents' permission, the researchers asked educators to describe the school performance of each child as being in the top 50% or lower 50% of the student's class. The data appear at left.

What do the results of your r_{pbi} analysis tell you about the relationship between academic performance and video game/TV behavior?

Video Hours	**Class Rank: Top / Bottom 50%**
21	T
18	T
25	B
31	B
23	B
15	T
19	T
21	T
37	B
34	B
41	B
17	T
15	B
31	B

Exercise 3-6: Linear Regression

When we calculate the correlation between two behavioral variables, we are unlikely to see a perfect linear (straight line) function, such as the one shown on the "perfect" worksheet of workbook 3-6. When the correlation *is* perfect between two variables, we may predict one variable from the other without any possibility for error. But when there is an underlying, though less than perfect, linear relationship between two variables, we do not see a straight line in the chart. Instead, we see a scatterplot. The dots suggest a positive or negative trend rather than the perfection of a straight line. (See "r positive" and "r negative" worksheets for demonstrations of such scatterplots.)

Regression analysis allows us to represent the trend in a scatterplot with a best-fit line. In a sense, the best-fit line is the mean of the scatterplot. Just as the mean represents the typical or average value in a distribution, the regression line represents the general trend of the scatterplot. The higher the correlation is between variables X and Y, the more pronounced the trend will be (i.e., the more the scatterplot will resemble a straight line), and the greater the accuracy will be when using the best-fit line to predict Y from X.

After you have digested the contents of workbook 3-6, you should be able to provide answers to the following questions and fill-ins.

---

1. In order to fit the best-fit "regression" line to a scatterplot, we must compute two constants from the data. These two constants are called the _______ and the _______.

2. The Pearson ***r*** statistic quantifies, on a scale of zero to one, the association that is present in a bivariate data set – two measures, X and Y, on the same people. The r^2 statistic, also called the *coefficient of determination*, tells us…

3. In the context of regression analysis, variable X is called the predictor because we use it to predict Y, the __________ variable.

4. We make predictions by solving the equation for the best-fit line. $\mathbf{Y' = a_y + b_yX}$ is the equation for a straight line. In words, the predicted value of variable Y equals the value at which the best-fit line intercepts the Y axis (the $\mathbf{a_y}$ term) plus the slope (the $\mathbf{b_y}$ term) times the value of **X**. The Y subscripts remind us that the equation is set up to predict variable ___ with the knowledge of variable ___.

Thus, once we know the values of the two regression constants, the Y intercept and the slope, we can substitute any value for X and solve the equation for Y. So, if the regression analysis shows that the intercept equals 10 and the slope = 1.5, when X=20, the predicted value of Y will be _______.

5. The standard error of estimate statistic, $\mathbf{S}_{est\ y}$, is a measure of…

6. The workbook shows a formula for the slope of the regression for Y on X that is the ratio of two measures of variability, SP_{xy} and SS_x. That formula is…

7. For the following data, use the appropriate paste functions to compute the correlation between X and Y, the slope of the regression line for Y on X, the Y intercept of the regression line for Y on X, the standard error of estimate for the regression of Y on X, and the coefficient of determination. Place the answers in the box below.

Pair	X	Y
A	4	53
B	25	99
C	27	86
D	12	69
E	10	89
F	48	64
G	36	45
H	66	31
I	44	60
J	47	39
K	55	31
L	40	65
M	31	67
N	36	29
O	84	9
P	80	48
Q	79	44
R	77	11
S	88	12
T	69	13

Correlation = __________
Slope = __________
Y intercept = __________

The formula for the regression "best fit" line is __________.

The standard error of estimate equals ________.

The coefficient of determination equals ________.

8. Repeat the analysis of the data set using the regression tool. You do NOT need to retype the data. Just run the regression tool on the same worksheet as the data. Do your answers check?

9. Use the FORECAST function to predict Y when X=50.

10. Regression analysis allows us to divide the total variability among the Y scores into two components: that which is predictable with the knowledge of X and that which is unpredictable. The predictable variability is called _________ and, for these data, equals _______.

11. The remaining variability among the Y scores is unpredictable. It is called __________ and for these data equals __________.

12. What value from the ANOVA table of the regression tool output tells us if the regression of Y on X is significant (i.e., unlikely to be a chance event)?

____

13. Label the following expressions as SS_{total}, $SS_{regression}$, or $SS_{residual}$.

$\Sigma(Y-\overline{Y})^2$ $\Sigma(Y-Y')^2$ $\Sigma(Y'-\overline{Y})^2$

__________ __________ __________

14. Explain why the predictions from X to Y are likely to be more accurate when the correlation between X and Y is high.

Periodic Review 1:

Practice Problems for Correlation and Regression

I. The data below are three measures on a group of workers: score on a mechanical aptitude test (variable X), on-the-job errors (variable Y), and the supervisor rating of the worker (variable W). Process these data as needed to answer the following questions.

X	Y	W
Mechanical Aptitude Test	**On-the-Job Errors**	**Supervisor Job Rating**
90	2	89
50	14	61
82	5	45
93	5	69
60	7	55
45	6	80
43	13	70
40	9	74
60	11	91
73	8	65
60	3	50
83	9	80
30	13	40
70	6	60
78	11	75

1. Using the appropriate statistical procedure (Pearson ***r*** or Spearman ***rho***):

   a. The correlation of X with Y equals ________.

   b. The correlation of X with W equals _______.

   c. The correlation of Y with W equals _______.

   d. Which of these (if any) is significant? How do you know?

2. After having completed the regression analysis for **Y** on **X** (remember, X is the predictor or "independent" variable, and Y is the dependent or "criterion" variable) fill in the blanks in the following questions:

a. The proportion of variability in on-the-job errors (Y) that is predictable with the knowledge of mechanical aptitude scores (X) equals ___________.

b. The coefficient of determination equals _____________.

c. The slope of the best-fit regression line equals ________.

d. The Y intercept of the best-fit regression line equals _______.

e. The standard error of estimate equals ______________.

f. The equation for the best-fit line is Y′ = ______________________.

3. If a person got an aptitude score of 85, we would predict an on-the-job performance score of ___________. But if the aptitude score was only 60, we would predict an on-the-job performance of _______.

4. The total Sum of Squares for variable Y is ______, and of that, _______ is predictable and _______ is unpredictable.

5. What feature of the bivariate data is revealed by the standard error of estimate?

6. How do we know if the degree to which we can predict Y from X is significant (i.e., better than chance)? Report the value on your output that tells you whether or not the regression is significant.

7. Using Excel, prepare and print out a well proportioned scatterplot for variables X and Y along with a trendline superimposed on the scatterplot (Select the chart by clicking inside the outer border, click Chart on the menu bar, click add trendline, and click OK)

II. A consumer researcher wanted to see if there was a relationship between customers' annual DVD purchases and purchases of music downloads. The data are below.

	X	Y
Consumer	**DVD Purchases**	**Music Downloads**
A	10	22
B	22	40
C	40	65
D	15	35
E	20	30
F	30	25
G	34	55
H	18	60
I	18	18
J	27	45
K	19	45
L	30	70
M	40	45
N	12	32

1. Compute the correlation statistic that best represents how much association there is between the X and Y variables. Be sure to include the name of the statistic (Pearson ***r*** or Spearman ***rho***) and its degrees of freedom.

____

2. The ***p*** value for the correlation is **<.05 / >.05** (**circle one**).

3. What do you conclude about the association between the X and Y variables? Offer an interpretation of your statistical results.

4. Enter the X-Y data in Excel. Select the data and, using Chart Wizard, create a scatterplot. As you can see from the scatterplot, the positive trend between X and Y stands out. Write the equation of the linear function that best represents that trend. Be sure to provide the <u>numerical</u> values for the a_y and b_y values in your statement of the equation in the form $Y' = a_y + b_y X$.

5. If a consumer bought 15 DVDs in a year, the predicted number of music downloads that consumer would purchase equals _______.

6. If a consumer bought 52 DVDs in a year, the predicted number of music downloads that consumer would purchase equals _______.

7. From the Analysis of Variance Summary Table that is included in the regression analysis output, the specific numerical value (a probability) that shows the significant correlation between X and Y (as well as significant regression of Y on X) equals _______.

8. Look at the Analysis of Variance table in your regression analysis output. The regression analysis for Y on X reveals that:

   a. the total variability among the Y scores equals ______.

   b. For the present data we see that some of the variability in Y is predictable if we know X, and some is not predictable. Together, the predictable ("regression") and unpredictable ("residual") components add up to the total variability. Your analysis of the above data shows that the predictable portion equals ________, and the unpredictable portion equals ______.

9. Find the value on your output that quantifies the degree to which the scatterplot dots are spread out around the regression (best-fit) line.

____

10. Complete the following statement. According to my output, the proportion of the variability in Y that is predictable with the knowledge of X equals ________.

11. Given the results of the analyses, would an advertiser want to target people who buy DVDs in a media campaign to get them to purchase music downloads? Why or why not?

Exercise 4-1: The Binomial Sampling Distribution

Evaluate your understanding of the material in workbook 4-1 by answering the following questions.

1. What is a sampling distribution?

2. What is the difference between a theoretical sampling distribution and an empirical sampling distribution?

3. What does it mean to refer to a statistic (e.g. heads versus tails) as dichotomous?

4. What does it mean to describe two events as mutually exclusive?

5. In a binomial sampling experiment, such as tossing a coin 5 times and counting the number of heads that occur, what very short mathematical expression tells us how many different tallies (outcomes) are possible?

6. In a binomial sampling experiment (e.g., tossing a coin 5 times and counting heads) how many different patterns ("permutations" or different arrangements) of results are possible? The answer is another very short mathematical expression.

7. In general, what information must we have at hand to determine the sampling distribution of mutually exclusive and dichotomous events? (Hint: see the sampling distribution of the number of heads that occur in 5 tosses of a fair coin.)

8. Do the "Bernoulli" experiment in workbook 4-1. Did your experimental results appear to be reasonably close to the theoretical predictions? If not, what accounts for the discrepancies you see between the theoretical and empirical output?

9. Perform the binomial experiment on the "any p q values" worksheet. On the next "goodness of fit" worksheet, the χ^2 test compares the empirical distribution of the heads statistic to the theoretical frequency distribution. Assuming that only chance is influencing the empirical outcome, what does it mean if the χ^2 statistic is significant?

10. Even when only chance is operating in a coin-flipping experiment (the coin is fair and unbiased), the differences between the empirical and theoretical frequencies will, on occasion, be too extreme to retain the assumption that only chance is operating. According to convention, we reject chance as the likely explanation for a rare event when the probability of that event is less than or equal to _____. When, despite the reality that only chance is operating, a very rare event *does* occur, the incorrect inference that more than chance was involved is a Type ___ error.

11. Do the binomial experiment on the "any p q values" worksheet using p=.5 and a random seed = **6519**. Now repeat the experiment with a random seed = **6520**. Which random seed yields results that are consistent with the conclusion that only chance is operating? Which random seed yields results that appear to show that something other than chance is affecting the coin-flipping results?

12. Repeat the "any p q values" experiment with $p \neq q$. What do you notice about the pattern of theoretical frequencies when $p \neq q$? Specifically, is the theoretical frequency distribution still symmetrical?

13. In the "goodness of fit" worksheet, what "fit" is being evaluated?

14. In the "five flips" experiment, each of the most extreme outcomes (zero heads or five heads) will, theoretically, occur three times in 100 repetitions of the five-flip sampling experiment. But in the "ten flips" table, the approximate expected frequencies of the most extreme outcomes (zero heads and ten heads) are listed as "maybe none." Why, in this experiment, are you unlikely to see *any* occurrence of either no heads or all heads in ten flips of a coin? Hint: use the BINOMDIST paste function to determine the probability of exactly zero heads or exactly all heads in ten flips of a coin.

Exercise 4-2: An Empirical Demonstration of the Central Limit Theorem

Workbook 4-2 includes an experiment that tests the predictions of the central limit theorem. The predictions are presented in the workbook along with the template for the experiment. Why go through this process? This is one of those occasions in the study of statistics when the best temporary course is to be content with the abstract nature of the theorem's predictions without wondering about the ultimate usefulness of the information. With that in mind, do your best to complete the following items.

Circle the correct selection and/or fill in the blank.

1. No matter what the sample size, the mean of every sample of data from the "Li" population (μ=50, σ=10) has an expected value of _____.

2. Given the way in which we are conducting our sampling from the Li population, any difference between a sample mean and the Li population mean must be a result of chance / computational error.

3. The larger the sample size you use (9, 16, 25, or 100), the more tightly / less tightly the sample means cluster about the mean of the Li population.

4. The deviation measure of a distribution of raw scores is called the standard deviation, but the deviation measure of a distribution of sample means is called the standard __________.

5. Theoretically, the mean of the distribution of sample means will stay the same with increasing sample size. The standard error will get smaller / larger / unstable with increasing sample sizes.

6. Assume a population has a standard deviation equal to 5 and we take a large number of samples from that population. If n=25, theoretically, the standard error of the distribution of sample means should equal ______.

7. Generate "your data" output for each sample size (9, 16, 25, and 100) and report below the mean and standard error of the resulting distribution of sample means. Inspect these data. What do you think they say about the influence of sample size on the standard error and on central tendency?

Sample Size	**9**	**16**	**25**	**100**
Mean	______	______	______	______
Standard Error	______	______	______	______

8. Run the sampling experiment in workbook 4-2 for n=25. Were the empirical results reasonably close to your expectations? If not, why not?

9. In workbook 4-2 on the "your parameters" worksheets (n=9, n=16, n=25, n=100), set the mean = 75 and the standard deviation = 9 and run the experiments.

a. How did the steadily increasing sample sizes affect the distribution of sample means? Specifically, did the means increase, decrease, or stay the same?

b. Did the standard error of the mean increase, decrease, or stay the same? The answer should provide evidence regarding the relationship between sample size and the standard error of the mean. As the sample size grows, the size of the standard error . . .

c. What were the specific values of the four means in these four experiments?

d. What did you *expect* the values to be?

Exercise 5-1: Computing Probability

Because statistical decisions are made on the basis of probability, it is important to have a reasonable grounding in probability fundamentals. The problems below require probability determinations in the context of both binomial and continuous variables. Use paste functions (covered in workbook 5-1) as necessary to arrive at the solutions to the following questions.

1. A ball rolls down a chute, bounces around randomly, and finally falls into one of 6 holes. Three of the holes are trimmed in black, and the other three are trimmed in white. If the ball is equally likely to rest in any of the 6 holes, what is the probability that the ball will come to rest in a black-trimmed hole?

2. If we repeat the process 8 times, what is the probability that the result will be a black-trimmed hole:

   a. in exactly 3 out of the 8 trials?

   b. in 3 or more of the 8 trials?

   c. in at least 4 trials?

   d. in fewer than 6 trials?

   e. in more than 6 trials?

   f. in 4 or fewer trials

3. A group of 300 military pilots has just completed jungle survival school. On the final evaluation, the mean survival test score for the group was 88 out of 100 possible points. The distribution of scores had a standard deviation of 4.0. Assume you must prepare a report about the graduating class for your superior officer. Answer the following questions with the appropriate Excel paste function.

   a. What proportion of students scored 85 or lower on the examination?

   b. What proportion of students scored 92 or higher?

   c. What proportion of students scored 90 or higher?

   d. What proportion of students scored 85 or higher?

   e. What proportion of students scored between (and including) 84 and 92?

Exercise 6-1: Estimating Error

1. When we use the value of the sample mean, $\overline{X}$, to estimate μ, the mean of a population, such an estimate is described as "unbiased." What property of the sample mean allows us to declare that it is an unbiased estimate of the population mean?

2. Assume we have drawn a small sample from a large population. If we use the following formula to compute the standard deviation of the sample data:

$$\sqrt{\frac{SS_X}{n}}$$

the solution will be a "biased" estimate of the population standard deviation. What property of this descriptive statistic makes it a biased estimate of the population standard deviation?

3. Why does the variability present in a sample tend to underestimate the variability that is present in the population from which the sample was drawn?

4. Do the exercise on the "experiment" worksheet of workbook 6-1 and report your results below. Are your results consistent with the theoretical expectation that the variability computed from a small sample tends to underestimate the variability of the much larger population from which the sample was drawn?

Sample 3 results: STDEV**P** = ________ STDEV = ___________

Sample 4 results: STDEV**P** = ________ STDEV = ___________

Which paste function, STDEVP or STDEV, gave a more accurate estimate of the standard deviation of the population (σ=10)?

If STDEV was, as expected, more accurate, what element of the formula was the key to its increased accuracy and designation as "***un***biased"?

Exercise 6-2: Rationale of the Single-Sample *t* Test

Introduction

The problems for which the *t* test is appropriate specify μ, the mean of some population, along with data that may or may not have come from that population. When $\overline{X}$, the mean of the sample data, is somewhat different from the value of μ, it is reasonable to question whether or not the sample truly did come from a population with a mean = μ. Why? Because, as the central limit theorem demonstration showed (workbook 4-2), the expected value of any sample mean is μ, the mean of the population from which the sample was drawn.

The single-sample *t* test (see workbook 6-2) allows us to evaluate which is the better of two possible explanations when the mean of a single sample is different from a specified value of μ:

the explanation offered in the **null hypothesis**: The sample was drawn from a population with a mean = μ and any deviation between the sample mean and μ is just chance;

or

the explanation offered in the **alternative hypothesis**: The sample was *not* drawn from the population with a mean = μ. Rather, the sample was drawn from a different population that has a mean ≠ μ . It is the generally higher (or lower) values in that different population, not chance, that explains why the mean of the sample data is above or below the μ specified in the null hypothesis.

The Two Possible Decisions

The key issue, of course, is how different does the sample mean have to be from μ before we defer to the alternative hypothesis and conclude that the sample was drawn from a population with a mean ≠ μ?

When the difference between a sample mean calculated from available data ($\overline{X}$) and the mean of some specific and known population (μ) is "slight," it is reasonable to attribute the difference to chance. Perhaps through chance alone, the random sample contained a slight imbalance of high data values, which would result in a sample mean that is > μ. Or perhaps the sample contained a slight imbalance of low data values, which would result in a sample mean that is < μ.

Assuming that the inequality between $\overline{X}$ and μ is "slight," it seems reasonable to retain the null hypothesis assumption that the sample was drawn from the known population.

If, however, the $\overline{X}-\mu$ difference is "substantial," it makes less sense to conclude that the difference arose by chance. In fact, the more different $\overline{X}$ is from μ, the less plausible it is that chance is a reasonable explanation for the difference. When the difference is large, it makes better sense to reject the null hypothesis, regard the difference as *significant*, and thus take the position that the sample was drawn from a population with a mean $\neq \mu$.

Chance versus Significance: The Tipping Point

But how do we decide if a difference is "slight" and insignificant versus "substantial" and significant? A core concept underlying the logic of hypothesis testing is that we answer the latter question on the basis of probability.

We approach the decision of significance (or the lack thereof) by initially assuming that the sample was indeed drawn from the known population (mean = μ). This assumption, as mentioned above, is called a *null hypothesis*. The logical consequence of the null assumption is to regard any $\overline{X}-\mu$ difference we see in the data as a chance phenomenon. Remember, we expect $\overline{X}$ to equal μ when a sample is drawn from a population with a mean = μ.

If $\overline{X} \neq \mu$, the reason put forth under the null assumption is that the inequality must be a chance event – a result of the random nature of the sampling process.

To Reject or Not to Reject: The Statistical Solution

The ***t*** test allows us to determine the probability that the difference between our single sample mean and μ is due to chance. Whenever the probability of the obtained difference is determined to be > .05, we retain the null hypothesis. Simply put, the difference is small enough to write off as a chance phenomenon, so we retain the assumption that the sample was drawn from the specified population.

When the probability of the obtained difference is determined to be ≤ .05, we reject the null hypothesis. That is, the difference is too large to assume that chance alone is responsible, so we reject chance as a reasonable explanation for the difference. By doing so, we default to the alternative hypothesis, which is that the sample was drawn from a population with a mean unequal to μ.

Naturally, the greater the $\overline{X}-\mu$ difference is, the more likely we are to reject the null hypothesis. You will be able to see this for yourself when you run the "calculations" worksheet in *ESC* workbook 6-2.

Finding *p*

Using the single-sample ***t*** test, we know we have reached the point of significance ($p \leq .05$) when the absolute value of the computed ***t*** statistic is *as large or larger than* the critical value of ***t*** as published in a statistical table. Thus, reaching the critical value of the ***t*** statistic marks the tipping point at which we transition from an evaluation of the $\overline{X} - \mu$ difference as insignificant to significant.

ESC Workbook 6-2

1. After familiarizing yourself with the information on the first five worksheets, click the tab for the "calculations" worksheet. We assume the data in column A of the Excel worksheet were drawn from a population with a mean = 50. According to the data, should we retain that assumption? The sample mean is 52, not 50. But, as you can see from the ***t***-test analysis of the data, the computed ***t*** is less than critical ***t*** value, so the difference between the expected value of 50 and the obtained value of 52 is too small to be considered significant. Nothing other than chance is assumed to be responsible for the two-unit difference between the sample mean of 52 and the population mean of 50, so we retain the assumption that the sample was drawn from a population with $\mu = 50$.

2. Now systematically change the data in column A by adding a constant to or subtracting a constant from every value in the column.

3. How deviant from 50 did your mean have to be before the analysis determined it to be significant?

4. After getting a significant result, what happens when you maintain the value of the value of the sample mean as a constant but increase the within-sample variability? Systematically increase the within-sample variability by following the instructions on the worksheet. What did you discover about the relationship between within-sample variability and the determination of statistical significance?

5. What happens when the analysis does ***not*** show a significant $\overline{X} - \mu$ difference and you change the data to <u>decrease</u> the within-sample variability? What did you discover about the relationship between within-sample variability and the determination of statistical significance?

6. The next worksheet provides a template for a variety of sampling experiments, some of which are outlined below. You are likely to discover some important statistical facts about power and sample size that relate not only to the test at hand but to other more advanced statistical analyses as well.

The "Experiment" Worksheet in Workbook 6-2:

1. Use a sample size of 10 (***n***=10) and take one sample from each population. Did the statistical test get it right? Was any mean from samples 2, 3, or 4 significantly different from 50, the mean of the Null? A failure to find a significant difference is an example of a Type __ error.

2. Use ***n***=25 and take one sample from each population. Did the statistical test get it right? Was any mean from sample 2, 3, or 4 significantly different from 50, the mean of the Null? A failure to find a significant difference is an example of a Type __ error.

3. Use ***n***=10 and take all 4 samples from the Null population. Did the statistical test get it right? Was any sample mean significantly different from 50, the mean of the Null? Any finding of a significant difference is an example of a Type ___ error.

Exercise 6-3: Confidence Intervals

Assume the existence of a population distribution the mean of which (μ) is unknown – perhaps even unknowable in any practical sense. For example, imagine the difficulty in finding the mean IQ of <u>all</u> college graduates in the year 2005. When it is unrealistic or very difficult to obtain the exact value of μ, we usually settle for an estimate computed from the data of a representative sample.

<u>The Point Estimate</u>

The demonstrations in workbook 6-1 show that the sample mean is an unbiased estimate of μ, the population mean. The estimate is unbiased because the sample mean will, on average, equal the mean of the population from which the sample was drawn. When used in this way, the sample mean is a *point* estimate of μ.

<u>The Interval Estimate</u>

Another approach for estimating μ is to specify a *range* of values that we believe contains μ. That is, instead of attempting to pin down the *exact* value of μ, we compute an interval that *probably* contains μ. How wide apart the upper and lower limits of the interval turn out to be depends on the degree of confidence we have in mind for the interval. The most widely used confidence interval format reads as follows:

> "I am 95% confident that μ, the mean of the population, falls within the interval <lower limit> through <upper limit>."

Unlike the point estimate, the interval estimate does not assign a specific value to the estimate of the population mean. Rather, the idea is to specify a range within which μ probably lies. Also, expressing confidence as a probability (".95") means that although the confidence interval is very *likely* to contain μ (p=.95), there is also a small probability (p=.05) that the confidence interval does *not* contain μ.

<u>An Empirical Verification</u>

The "sampling experiment" worksheet of workbook 6-3 allows us to test empirically if .95 is indeed the probability that an interval contains μ. In this sampling experiment, Excel draws 100 samples from a known population and computes one hundred 95% confidence intervals – one for each sample. After completing *ESC* workbook 6-3, answer the following questions.

1. Of the 100 intervals displayed in the sampling experiment, how many *should* contain μ?

2. Of the 100 intervals, how many should *fail* to contain μ?

3. If the empirical results you predicted were not realized, what is the explanation?

4. In the demo 1 worksheet, what happens to the width of the computed confidence interval if you increase the variability that is present in the sample?

5. In the demo 1 worksheet, what happens to the width of the computed confidence interval if you decrease the variability that is present in the sample?

6. Complete exercise 1 in workbook 6-3 for sample sizes 10, 25, and 50. What is the relationship between the sample size and the width of the 95% confidence interval? Which sample size resulted in the most precise (smallest width) estimate of μ?

Exercise 6-4: Testing the Pearson *r*

Introduction

From the workbooks in Folder 3 (correlation and regression) you learned that even when there is no underlying association between two variables (X and Y), an incorrect determination of significant association between variables X and Y will occur 5% of the time (a Type 1 error). One can get a visual representation of such an event by looking at the "distribution" worksheet in workbook 6-4. It shows the distribution of possible values that can result from an analysis of bivariate sample data when there is ***no*** underlying X-Y association. In such an instance, we *expect* the Pearson ***r*** to equal zero, the midpoint of the distribution. But when the computed ***r*** is, by chance, far away from zero either on the right tail (positive) or left tail (negative), a determination of significant association may result even when none truly exists. How far from zero does ***r*** have to be before we discount chance as an explanation for the apparent association? The most widely used standard is when the ***p*** value for the ***r*** statistic is $\leq .05$.

Published statistical tables provide the critical values for the ***r*** statistic for p=.05 or p=.01, but we can use Excel to find the exact ***p*** value. As shown on the "automatic p value" worksheet of workbook 6-4, after inputting the degrees of freedom (the number of X-Y pairs minus 2) and the value for the Pearson *r* statistic, Excel will output the ***p*** value. (Using a simple formula, the worksheet converts the Pearson ***r*** to a ***t*** statistic, and then uses the TDIST paste function to output the ***p*** value.)

Using information on the "example" and "automatic p value" worksheets, let's make a table that shows the values for ***df***, t_{crit} and ***p*** for various sample sizes. Assume the Pearson ***r*** = .45.

n	*df*	t_{crit}	*p*
10	_____	_____	_____
15	_____	_____	_____
20	_____	_____	_____
25	_____	_____	_____
30	_____	_____	_____

What do your results tell you about the relationship between sample size, r_{crit}, and the ***p*** value for the ***r*** statistic?

Periodic Review 2:

Introduction to Hypothesis Testing

Part I: What Is Hypothesis Testing?

The fundamental task in hypothesis testing is to compare a statistic computed from sample data (the number of successes that occurred, the mean of a single sample, the difference between the means of two samples, the extent of relationship between two variables, and so forth) to what we would expect to find *assuming only chance is operating.*

In general, statistical tests allow us to determine whether chance alone is or is not a reasonable explanation for certain measurable characteristics of data. If we use a statistical test that is appropriate to the research question being asked and compatible with specific properties of the research data (for example, whether the scaling of the data is nominal, ordinal, interval, or ratio), our conclusion about the contribution of non-chance factors to the data will be logical and defensible.

Gaining an understanding of hypothesis testing is best accomplished by – you guessed it – practicing! As explained below, the process begins by framing the research question in a way that makes it testable. Following that initial discussion, you will come upon several examples that relate to the statistics covered in *ESC* folders 1 through 6. The last section of this review contains problems of various types that will allow you to practice your hypothesis testing skills. Specifically, you will practice choosing the statistical test that is appropriate both for processing the research data and answering the research question described in the problem.

Framing the Question

The ***null hypothesis*** is a formal statement of the conditions that we assume were in force when the sample data were collected. Null hypotheses we have encountered or will soon encounter include:

a. The coin used to collect heads/tails data was unbiased [p(head)=.5]. (…and any departure from an even 50-50 split is due to chance.)

b. The sample was drawn from a population with a mean equal to μ, as in $\mu_0=50$. (…and any difference between the sample mean and μ is due to chance.)

c. The difference between the mean from which the first sample was drawn and the mean of the population from which the second sample was drawn is zero, as in $\mu_1 - \mu_2 = 0$. (...and any difference between the two sample means is due to chance.)

d. The relationship between X and Y is zero, as in $\rho=0$. (...and any apparent correlation between the variables is just chance.)

In all the above examples, chance alone is assumed to account for any difference between what we expected to find and what we actually found in the analysis of the sample data.

Similarly, the ***alternative hypothesis*** describes a scenario in which *more* than chance is operating. Alternative hypotheses we have encountered or will soon encounter include:

a. The coin used to collect heads/tails data was biased [p(head)$\neq$.5]. (...and any departure from an even 50-50 split is because of that bias.)

b. The sample was <u>not</u> drawn from a population with a mean equal to μ. (...and any difference between the sample mean and the value for μ specified in the null hypothesis is because the sample was *not* drawn from a population with a mean = μ.)

c. The difference between the mean from which the first sample was drawn and the mean of the population from which the second sample was drawn is ***not*** zero, expressed as $\mu_1 - \mu_2 \neq 0$. (...and any difference between the two sample means is not chance. Rather, it is because the two samples were drawn from different populations.)

d. The relationship between X and Y is ***not*** zero, as in $\rho\neq0$. (...and the apparent correlation between the variables is real, not just a chance occurrence.)

In general, when statistical analysis of the sample data reveals information that is substantially inconsistent with the null hypothesis statement, the finding is "significant" and we reject chance as an acceptable explanation for the inconsistency.

<u>When Does "Somewhat Inconsistent" Become "Substantially Inconsistent"?</u>

Let's examine the concept of significance in the case of a binomial sampling experiment to evaluate the fairness of a coin. In 10 tosses of a fair (unbiased) coin, the most common result is 5 heads and 5 tails. The probability of finding this even split equals .246 and is more likely than any other result. So, if we do the coin-toss experiment, we can reasonably ***expect*** to see the 5 head-5 tail result.

But let's say we flip a coin ten times and our data reveal a 6-4 split instead of the expected 5-5 split. Do we confidently infer that *more* than chance (i.e., some bias) affected the outcome? We would likely regard chance as the more accurate explanation because a 6-4 split is a fairly common outcome in the 10-toss experiment. In fact, the probability of either a 6 head-4 tail split or a 4 head-6 tail split using a fair coin equals .41 (.205 for the 6-4 split plus .205 for the 4-6 split).

When, however, the difference between expectation and reality is extreme (say, 10 heads and no tails versus the expected 5-5 split), we would understandably be reluctant to retain the null-hypothesis assumption that chance alone is responsible. In the face of such an extreme result, it would make much more sense to infer that the coin was biased. Why? A 10 head-0 tail split will happen in only 1 of 1000 repetitions of the coin-flip experiment. If you got 10 heads in a row, would you believe that by an odd stroke of chance you just happened to get that 1 in 1000 result (p=.001), or would it make more sense to question the fairness of the coin?

How inconsistent with the null-hypothesis expectation does a statistical result have to be before we reject chance as the explanation for that result? By convention, if statistical analysis reveals that the probability of the obtained result *or one even more extreme* is ≤ .05, we reject the null hypothesis and pronounce the difference between the actual result and the null hypothesis expectation to be ***significant***. If the probability turns out to be > .05, we retain the null hypothesis assumption that only chance is operating. That is, we view the difference between actual results and the expectation as stated in the null hypothesis to be ***in***significant.

Although all the various tests that make up inferential statistics are vehicles for deciding whether chance or something other than chance is the better explanation for certain statistical features of the data, choosing a specific analytical approach for the data must be done with great care. We must consider the scaling of the data (nominal, ordinal, or interval/ratio), the statistical feature of the data on which we are focusing (comparing means, comparing frequencies, assessing relationships, making predictions, etc.), and whether the data conform to various assumptions. Nevertheless, the underlying logic and procedures are virtually the same no matter what statistical analysis is used.

Testing Hypotheses

We start the testing process by framing the question, which involves stating the null hypothesis (H_0), the alternative hypothesis (H_1), and the criteria we will apply for the determination of significance (.05 versus .01).

After that is done, we follow the Five Steps of Hypothesis Testing.

1. Collect the data.

2. Compute a statistic from the data.

3. Locate the statistic on its theoretical sampling distribution. (The theoretical sampling distribution of the statistic is the distribution that would result under the condition that H_0 is true.)

4. Determine the probability of obtaining the computed statistical value.

5. Compare the latter probability to the criterion for significance (usually .05 or .01).

Let's apply these steps to some problems.

1. Eleven separate parcels in Oswego County yield an average of 50 bushels of lettuce per season. Of course, some years are better than others, but some variability in yield is normal from one year to another because of variations in the weather, soil moisture levels, and the quality of the seed. The Cooperative Extension obtained an agreement from the owners of the parcels to make some systematic changes to their cultivation practices during the 2004-2005 growing season. After the final harvest, it was determined that the 11 parcels yielded an average of 52 bushels per acre. Was the increase in yield (over the traditional 50) significant? **The data appear on the "calculations" worksheet of workbook 6-2**.

How high above 52 did the mean have to be for the increase in yield to be significant? As you shall see, the answer to the latter question is not a simple one. It depends not only on how much of an increase there was in the crop yield, but also on the variability among the 11 data values. Let's make some systematic changes to the data to reveal the important relationships between features of data and statistical significance.

2. Using single digits, add a constant of your choice (for example, first try 3, then 5, then 7, etc.) to every value of the original "calculations" data array. How high does the mean have to be to achieve significance? What happens if we keep the mean at its present value and change the data in a manner to increase the variability? (Instructions are on the "calculations" worksheet of workbook 6-2.)

3. Now subtract 4 units from each value of the significant data set. This will likely render the analysis insignificant. But is it because the mean increase is too small or because there is excessive variability? If this were *your* research project, what measures could you take in an attempt to minimize the variability in yield among the parcels? (Think of variables that are likely to contribute to crop yield that are under the farmer's control, such as weed control, spacing of plants, pest control practices, etc.)

4. The "calculations" worksheet allows us to simulate a successful effort to reduce variability among the parcel crop yields. First let's record the value of the mean that is, for the time being, too close to 50 to be significant. Next, following the instruction on the worksheet, systematically reduce the variability in the data array. What happens to the ***t***-test result when we reduce the variability among the data values? What does this tell you about the importance of precision in research?

5. Regard the original data as the marksmanship scores of a random selection of 11 soldiers of a boot-camp brigade. They must average significantly better than the mean of 50 that they achieved on the previous day before the lieutenant will let them return to barracks. What will have to happen for the 11 soldiers to be successful? Can the good shooters "carry" the less skilled ones, or will they all have to improve in order to return to barracks? (maximum possible target score = 100). What if all their scores were uniformly in the mid 50s as opposed to the large spread in the skill they exhibited in their first set of 11 targets (see original data on "calculations" worksheet)?

Part II: Practice Testing Hypotheses

The following problems go beyond the single-sample ***t*** test used in the previous example. Other statistics covered in earlier folders (correlation [***r***], the binomial, and ***z***) are also suitable for testing certain kinds of hypotheses. Keep in mind that the statistical analysis you use for each specific problem will depend on the nature of the data and the question you are seeking to answer.

After reading each problem, state the null hypothesis (what the relevant statistic *should* equal if only chance is operating) and the alternative hypothesis, which supposes something *in addition* to chance is reflected in the data. The test you choose to run should enable you to decide whether it makes more sense to retain or reject the null hypothesis. By convention, we reject the null hypothesis when the ***p*** value yielded by the analysis is ≤ .05.

1. Suzy says she can pass any true-false test. She writes a "T" on the tip of her right index finger and an "F" on the tip of the middle finger. She claims that when she does not know the answer to a test question, she calls on her guardian spirit for help. Soon, one of her fingertips, the T or the F, will tingle to provide the answer.

To see if Suzy's method was really better than guessing, a researcher gave her a true-false test with 20 items in a subject Suzy knew nothing about – the physics of super conductivity. Suzy got 7 correct out of 20.

a. Does the outcome support the interpretation that Suzy is indeed being helped by a spirit?

b. How many items would Suzy have to answer correctly before you would be convinced that more than chance (Suzy's guardian spirit?) governed Suzy's answers on the test?

2. Fred has been training seals for many years. His carefully recorded and complete records indicate that seals take an average of 25 hours to learn a complex ball-toss trick. The standard deviation of the distribution of learning times equals 5. A recent group of 16 seals took an average of 28 hours to learn the trick. Was the mean 28-hour learning time significantly different from normal? Is the longer time (28 hours versus the usual 25) just a random event, or were the times for this last group of seals significantly longer than the historical average?

Let's compare the latter problem to #3.

3. Fred has been training seals for many years. Based on his experience, he hypothesizes that it will take the seals 25 hours to learn a complex ball-toss trick. A recent group of 16 seals learned the trick, and times to learning criterion were recorded. Was the actual mean time significantly different from the normal 25 hours? The data (hours to learning criterion) are below.

35, 27, 21, 24, 29, 27, 26, 28, 22, 24, 30, 28, 26, 31, 28, 33

4. Fred has been training seals for many years. Based on his experience, he hypothesizes that it will take the seals 25 hours to learn a complex ball-toss trick. A recent group of 50 seals learned the trick and times (in hours) to learning criterion were recorded. Was the average learning time significantly different from Fred's hunch? Here are the data for the 50 seals:

28	33	32	28	29	35	37	19	29	30
30	28	18	23	23	21	26	27	16	35
34	26	26	23	26	25	31	23	31	24
28	31	25	24	20	24	25	20	28	26
17	23	19	32	19	31	29	22	20	29

5. Fred has been training seals for many years. Based on his experience, the norm is for half the seals to learn a complex ball-toss trick within 20 hours of training. At the end of the 20 hours of training, 14 of the 20 seals had learned the trick. Did this most recent group of seals differ from the norm?

6. Fred kept careful records of how long it took a group of seals to learn a ball-toss trick. Then he trained them on a jumping trick. Was there a significant relationship between the ball-toss times and the jumping times? Will knowing how long it takes to teach a seal the ball-toss trick help to predict how long it will take that seal to learn the jumping trick?

	A	B	C	D	E	F	G	H	I	J	K	L	M	N	O	P
Ball Toss	35	27	25	24	29	27	26	32	30	24	30	33	26	31	28	33
Jump	33	15	15	22	32	30	23	20	26	25	35	29	23	34	32	37

7. Remembering the names of people we meet is difficult for some people. A new memory strategy is reputed to greatly enhance the retention of names. To test the method, a research participant who had been trained in the new memory technique was shown photographs of 25 faces along with the first name of the person in the photo. Each photo appeared for only two seconds. After a 30-min break, the same photos were randomized and shown again to the participant. This time, however, each photo was shown with TWO names – a correct name and an incorrect name. The task for the participant was to choose the correct name for the person in the photo.

a. If the participant correctly named 12 individuals, would you be convinced of the value of the new memory technique?

b. If the participant correctly named all 25 individuals correctly, would you be convinced of the value of the new memory technique?

c. What if 15 out of the 25 people were named correctly?

d. How many correct names would the participant have to choose before you were convinced that more than guessing was involved?

8. Absenteeism does vary from week to week in Creighton High, but over many years the average has been a fairly stable 36 per week. The standard deviation of the distribution of weekly absence scores is 5.0. Over the past 25 weeks, however, the average absenteeism was recorded as 38. Has absenteeism increased significantly, or is the rise a random "blip."

9. A dowser ("water witch") agreed to a scientific evaluation of her supposed ability to detect underground sources of water for drinking and irrigation. Twenty 500-gal. drums were buried in a 5 x 4 grid at a desert location. Each burial site was 100′ distant from the next closest one. Half of the drums were filled with water before closing the burial hole, and the other half remained empty. As the dowser walked the grid and passed over the barrels, she declared whether or not there was water below. Out of the 20, 15 barrels were correctly assessed as either empty or containing water. The dowser gave incorrect answers for the other five. Can the dowser really divine the presence of water to an extent more than just luck (chance) would predict?

10. The manufacturers of the 2002–2003 flu vaccine claimed that 80% of injected patients would pass through the flu season without getting sick. Out of 15 randomly selected people who received the shot, 6 got sick with the flu. Is what actually happened (40% got sick) compared to what was predicted to happen (20% get sick) explainable by chance alone, or was the 80% claim of the vaccine's effectiveness exaggerated?

11. The sick-leave data of one population of General Appliance factory workers show that on average they take 10 days of sick leave per year. (The distribution has a mean of 10 and a standard deviation of 3.) In an effort to shrink this number and add to company productivity, a pilot wellness program was initiated (group exercise and programming related to the use of drugs, alcohol, smoking, speeding, etc.). After one year, the sick-leave data of a random sample of 16 workers were retrieved from company files. The data showed that the mean sick leave taken by the sample was 8.5 days.

a. Do these data indicate that the wellness programming changed sick leave absences?

b. Redo the test of the hypothesis using alpha = .01 and assuming a sample size n=36 and the same mean absentee rate of 8.5 days. Consider "the cost of Type 1 error" as the criterion for using .05 versus .01.

c. What if the sample mean equaled 11.5 days? How could we account for a significant <u>increase</u> in absenteeism?

12. A manufacturing facility has historically put out an average of 70 widgets per worker per day. The plant manager thought she could improve productivity by introducing some changes to the assembly-line procedures. A group of 16 workers was randomly selected from the labor force and given special training. They then went back to work, and their widget assembly scores were recorded for one full day. The data appear below. Is there an indication that widget output went up to a significant degree following the training session?

79, 75, 73, 80, 81, 90, 71, 67, 68, 78, 76, 92, 73, 63, 61, 73

a. What is the null hypothesis?

b. What is the alternative (experimental) hypothesis?

c. What is the sample mean?

d. If the null hypothesis is true, what should you expect the sample mean to equal?

e. Is the difference between the sample mean and the value of the population mean (stated in the null hypothesis) a significant difference? Show the data analysis to support your conclusion, including the computed value for t, the critical value for t, and the p value for the t statistic.

f. What do the results of the statistical tests mean in the context of this problem? Based on these data, state your conclusions about the effect of the plant manager's changes on worker productivity.

g. Using the sample data above and the procedures described in workbook 6-3, construct an interval estimate of the mean of the population from which the sample was drawn.

Exercise 7-1: Inside the *t* Test

Introduction

The ***t*** test is likely to be the first statistical procedure that a student researcher in the behavioral sciences applies to real experimental data. That is because the ***t*** test accomplishes the objective of what is arguably the most fundamental of experimental designs: the comparison between two independent groups.

In one version of that design, subjects are randomly assigned either to a control group, which ***is not*** exposed to the experimental condition, or an experimental group, which ***is*** exposed to the experimental condition. Data are collected for the two groups (presumably some measure of behavior), and the task is to decide if the behavior of the two groups differed to a significant degree. If exposure versus no exposure to the experimental treatment is the only systematic difference between the two groups, any difference between the two group means is likely to be a consequence of the treatment rather than just chance.

But how big a difference must exist before we make the inference that there is a *significant* treatment effect? *Some* difference is likely to occur just through chance. Is the difference large enough to discount chance as a reasonable explanation? That is where the ***t*** test comes in. When two samples have different means, the ***t*** test is used to determine the probability that the difference between those means arose from chance. If the probability is $>.05$, we conclude that the difference between sample means *did* arise from chance. Expressed another way, when $p>.05$, it makes better sense to conclude that both samples came from the same population, and any apparent difference between the sample means is too small to attribute to an experimental effect.

But when the probability of the obtained difference is $\leq .05$, the difference between means is too large to regard as a chance phenomenon. Instead, we conclude that the samples came from two differently behaving populations: the population of treated participants and the population of control participants. In short, when the probability that an event will occur by chance is very low yet the event occurs *anyway*, it is more logical to conclude that something other than chance led to the event rather than conclude that chance alone was responsible.

Let's Flip

Consider how a coin-flipping experiment illustrates this basic concept. If a person tossed 10 heads in a row (an event with a probability of .001) it would make more sense to conclude that the coin was biased for heads than believe that the highly improbable event of 10 heads in a row had occurred. If the split were 6 heads and 4 tails (an event with a relatively high probability of .20), we would feel comfortable assuming that the outcome was driven by chance alone.

The initial assumption, that only chance is responsible for any difference between sample means, is called the *null hypothesis*. Rejection of the null hypothesis (because $p \leq .05$) leaves only the *alternative hypothesis* – the position that *something other than chance* is responsible for the difference between the sample means.

Review of the Contents of Workbook 7-1

1. One group of laboratory rats was treated with an experimental tranquilizer, and another group was treated with a placebo. The dependent variable was running-wheel activity.

a. The null hypothesis would be…

b. The alternative hypothesis would be…

2. The Cohen ***d*** statistic and the ω^2 statistic both quantify *effect size*, the degree to which the different treatments experienced by the two groups are responsible for the different values of the sample means. Complete the following items by circling the correct response.

a. As the difference between sample means grows larger, the computed *effect size*

is unaffected gets larger gets smaller

b. As the within-sample variability grows larger, the computed *effect size*

is unaffected gets larger gets smaller

3. It is possible for the difference between means to be quite large without achieving statistical significance. What feature of data would lead to that outcome? Check your answer using the "variability" worksheet of workbook 7-1. What circumstances in the research environment could lead to the undesirable situation of excessive within-treatment variability?

4. It is possible for the magnitude of the difference between sample means to be very small and yet achieve statistical significance. What feature of data would lead to that outcome? Check your answer using the "variability" worksheet of workbook 7-1. What circumstances in the research environment could lead to the desirable situation of minimal within-treatment variability?

5. The worksheets refer to a "critical value for ***t***." What must the relationship be between t_{obt} and t_{crit} for the comparison between sample means to be significant?

6. On the "treatment effect" worksheet what happened to the value of the ***t*** statistic as you increased the treatment effect? What happened to the ***p*** value?

7. On the "variability" worksheet, what happens to the effect size and the value of the ***t*** statistic when you

a. increase the **within**-sample variability?

b. decrease the **within**-sample variability?

8. On the "variability" worksheet, what happens to the values of the ***t*** statistic and ***p*** value when your changes to the data

a. increase the **between**-sample variability (i.e., increase the magnitude of the difference between means)?

b. decrease the **between**-sample variability (i.e., decrease the magnitude of the difference between means)?

9. A researcher compared two methods of toilet training baby girls by randomly assigning mothers who volunteered for the study to use either method A or method B.

a. State the researcher's null hypothesis.

b. After doing the *t*-test analysis, the decision was to reject the null hypothesis. What is the logical conclusion regarding the observed difference between the Method A (Group 1) and Method B (Group 2) means? Was the difference just chance? Were the means too close in value to suggest any difference between the two groups? Or was one method truly superior to the other?

c. Does the low ***p*** value and consequent rejection of the null hypothesis guarantee the accuracy of the conclusion? Have we "proven" that one method is better than the other? Explain.

10. Which choice below correctly completes the following sentence:

The expressions $\mu_1 - \mu_2 = 0$ and $\mu_1 = \mu_2$

a. represent the idea that both samples came from the same population.

b. represent the idea that the means of the two samples differ only because of chance, not because of an effect linked to the experimental treatment.

c. are two ways to state the null hypothesis in the context of the two-sample t test.

d. all of the above.

11. If you complete the demonstration that allows you to hold the difference **between** sample means constant while letting the **within**-sample variability grow larger, the likelihood of achieving statistical significance will grow (smaller / larger).

12. Determining the value of "degrees of freedom" is a necessary step for determining the critical value for the ***t*** statistic. How are degrees of freedom (***df***) computed for the two-sample ***t*** test?

Exercise 7-2: Estimating Error

1. Theoretically, when the null hypothesis is true, the mean of the distribution of $\overline{\mathbf{X}}_1 - \overline{\mathbf{X}}_2$ difference scores will equal ________. The deviation measure of the distribution of difference scores, the "standard error of the difference," can be computed using the expression (write the formula in the space provided):

2. What feature of the SE_{diff} formula reveals that the SE_{diff} is computed by "pooling" information about variability from the two separate samples?

3. Rerun the "experiment" worksheet in workbook 7-2 three times. Report the random seed you used, the estimate of the standard error of the difference (SE_{diff}) that emerged from your data, and the mean of the distribution of difference scores.

Random seed = _______ SE_{diff} = _______ Distribution mean = _______

Random seed = _______ SE_{diff} = _______ Distribution mean = _______

Random seed = _______ SE_{diff} = _______ Distribution mean = _______

4. As instructed on the "error term" worksheet, copy and paste two samples from the "experiment" worksheet. Record the output of the SE_{diff} formula. Repeat the process 5 times. How close did you get to the theoretically expected value of 4.472? Did your formula outputs tend to overestimate or underestimate the theoretically expected value?

Exercise 7-3: The Paired-Samples *t* Test

1. As explained on the first worksheet of Exercise 7-3, we assume correlation is present between two samples when the data are collected on the same participants or on pairs of participants who have been matched on some personal attribute or performance measure. Is this a reasonable assumption? Why would you expect students who do well on a midterm to continue to do well on the final examination?

2. When you changed data values as suggested on the "switch" worksheet, the computed value of the *t* statistic also changed. What did that change tell you about the impact of between-sample correlation on the results of the paired-samples *t* test?

3. Did anything happen to the computed value of the *t* statistic when you completed the same suggested switch of data values on the "independent" worksheet?

4. Why did the same change of data values have different effects on the two versions of the *t* test?

5. If the null hypothesis is true (both samples selected from the same population), we expect the difference between the two sample means to equal _______.

6. On the "computations" worksheet, what Excel paste function did the formula (in blue) use to compute the variability (Sum of Squares or "SS") among the difference scores?

7. With the SS value in hand, what further mathematical operations were required to compute the standard error of the difference?

8. For the analysis on the computations worksheet, the computed value of the *t* statistic (t_{obt}) must be ________ units above or below zero to be significant.

9. From the *t*-test results shown on the computations worksheet (original data), what would your interpretation be regarding the relative difficulty of the two examinations?

10. Use Excel's TTEST paste function to check your ability to arrive at the same result shown in cell **I10**. Then take the TTEST output, which is a probability value, and use the TINV function to find the value of t_{obt}. Are your test results the same as shown on the worksheet? (Select cells **I10**, **I11**, and **I12**, then click f_x. The three dialog boxes will appear with the correct entries.)

11. What happens to the results of the paired-samples *t* test as within-sample variability increases?

12. On the "M1-M2 difference" worksheet, did the standard error (denominator of the *t* formula) change as you increased the effect size between the samples? If not, why not?

Exercise 7-4: Statistical Power

The power of a test refers to its ability to show a statistically significant result when the null hypothesis is false and should be rejected. Workbook 7-4 encourages you to explore how specific features of data affect statistical power. Here are several settings for the workbook 7-4 experiments that, together, demonstrate the key relationships between effect size, within-sample variability, and power. The first five experiments use worksheet "n=10" in *ESC* workbook 7-4.

	Population Mean	Treatment Effect	Within-Treatment Variability	Comments
Experiment **1**	50	0	20	The null hypothesis is true. Look for Type 1 errors.
Experiment **2**	50	5	50	Weak effect, high variability. Look for Type 2 errors. Out of 20 data sets, how many $\overline{\mathbf{X}}_1 - \overline{\mathbf{X}}_2$ differences were large enough to be statistically significant?
Experiment **3**	50	5	10	Weak effect, low variability. Out of 20 data sets, how many comparisons were significant? Was power held down by weak effect and small sample size?

Compare the results of experiments 2 and 3. In which experiment was power more evident – in the weak effect-high variability configuration or the weak effect-low variability configuration?

Experiment **4**	50	20	50	Strong effect, high variability. Look for Type 2 errors. Did the high variability result in many Type 2 errors? Compare the frequency of Type 2 error to Experiment 3, which had the same variability, but a weak treatment effect.
Experiment **5**	50	10	25	Moderate effect, moderate variability. Power will be relatively low because of the small sample size. When you redo the experiment on the next worksheet using a larger sample size, you will see fewer Type 2 errors.

Now switch to the "n=20" worksheet in *ESC* workbook 7-4.

Experiment **6**	50	10	25	Compare these results with the previous experiment (5), which had the same settings but a smaller (***n***=10) sample size.
Experiment **7**	50	5	10	Compare these results to those of experiment 3, which used the same settings but a smaller (***n***=10) sample size.
Experiment **8**	50	5	50	Compare these results with those of experiment 2, which used a small treatment effect and high variability. Are there fewer Type 2 errors here with ***n***=20?

Now switch to the "n=50" worksheet in *ESC* workbook 7-4.

Experiment **9**	50	5	50	To what extent did this large sample size (***n***=50) overcome the weak effect and the high variability that was evident in Experiment 2? Do you see as many Type 2 errors here?
Experiment **10**	50	0	50	Here, the treatment effect is zero (null is true), but ***n*** is large. When the sample size is large, are you any less vulnerable to Type 1 error?

As you change from relatively small to large sample sizes,

a. do the sample means tend to be nearer to the population mean of 50?

b. does the difference between the two sample means become smaller as the sample sizes grow larger?

Both of the latter results are expected because the sample mean becomes a more precise estimate of the population mean as the sample size grows larger (see workbook 4-2).

After completing the workbook 7-4 experiments, review by answering the following questions.

1. In your own words, explain the concept of statistical power.

2. What properties of data are consistent with a high degree of statistical power?

3. What characteristics of data are consistent with a low degree of statistical power?

4. When a high level of power is present, how does that affect the likelihood of making a Type 2 error?

5. When a low level of power is present, how does that affect the likelihood of making a Type 2 error?

6. In ESC workbook 7-4, what tends to happen to the value of the ***t*** statistic and the effect size statistic when, for a specific $\overline{\mathbf{X}}_1-\overline{\mathbf{X}}_2$ treatment effect,

   a. you set the within-sample variability to a higher level?

   b. you set the within-sample variability to a lower level?

7. In ESC workbook 7-4, what happens to the value of the ***t*** statistic and the effect size statistic when, for a specific level of variability,

   a. you increase the $\overline{\mathbf{X}}_1-\overline{\mathbf{X}}_2$ treatment effect?

   b. you decrease the $\overline{\mathbf{X}}_1-\overline{\mathbf{X}}_2$ treatment effect?

8. In ESC workbook 7-4, what tends to happen to the value of the ***t*** statistic and the effect size statistic when you increase the sample size from 10 to 50 but hold the treatment effect and variability inputs constant?

9. In ESC workbook 7-4, what tends to happen to the value of the ***t*** statistic and the effect size statistic when you decrease the sample size from 50 to 10 but hold the treatment effect and variability inputs constant?

Exercise 7-5: Independent Groups versus Paired Samples

Workbook 7-5 explains how the ***t*** test we use to compare two independent groups differs from the ***t*** test we use when the design includes repeated measures or matched groups. The two samples shown below in problem 1 are independent groups of research participants, and the two samples in problem 2 are paired samples – repeated measures on the same participants. Before performing the ***t*** tests on these data sets, the questions below direct you to engage in the same partition of total variability that was demonstrated in workbook 7-5. This experience will make you more aware of how truly different the two versions of the ***t*** test are and why it is important to select the correct version for the analysis of a two-treatment experiment.

Behavior Modification	Drug Therapy
70	63
71	61
66	62
54	48
56	52
65	61
63	59
66	62
74	52
57	71
80	75
66	62
54	50
71	75
68	62

1. A researcher compared the effectiveness of two treatment protocols for Attention Deficit Disorder in children. Thirty children identified as ADD were randomly assigned to one of two treatment conditions. In the behavior modification condition, inappropriate behaviors were ignored, and appropriate behaviors were rewarded. The hope was that the ADD children could learn to replace their inappropriate behaviors with appropriate behaviors.

The second therapeutic approach was biologically based. The children took a drug to help them stay on task more effectively. After two weeks of behavior modification or drug therapy, a psychologist tested the children and assigned an attention score (on a 100-point scale). The higher the score, the more the children were able to stay on task.

a. Treat the 30 data values of the experiment as one combined set and compute the Sum of Squares. Using the DEVSQ paste function on the 30 values, SS_{Total} = __________.

b. Use DEVSQ to determine the $SS_{within\ treatment}$ separately for the 15 behavior modification scores (sample 1) and the 15 drug scores (sample 2): SS_1 = __________ and SS_2 = __________.

Now **add** the SS_1 and SS_2 values and write the $SS_{within\ treatment}$ here: ________________.

c. Next, using the AVERAGE paste function, compute the means of the two samples.

The means are _______ and _________.

d. Use DEVSQ to compute the Sum of Squares for the two sample means. Remember, we must multiply the output of DEVSQ by ***n***, the sample size (here, 15) as described on the "DEVSQ" worksheet of workbook 7-5. This step is necessary because we put <u>*means*</u> into the DEVSQ function and we must express the variability in <u>*raw score*</u> terms just as we did above for the $SS_{within\ treatment}$. ____________

e. Does the sum of the answers you filled in to items **b** and **d** above equal the answer you gave to item **a**, the SS_{Total}?

f. Which of the two measures of variability, the $SS_{within\ treatment}$ or the $SS_{between\ treatment}$, is considered "error" variability and which reflects the magnitude of the treatment effect?

g. The independent groups ***t*** test on these hypothetical data shows that ...(Be sure to back up your conclusion with the results of the independent groups ***t*** test.)

Before going on to problem 2 (next page), keep in mind that in the independent groups design we partitioned the SS_{Total} into only *two* parts: the $SS_{within\ treatment}$ and the $SS_{between\ treatment}$.

2. Now consider the following paired-samples scenario. We have two sets of examination scores from a class of 15 students. Each row of the table represents the grades of one student. *As you may have noticed, the values used to represent the examination scores in problem 2 are the same values used for the attention data in problem 1.*

Was performance on the two examinations essentially the same, or did student performance differ? Before testing that hypothesis, let's partition the variability of these data in a fashion similar to what we did above for the independent-groups experiment. (See the "related" worksheet in workbook 7-5.)

Exam 1	**Exam 2**
70	63
71	61
66	62
54	48
56	52
65	61
63	59
66	62
74	52
57	71
80	75
66	62
54	50
71	75
68	62

a. The SS_{Total} = ____________.

b. The $SS_{between\ exams}$ = ____________.

c. Compute a mean for each row of data. As you may remember, an easy way to do this in Excel is to paste the AVERAGE paste function in the cell to the right of the first row of data, then drag the cell's fill handle (lower right corner of the cell) down to the last row of the table. This operation copies the formula to all 15 cells.

The row means are: ______________________________.

d. Now put the 15 row means into the DEVSQ function and multiply the DEVSQ output by **2** to restore the SS value to raw score terms. (Each row mean is the mean of **2** data values.)

The variability (SS) among the row means is ________. This value represents that portion of the SS_{Total} that is attributable to **systematic individual differences**.

e. Now add the SS values you recorded as your answers to questions **b** and **d** and subtract the sum from the SS_{Total}. This is the residual component – the variability that is left over or unaccountable (due neither to the column variable [exam 1 versus 2] or systematic individual differences. The residual (error) equals ________.

f. Compare the estimate of error you computed above ("residual") to the estimate of error you computed for item **b** in problem 1, the $SS_{within\ treatment}$. Given that the two data sets contained identical values, what accounts for the two different estimates of error?

g. Do the answers to **b**, **c**, and **d** add up to the SS_{Total} that you computed for item **a**?

h. What are the null and alternative hypotheses regarding the comparison of the two sets of examination scores?

i. Using the paired-samples ***t*** test, compare the mean on Exam 1 to the mean of Exam 2. What is your conclusion? Be sure to back up your conclusion with the results of your paired-samples ***t*** test.

j. Given that the hypothetical data used for problems 1 and 2 are identical, why was ***t*** significant for problem 2 and not for problem 1?

Periodic Review 3:

Two-Treatment Practice Problems

Start each problem by stating the null and alternative hypotheses along with a justification for your choice of data analysis (independent or related samples). Then explain how the results of your data analysis reflect on the research issue at hand.

1. A pharmaceutical company research team compared two drugs that have chemical properties consistent with an anti-anxiety effect. An animal model (the laboratory rat) was used to collect behavioral data relating to the two drugs. Twenty animals were randomly divided into two groups. Group 1 was treated with Drug A, a medication currently on the market for use in lowering anxiety. Group 2 was treated with Drug B, an experimental drug that has not yet been approved for use by humans.

Rats tend to be inactive when anxious and may even freeze in position when stressed. Calm rats explore and move about much more readily. Therefore activity may be used to reflect underlying anxiety. The data are the activity scores for the 20 animals. Did the activity of the two treated groups differ?

Drug A	**Drug B**
60	57
87	69
92	56
62	66
48	42
55	54
93	89
74	56
39	44
88	74

2. Ten retail stores in Central City reported their average monthly gross sales (in thousands) for the six months before and after the opening of a "big-box superstore" in the community. Did their gross sales change after the new superstore opened?

Store	**First 6 months**	**Second 6 months**
A	40	57
B	67	69
C	72	56
D	42	66
E	28	42
F	35	54
G	73	89
H	54	56
I	19	44
J	68	74

3. The Defense Department ordered a study of the relative effectiveness of two seasickness remedy delivery systems. Once in rough seas, personnel on 10 randomly chosen ships of a 20-vessel U.S. Navy convoy wore a special medicated patch behind an ear. Personnel on the other 10 ships took the same medication orally. The data reflect the percentage of sailors on each ship who suffered from seasickness one or more times during the rough-seas test interval. Was there a difference in seasickness between the Patch and Pill groups?

Patch	**Pill**
50	41
45	26
72	36
22	46
59	27
45	34
41	19
27	26
34	49
78	22

4. A botanist controlled an experimental plot that contained 20 five-year old blueberry bushes – two bushes for each of 10 different hybrid varieties. One randomly selected bush of each variety was treated with Acidophile, a newly developed liquid fertilizer for acid-loving plants. The second bush of each pair received the usual granular fertilizer. The data represent the number of blueberries harvested from each of the 20 bushes. Did the Acidophile-treated bushes yield more fruit?

Hybrid	Acidophile	Granular
A	120	117
B	147	129
C	152	116
D	122	102
E	108	102
F	115	114
G	153	149
H	134	104
I	99	104
J	148	134

5. A group of 22 female infants was randomly divided into two groups. The mothers of Group A agreed to use the Conte method for toilet training their children, and the mothers of Group B agreed to use the Finkel method. The data (next page) represent the months of age it took the girls to achieve one "accident free" week. Was there a difference between the two methods with respect to the age at which toilet training was achieved? Use α=.05. Why were the participants restricted to one gender?

Training Method	
Conte	**Finkel**
26	24
18	19
19	18
26	24
30	26
17	14
34	26
28	25
24	21
27	24
22	24

6. The Director of Security for a chain of eleven retail stores did a study comparing arrests for shoplifting for a one-month period prior to the installation of a new high-tech security system to the number of arrests in the same stores for the one-month period following installation of the new system. Substantial publicity accompanied installation of the new system. ("To control costs and better serve our shoppers we are installing...") Analyze the data in the following table to evaluate the effectiveness (or lack thereof) of the announced change in security systems. Use α=.05

	Security System	
Store	**Old**	**New**
1	34	26
2	28	25
3	24	21
4	27	24
5	22	24
6	26	24
7	18	19
8	19	18
9	26	24
10	30	26
11	17	14

7. Thirteen laboratory rats were tested twice for activity in a running-wheel apparatus. (Each row of the table represents the scores of one animal.) The data reflect the number of wheel revolutions the rats ran during each of the

Trial 1	Trial 2
70	65
74	59
81	62
63	48
56	37
65	73
47	32
66	42
54	62
57	66
80	86
66	52
54	44

testing periods. Was there a significant change in activity level from trial 1 to trial 2?

For this research problem:

a. The null hypothesis is:

b. The alternative hypothesis is:

c. I analyzed these data using the ______________________ test because …

d. State your conclusions in the context of the problem, being careful to back them up with the appropriate statistics.

Exercise 8-1: The ANOVA Model

Introduction

Workbook 8-1 demonstrates the underlying model of the single-factor analysis of variance ("ANOVA"), which is used to compare the means of multiple independent groups. In the special environment of the Excel spreadsheet, you will be able to manipulate the size of treatment effects, the extent of within-sample variability, and the sample size so you can see instantly how these features of data are reflected in the ANOVA's statistical output.

Relevance to Research Design

Of the three features subject to manipulation in these Excel worksheets (sample size, treatment effect, and within-sample variability), all are under some degree of control in a real research environment. Using precise, consistent, and carefully crafted research methodology can have a substantial impact on within-sample ("error") variability. Sample size is often limited by practical considerations (time, money, and other limited resources). But once you see how important adequate sample size is for power, you may be encouraged to make the extra effort to ensure an adequate sample size. The decision about what the different treatments will be in your experiment (for example, what doses to give the different groups in a drug study) will clearly affect the ANOVA for your data. It is necessary to become as familiar as possible with published research related to your project so you will have the knowledge base necessary to guide your selection of treatment conditions.

After digesting the content of workbook 8-1, tackle the following questions.

---

1. The theoretical model of the one-way analysis of variance represents the value of each individual datum as a composite of three entities:

   a. the value of the population mean from which the datum was drawn,

   b. the contribution of a treatment effect, which, if present, acts to increase or decrease the value of the datum, and

   c. the contribution of any random factors (chance) that affect the value of the datum.

In the space below, write the formula that represents this theoretical model.

2. The one-way ANOVA allows us to evaluate whether

a. several samples were all drawn from the same population

or

b. one or more of the samples was/were drawn from different populations.

Which statement, **a** or **b**, represents the null hypothesis?

3. What characteristics of data affect the ability of the one-way ANOVA to retain or reject the null hypothesis?

4. On the "interactive demo" worksheet, each press of the <**delete**> key generates new sample data. The instructions specify the selection of cell D5 before typing <**delete**> so users will not arbitrarily select just any empty cell and possibly experience unintended scrolling away from the main display. Otherwise, there is nothing special about cell D5.

You will notice that, with the original settings for the treatment effects (0, 2, and 5) and error variability (20), some experiments show a significant difference among the samples, and others do not. The failures to find a difference among the sample means are examples of Type ___ errors.

5. If you change the treatment effects (τ_j values) so that all three are the same and the comparison among the sample means, nevertheless, shows a statistically significant difference between treatments, that is a Type ___ error.

6. With equal treatment effects, out of 20 sets of computer-generated data (i.e., 20 presses of the <**delete**> key) we expect ____ experiment(s) to show statistical significance among the treatments just by chance.

7. Try increasingly diverse values for the treatment effects until you can reliably get the experiments to show statistical significance ($p \le .05$). Then increase the value for variability (ε_{ij}) and generate several new sets of data – by selecting cell D5 and typing the <**delete**> key. What happened to the frequency of statistically significant results? Were there more or fewer significant outcomes?

8. Reduce the differences among the treatment effect (τ_j) values until, with repeated experiments, you obtain only an occasional instance of statistical significance. Then reduce the value for variability and generate several sets of new data by selecting cell D5 and typing the <**delete**> key. What happened to the frequency of statistically significant results?

For 9 to 13, circle the correct answer to complete the sentence.

9. When you used treatment-effect values that were numerically close to each other, statistical significance was possible to achieve only if the within-sample variability was *large / small*.

10. When the within-sample variability is high, the differences among the three values for treatment effect must be *minimal / large* to have a chance at achieving statistical significance.

11. Given the existence of some treatment effects, the computed effect size will tend to *decrease / increase* as the within-sample variability increases, and the ***p*** value will *increase / decrease*.

12. Given the existence of some treatment effects, the computed effect size will tend to *decrease / increase* as the within-sample variability decreases, and the ***p*** value will *increase / decrease*.

13. For a given degree of random variability, the computed effect size will *increase / decrease* as the treatment effects grow, and the ***p*** value will *increase / decrease*.

---

14. What Excel paste function is applied in the "interactive demo" worksheet to compute the within- and between-sample variability for the sample data?

15. In words, explain how the ***df*** values, the MS values, and the ***F*** values that appear in the ANOVA Summary Table are computed.

16. When the null hypothesis is true (i.e., there are no treatment effects, so all samples are drawn from the same population), what is the expected value of the ***F*** statistic?

17. In the "your sample size" worksheet you are invited to take one sample from each of three populations. The means of the three populations are, respectively, 50, 54, and 58. Do an experiment with a small sample, and then do another with a large sample. Analyze both data sets using Excel's ANOVA: Single Factor tool. How does sample size affect the ANOVA's capacity to show that the three samples were drawn from different populations?

Exercise 8-2: The Single-Factor ANOVA: Related versus Independent Samples

Introduction

Workbook 8-2 presents data from four trials of a memory task. The pie charts in the display represent the total variability among all the data values. Depending on whether the data are cast in the model of independent groups or related samples (repeated measures on the same participants), the ANOVA slices up the pie of total variability differently. The most noteworthy end result is the two different methods for calculating error variability. In your coverage of workbook 8-2 be sure to note the objectives that are on the last ("Summary") worksheet. Go back as necessary to view the relationships between the data and ANOVA results noted in the summary.

For the experiment described in Workbook 8-2:

1. State the null hypothesis in your own words.

2. State the alternative hypothesis in your own words.

3. The conclusion for the related samples design (using the original data) is:

4. The conclusion for the independent groups analysis of the same original data is:

5. What accounts for the two different sets of ANOVA results? (Clearly, it is not due to any difference in the treatment effect, which is the same for both analyses.)

6. What output value in the two ANOVA output tables (independent and related) reflects the variability attributable to differences among the sample means?

7. What output value in these same two tables reflects the variability among the data values that is from random sources (error)?

8. The result of the independent groups analysis of the original data is not significant. Without changing the values of the column means, what feature of the data would have to change in order for the independent groups analysis to yield a significant result? (See "Preview" worksheet.)

Exercise 8-3: Unplanned Comparisons

Introduction

After using a single-factor ANOVA to compare the means of multiple samples and finding a significant ***F*** ratio, we know at that point that there is at least one sample mean that is significantly different from some other sample mean. We do not, however, know the specific pattern of significant and insignificant differences among the sample means. As the introduction to workbook 8-3 points out, we can often make an educated guess about which difference(s) contributed to the significant ***F*** statistic by inspecting the treatment means. The two treatment means that are furthest apart are likely to stand out as major contributors to the significant ***F*** ratio.

Workbook 8-3 begins with an examination of what can happen when the smallest and largest means alone are compared without due consideration as to whether the comparison was planned or unplanned. The planned versus unplanned distinction is important because the probability of Type 1 error climbs dramatically as the number of unplanned comparisons increases.

Statisticians have devised a number of solutions for the problem of alpha level inflation. The workbook presents one such solution, the Tukey HSD test. The workbook includes examples for both the independent and repeated measures scenarios. After running *ESC* workbook 8-3, test yourself with the following questions.

1. Comparisons between treatment means that were not planned prior to running the experiment and/or are not logically linked to the experimental hypothesis are called

   a. post hoc comparisons.
   b. a posteriori comparisons.
   c. after-the-fact comparisons.
   d. all the above

2. The more unplanned comparisons we make between pairs of treatment means, the greater will be

   a. the probability of making a Type 1 error.
   b. the probability of making a Type 2 error.
   c. the revelation of valuable information.
   d. the power of the test.

3. When doing all possible comparisons between pairs of means,

   a. the Tukey HSD test limits the probability of Type 1 error to .05.
   b. at least one comparison will show statistical significance.
   c. all will show statistical significance if the ***F*** ratio is large enough.
   d. never do more than k-1 comparisons.

4. When doing all possible unplanned paired comparisons among 6 treatment means, _____ comparisons are possible and the probability of a Type 1 error equals _____. (See the "real alpha level" worksheet.)

5. When you followed the directions on the "experiment" worksheet, what was the ***p*** value for the ***t*** statistic that compared the treatment conditions with the smallest and largest means? Was it significant?

6. What was the ***p*** value when you computed the ***t*** statistic for ***any*** two samples selected at random from the set of 10? Was it higher than the ***p*** value reported in answer to question 5? Was it significant?

7. Chances are your answers to 5 and 6 above are quite different. Do you know why?

8. For each ANOVA in "Periodic Review 4" for which you find a significant ***F*** ratio, use the Tukey HSD to compare all possible pairs of treatment means. Consult the last two worksheets of workbook 8-3 ("independent" and "related") as necessary to complete the HSD computation.

Periodic Review 4:
Single-Factor ("one-way") ANOVA

I. A researcher conducted a field trial on an experimental medication for people who suffer from insomnia. Participants were randomly divided into 5 groups: Untreated, Placebo, Low Dose, Moderate Dose, and High Dose, as shown in the table below. The participants slept for 5 consecutive days in a special laboratory where their sleep was physiologically monitored by an EEG machine. The DV was the number of minutes spent in Stage 4 sleep.

First, state the null and alternative hypotheses. Then analyze these data and offer your conclusions concerning the effectiveness of the sleep medication to induce stage 4 sleep. Be sure to back up your conclusions with the appropriate statistics from the ANOVA and Tukey tests.

Untreated	Placebo	Low Dose	Moderate Dose	High Dose
65	54	86	101	71
59	57	71	78	96
65	52	39	73	108
68	80	80	76	100
63	92	60	77	75
76	93	71	81	101
47	68	84	54	70

Null:

Alternative:

Conclusions:

With regard to problem I:

1. What are the numerical values of the means that you are evaluating for a statistically significant difference, and what number on your output tells you whether there is a significant difference among the means?

2. Your output shows that the means for the five drug conditions are not exactly equal. How does the null hypothesis account for the differences among the means?

3. When the null hypothesis is true, the expected value for the **F** statistic equals _______.

4. What specific number in your output reflects the portion of the variability among the 35 data values that is due to chance?

5. What specific number in your ANOVA table reflects the portion of the variability among the 35 data values that is due to the IV (different doses)?

6. Excel divided one variance ("MS") by another to compute the **F** statistic. Specifically, Excel divided ______ by _______ to compute the **F** statistic.

II. Some physical therapy, although ultimately effective, does not offer an immediate therapeutic effect. The patient must be treated over several weeks, or even months, before experiencing significant improvement. The data below track the progress of 6 patients who were undergoing therapy to increase range of motion following a knee injury. The range of motion of the "good" (uninjured) leg was used to estimate full range of motion. So, for example, a data point of 46 means that the injured leg had 46% of the range of motion of the patient's good leg. Analyze these data to evaluate the effectiveness of the therapy over the three biweekly periods.

		Weeks of Therapy		
Patient	**Baseline**	**Two**	**Four**	**Six**
1	46	64	63	61
2	60	55	66	71
3	61	41	52	49
4	55	48	58	61
5	51	60	68	64
6	62	60	66	76

Null:

Alternative:

Conclusions:

With regard to problem II:

7. What are the numerical values of the means (see your output) that you are evaluating for a statistically significant difference, and what number on your output tells you if there is a significant difference among the means?

8. According to your output, what is the probability that chance is responsible for the variability among the data values?

9. What specific value(s) reported in your ANOVA table represents the portion of the variability among the 24 data values that is due to the "weeks of therapy" IV?

10. What specific value reported in your output represents the portion of the variability among the 24 data values that is due to systematic individual differences among the research participants?

11. Differences among treatment means may be numerically very large without being statistically significant. This could happen if the error variability is …

12. The differences among the treatment means may be very small and still be statistically significant. This could happen if the error variability is …

Exercise 9-1: Interpreting Results

Introduction

Workbook 9-1 presents several possible outcomes of a fictional 2 x 4 factorial experiment along with a chart, ANOVA, and a statement pointing out a key feature of each data set. The two levels of Factor A are defined by the clients' receiving one-on-one therapy (A_1) versus group therapy (A_2), and the four levels of Factor B are defined by attendance at therapy once (B_1), twice (B_2), three (B_3), or four (B_4) times per week. As a two-factor experimental design, each participant experiences two treatments: one level of Factor A and one level of Factor B. Each factor can have many different levels, and this adds substantially to the potential complexity of research results.

Workbook 9-1 will give you the foundation for interpreting several possible patterns of research results. Then, in the next workbook (9-2), Excel's dynamic calculations will give you the opportunity to create, display, and interpret any number of hypothetical data sets. The objective of workbook 9-1 is to draw attention to features of data that reside in the ANOVA's statistical output and in charts of the cell means. Workbook 9-2 will help you understand how the features you incorporate into the data are reflected in the statistical output of the ANOVA. Interpreting statistical output can be quite challenging, and the workbooks in folder 9 will give you valuable practice and help you develop insight into the process.

---

1. What are the independent variables (IVs or "factors") and dependent variable (DV) for the experiment described in workbook 9-1?

2. What are the <u>null</u> hypotheses with respect to the main effects of the two IVs?

3. What are the <u>experimental</u> hypotheses with respect to the main effects of the two IVs?

4. In the context of the present experiment, which of the following describes a pattern of results that would be consistent with an interaction between the two IVs?

   a. One factor is influencing the DV more than the other.
   b. The influence of one factor on behavior differs (i.e., is inconsistent) across the levels of the second factor.
   c. The answer to the question, "Which therapy is best?" would be, "It depends on how many weeks of therapy the patients experienced."
   d. **b** and **c**, but not **a.**

5. What is the null hypothesis with respect to the interaction effect between the two IVs?

6. According to the **null** hypothesis, what accounts for the differences between the two row means and among the four column means of the AB Summary of Means table? (The AB Summary of Means table is at the bottom of the workbook 9-1 worksheets. Scroll as necessary to see these tables.)

7. According to the **experimental** hypotheses, what accounts for differences between the two row means and among the four column means of the AB Summary of Means table?

8. Assume the three null hypotheses are all <u>true</u>. Give as accurate a verbal description as you can of the chart you expect to see when you plot the cell means.

9. Assume that there is a significant A main effect. In your own words, describe the chart you expect to see when you create a chart of the eight cell means.

10. Assume that there is a significant B main effect. In your own words, describe the chart you expect to see when you create a chart of the eight cell means.

11. Assume that there is a significant AxB interaction. In your own words, describe the chart you expect to see when you create a chart of the eight cell means.

12. In a two-factor design for independent groups, how many sources of variability among the data values can the ANOVA identify? What are these sources of variability in the present problem?

13. Why run a **two**-factor experiment in which you manipulate two variables simultaneously? Why not just do two separate single-factor (one-way) experiments?

Exercise 9-2: Creating Patterns

Workbook 9-2 initially shows a hypothetical set of results from a two-factor experiment for which the null hypothesis is true: there is no main effect for either factor, and there is no interaction between the two factors. Then, using two separate approaches (the "quick change" and "your sample data" worksheets), workbook 9-2 allows you to introduce systematic changes to the original data to simulate main and interaction effects. Creating main effects and interaction effects on the demonstration worksheets will make you more likely to recognize and understand these effects when you encounter similar patterns in real research contexts. Refer back as necessary to workbook 9-1 to review the features of data that the ANOVA represents as significant main effects and interactions.

1. Using the "quick change" worksheet, alter the original data (for which the null hypothesis is true) so the ANOVA reports a significant A main effect.

2. Using the "quick change" worksheet, alter the original data (null hypothesis true) so the ANOVA reports a significant B main effect.

3. Using the "quick change" worksheet, alter the original data (null hypothesis true) so the ANOVA reports a significant AxB interaction.

4. Go to the "your sample data" worksheet. One by one, start subtracting a single-digit constant (5 is a reasonable choice) from the values in the second row ("Group Therapy") of the table until the F ratio for the A main effect just passes the threshold of significance ($p \leq .05$). Check the ANOVA Summary Table following each change to track your progress.

Then, to demonstrate the role within-sample variability plays in the determination of statistical significance, add a constant to the highest value in each cell and subtract that same constant to the lowest value in each cell. This will not change the Group Therapy cell means or the appearance of the chart on the "your chart" worksheet... but what happens to the A main effect? Check the ANOVA Summary Table. As you shall see, an increase in within-cell variability can mask an experimental effect, which is why researchers work so hard to keep it under control with precise and consistent administration of both independent variables.

5. Go to the "your sample data" worksheet. As you did for the previous

exercise, start subtracting a constant from the values in the second row ("Group Therapy") of the table, but stop before the A main effect passes the threshold of significance. Check the ANOVA Summary Table following each change to track your progress. Now subtract a constant from the highest value in each of the four Group Therapy cells and add that same constant to the lowest value. What effect did the reduction of within-sample variability have on the ANOVA results?

6. Pick an AB Summary of Means table and, using Excel's Chart Wizard, create a properly proportioned chart from the cell means.

Exercise 9-3: Computational Method for the Two-Factor ANOVA

Apply the computational method detailed in workbook 9-3 to the following problem.

Part I. After a person takes medicine, perceived relief from uncomfortable physical symptoms has long been known to be, at least in part, a psychological phenomenon unrelated to the medicine itself. It is called the placebo effect.

A researcher conducted an experiment to explore the possibility that the appearance of a medicinal tablet would influence perceived pain relief. Perhaps, the researcher hypothesized, an unusual shape (diamond, triangular, etc.) or unusual color would lead consumers to assume that the drug must be very new and the product of the most modern scientific efforts. This perception might, in turn, lead to an increased expectation that the therapy would have a powerful and desirable result and enhance the placebo effect.

The 16 participants were male volunteers all of whom had a medically necessary unilateral hernia repair within 2 hours before the beginning of the experiment. Participants were told to take 2 tablets and, one hour later, were asked, "What percentage of your original pain still persists?" Tablets were either round like generic aspirin tablets or diamond shaped. In addition, the tablets were either white or mixed color (blue on one side and green on the other). In all cases, the tablets consisted of ordinary Tylenol.

Do a statistical analysis to determine if there is any evidence that the appearance of the tablet affected the degree of post-surgical pain relief. Present the results of your data analysis using two tables: an AB Summary of Means and an ANOVA Summary Table.

		Shape	
		Round	**Diamond**
Color	**White**	73	85
		72	70
		76	55
		66	75
	Blue/ Green	81	50
		54	55
		75	60
		66	40

These data represent the participants' response to the researcher's question about pain relief.

Part II

1. What number from the ANOVA Summary Table tells you how much of the variability among the data values is attributable to the Shape IV?

2. Which of the three *F* ratios reported by the ANOVA is significant?

3. Write a statement of conclusion in the context of the present research problem, which is an exploration of the possible effect of shape and color on the placebo effect.

Exercise 9-4: The Mixed Two-Factor Design

A Mixed Experimental Design

At the beginning of the college semester, male sophomores were surveyed to identify students who would agree to take part in a weight-loss study. Factor A of the study was a low-carbohydrate versus a low-fat diet program, and Factor B was the duration of the diet program (four, eight, and twelve weeks). The table below shows the design along with total weight loss 4, 6, and 8 weeks after initiating the diet program.

		Time on Diet Program		
		4 weeks	**8 weeks**	**12 weeks**
Low Carb (Group 1)	Sam	14	17	34
	Alan	19	20	27
	Eric	18	20	28
	Jeff	7	17	29
	Tom	17	25	29
Low Fat (Group 2)	Alex	9	11	17
	Larry	9	12	9
	Pete	10	22	37
	Zack	14	11	8
	Matt	7	14	26

Use the techniques described in workbook 9-4 to complete the ANOVA Summary Table below. Then view the "practice problem" worksheet in *ESC* workbook 9-4 to see the ANOVA solution and a chart of the cell means. The 9-4 "practice problem" data are dynamically linked to the ANOVA, so for more practice you may enter different data for the problem, compute your own ANOVA, and check your answers against the solution on the "practice" worksheet (scroll right).

Analysis of Variance Summary Table

Source of Variation	**SS**	***df***	**MS**	***F***	***p* value**
Between Subjects	_____	_____			
Factor A (type of diet)	_____	_____	_____	_____	_____
Error (subjects within groups)	_____	_____	_____		
Within Subjects	_____	_____			
Factor B (weeks of dieting)	_____	_____	_____	_____	_____
A x B Interaction	_____	_____	_____	_____	_____
Error (B x subjects within group)	_____	_____	_____		
Total	_____	_____			

Exercise 10-1: The Chi-Square Goodness-of-Fit Test

Introduction

You may recall having first seen the chi-square goodness-of-fit test at the end of workbook 4-1. On that occasion the chi-square test was used to evaluate how close the fit was between the frequencies of a theoretical ("expected") binomial sampling distribution and the frequencies of an empirical ("obtained") binomial sampling distribution that were generated by a simulated coin-flipping experiment.

In general, the chi-square goodness-of-fit test determines if the fit between obtained and expected frequencies is good enough to attribute any lack of fit to chance, or so poor that chance is not an adequate explanation. If we determine that the probability of getting the obtained fit between expected and actual frequencies *by chance* is ≤ .05, we discount chance as the explanation for the poor fit and declare the deviation between expected and obtained frequencies to be statistically significant.

---

1. Complete the problem on the "practice" worksheet using either the formula method or Excel's paste functions. Then check your solution against the information in the "answers" worksheet.

   a. What do the results mean? Are some medical specialties more often targets for legal action than others?

   b. Next, gradually change the obtained frequencies to bring them more in line with the expected frequencies. The statistical output is dynamically linked to the data and will update instantly. What happens to the computed value of the chi-square statistic and the ***p*** value as you gradually improve the fit?

   c. Did the fit have to be perfect for retention of the null hypothesis?

   d. How do you interpret a "good" fit (p>.05) in the context of this problem?

2. The "Type 1 error" worksheet demonstrates the vulnerability of the chi-square statistic to Type 1 error by doing successive analyses on randomly generated frequencies. Each press of the <**delete**> key generates new data and statistics. Do 100 experiments (i.e., 100 presses of <**delete**>) and keep track of how many times ***p***≤.05. Did you find the anticipated (5% or 5 in 100) frequency of Type 1 error? In the long run, 5% of data sets will reveal a significant lack of fit between obtained and expected frequencies even though only chance is governing the data selection process.

Exercise 10-2: The Chi-Square Test of Independence

Introduction

The chi-square test of independence allows us to determine if two categorical variables are associated (dependent) or not associated (independent). Like the data we analyzed in workbook 10-1 using the chi-square goodness-of-fit test, the data analyzed by the chi-square test of independence are frequencies in categories. In the latter case, however, the data reflect categorical assessment of the research participants on **two** dimensions – a row variable and a column variable. The researcher enters a tally in the cell of the row-by-column table that most accurately describes the participant with respect to the two variables. Such a table is commonly referred to as a contingency table. At the end of the data collection process, the summary table of all participant tallies is ready for analysis by the chi-square statistic.

In workbook 10-2, for example, each participant was measured with respect to the variables: self-esteem (row) and degree of religious involvement (column). Naturally, accurate assignment of the participants to the cells of the contingency table depends on having developed operational definitions of "none," "low," "medium," etc., that are as precise and unambiguous as possible. So, for example, "none" for religious involvement might be defined as no attendance at worship services for the last two years.

---

1. The resident data on the "your data" worksheet show the state of dependence (or "contingency") between the row and column variables. There is a relationship between one's self esteem and one's religious involvement. Gradually change the obtained frequencies in a manner that will erode the state of dependence (i.e., increase the p value and decrease the value of χ^2. Once the p value exceeds .05, restore the state of dependence either by clicking the "undo" button on the tool bar or by manually restoring the original pattern of frequencies. Do you have a better sense of the patterns of dependence and independence?

2. Apply the skills you learned in workbook 10-2 to the following problem.

Single men and women were asked, "Would you be willing to marry a person that was younger than you by 5 or more years?" The table below summarizes the responses.

		Willing to Marry?	
		No	**Yes**
Gender	**Male**	30	53
	Female	42	33

Do the data reveal an association between the gender of a single person and his/her willingness to marry someone 5 or more years younger?

Exercise 10-3: The Mann-Whitney *U* Test

The nonparametric statistical tests covered in *ESC* Folder 10 (χ^2, Mann-Whiney ***U***, and Wilcoxon ***T***), allow us to test for association between variables and make comparisons between groups, just as their parametric cousins (***t*** test and Pearson ***r***) do. It may seem unnecessary to have a separate class of tests to serve equal statistical goals, especially when we consider that parametric tests are generally more powerful than their nonparametric equivalents. But in some situations nonparametric tests have a distinct advantage: they can address the issues of inter-group differences and association when the data are unsuitable for parametric analysis.

When doing a ***t*** test, for example, the data of the two samples are presumed to be normally distributed, have interval or ratio scaling, and have roughly equal within-sample variability ("homogeneity of variance"). Performing a ***t*** test without meeting one or more of these assumptions risks obtaining statistical output that misrepresent the information in the data.

The Mann-Whitney *U* Test

The ***U*** test is aptly described as the nonparametric alternative to the ***t*** test for independent groups. Perhaps the most common reason for deferring to the Mann-Whitney ***U*** over the ***t*** test is the need to compare two sets of sample data that have ordinal rather than interval or ratio scaling. Consider the following example.

Twenty-two children with a confirmed diagnosis of ADHD participated in a double-blind study to evaluate the effectiveness of Ritalin in reducing fidgety behavior. The 22 were randomly split into two groups. One group took prescribed doses of Ritalin, and a second group took a placebo pill on the same medication schedule. After one week of treatment, observers completed a behavioral checklist that enabled them to assign a fidgety rating to each of the 22 children. Low ratings on the 100-point scale are indicative of calm and focused behavior, and high values are indicative of fidgety and restless behavior. The data and a worksheet for computing the ***U*** statistic appear on the next page.

As subjective ratings, it is difficult to defend these data as having met the criteria for interval or ratio scaling. We cannot reasonably assume that the 10-unit difference between participants rated at 30 and 40 represents the exact same behavioral difference that separates participants rated at 90 and 100. Nor may we assume that the scale has a true zero point. (Does a rating of 90 really reflect exactly twice as much fidgety behavior as 45?)

Using the techniques presented in workbook 10-3, compare these two independent groups using the Mann-Whitney ***U*** test. The critical values of ***U*** with $n_1 = n_2 = 11$ are 30 and 91. To be significant, the ***U*** statistic must be ≤ 30 or ≥ 91.

Fidgety Ratings		**Ranks**	
Placebo	**Ritalin**	**(Placebo)**	**(Ritalin)**
44	35	____	____
71	50	____	____
91	37	____	____
61	43	____	____
68	58	____	____
53	53	____	____
76	26	____	____
55	73	____	____
93	75	____	____
82	47	____	____
90	28	____	____

$$U = n_1 n_2 + \frac{n_1(n_1 + 1)}{2} - R_1$$

$U =$ __________

$R_1 =$ __________

Exercise 10-4: The Wilcoxon Matched-Pairs Signed-Rank Test

The Wilcoxon **T** (capital T, not t) statistic is the nonparametric equivalent of the paired-samples (repeated measures) t test. The problem in this exercise addresses the same research issue as the problem in Exercise 10-3: Does Ritalin reduce fidgety behavior in ADHD children? Here, however, as you will notice in the table on the next page, each child is evaluated twice: once while under the influence of a placebo and again while taking Ritalin.

Six of the 12 participants took a placebo prior to their first behavioral evaluation, after which they were switched to Ritalin and evaluated again. Another 6 experienced the reverse: first Ritalin, then placebo. Neither the participants nor the behavioral evaluators knew what treatment was in force at the time of evaluation, neither was aware of the switch from placebo to drug or drug to placebo, and the children did not know when observers were completing the behavioral checklist because the assessments were made behind one-way glass.

The data are on the next page. Just as in the independent groups data of Exercise 10-3, we cannot defend subjective ratings as having met the criteria for interval or ratio scaling. Text in exercise 10-3 pointed out the difficulty in assuming that the 10-unit difference in fidgety behavior between two participants with ratings of 30 and 40 exactly equals the difference in fidgety behavior that separates participants with ratings of 90 and 100. Nor may we reasonably assume that the fidgety scale has a true zero point. (Does a rating of 90 really reflect exactly twice as much fidgety behavior as 45?)

As pointed out in *ESC* workbook 10-4, before calculating the Wilcoxon **T** we must discard any tied scores. We do have a tie (participant L), which leaves us with 11 matched pairs for the analysis.

Participant	Placebo	Ritalin	Difference	Rank of Difference	Signed Ranks
A	44	35	_____	_____	_____
B	71	50	_____	_____	_____
C	91	37	_____	_____	_____
D	61	43	_____	_____	_____
E	68	58	_____	_____	_____
F	53	54	_____	_____	_____
G	76	66	_____	_____	_____
H	55	73	_____	_____	_____
I	93	75	_____	_____	_____
J	82	47	_____	_____	_____
K	90	28	_____	_____	_____
L	75	75	_____	_____	_____

T = __________

A Wilcoxon problem in workbook 10-4 ("your data") also has 11 pairs. Therefore, you may check your answer to the current problem by entering the data on the "your data" worksheet.

Exercise 11-1: Test Selection

Name the appropriate statistical approach for each of the following diet studies.

1. A researcher wanted to compare the relative effectiveness of the South Beach and Atkins diets. She managed to round up a group of male volunteers all of whom had a BMI over 32 (obese). She randomly split the group in two. One group followed South Beach for two months and the other followed Atkins.

2. A researcher wanted to compare the relative effectiveness of the South Beach and Atkins diets. She calculated the BMI for her male volunteers and formed matched pairs using BMI as the matching criterion. One person of each matched pair was randomly assigned to follow the South Beach diet, and the other person followed Atkins.

3. A researcher wanted to compare the relative effectiveness of the South Beach, Atkins, and Weight Watchers diets. She managed to round up a group of male volunteers all of whom had a BMI over 32 (obese). She randomly split the group into three groups, assigning a different diet to each group.

4. A researcher measured a group of smokers with respect to two variables: Average Daily Caloric Intake (low – medium – high) and Smoking Habit (minimal –moderate – heavy). Is there an association between the degree to which people smoke and their eating habits? Were the frequencies across the three levels of Daily Caloric Intake (low-medium-high) even, or were there more people in one category compared to another?

5. A researcher repeated the experiment described above in question 1 with the addition of a gender variable. That is, equal numbers of males and females dieted either with South Beach or Atkins.

6. Driven by the idea that overweight people may be discriminated against in the workplace with respect to raises and promotions, a researcher collected data on BMI and annual salary among all the workers of a prestigious accounting firm who were employees for 8-12 years. His plan was to evaluate the data for evidence of a negative association between these two variables and, if he found one, to predict annual salary from BMI in this population.

Practice Problems

Do the data analysis that is both appropriate for the data and capable of answering the research question.Then state your conclusion supported by the appropriate statistics.

1. Data collected on a group of 12 students appear below.

Student	IQ	GPA
1	110	1.0
2	112	1.6
3	118	1.2
4	119	1.1
5	122	2.1
6	125	1.8
7	127	2.6
8	130	2.0
9	132	3.2
10	134	2.6
11	136	3.0
12	138	3.6

a. What proportion of the variability in GPA can be predicted from IQ?

b. Report the statistic that expresses the degree of relationship that exists between IQ and GPA.

c. Is there a significant relationship between IQ and GPA? Back up your conclusion with the appropriate statistics.

2. Monkeys learned to press a bar to hear a sound. The researcher wanted to evaluate the monkeys' preference for novelty. Pressing Bar 1 produced the same sound each time. Pressing Bar 2 produced a different sound. Did the monkeys prefer to press one bar more than the other?

Monkey	Bar 1	Bar 2
1	20	40
2	18	25
3	24	38
4	14	27
5	5	31
6	26	21
7	15	32
8	29	38
9	15	25
10	9	18
11	25	32
12	31	28

3. Does marijuana increase the appetite of AIDS patients? The data below represent the increase in average daily caloric intake for two groups of AIDS patients. One group was treated with a placebo and the other was treated with THC, the active ingredient in marijuana.

Placebo	THC
1051	872
1066	943
963	912
1179	1213
1144	1034
912	854
1093	1125
1113	1042
985	922
1271	1136
978	886
951	902

4. One hundred incoming freshmen from <u>each</u> of seven colleges were randomly selected for a study. After four years on campus, a determination was made to see how many of the original 100 qualified to graduate. The data are below. Is the graduation rate uniform across the colleges, or did some schools do better than others pushing their students out the door in the traditional 4 years?

	Graduate?	
College	**Yes**	**No**
A	72	28
B	55	45
C	44	56
D	57	43
E	80	20
F	65	35
G	52	48

5. Despite the effectiveness of modern birth control methods, cultural barriers exist in many primitive ("third-world") societies that limit the capacity or willingness of the women to follow the necessary medicinal regimen for birth control. A study was done to compare the relative effectiveness of four methods of birth control. The data represent the incidence of unplanned pregnancies per 100 ("UP/100") population over a 2-year period. Do the methods differ in effectiveness?

	Pill (daily)	**Pill (monthly)**	**Sub Cu Implant**	**Spermicidal Foam**
UP/100	27	14	6	32

6. A group of 6 medical school graduates was tested for short-term memory at the ages of 30, 40, 50, and 60. The data represent the number of correct responses on the short-term memory test. Did short-term memory capacity change as the subjects grew older?

	30 years	**40 years**	**50 years**	**60 years**
Sam	4	12	17	13
Joe	13	15	14	10
Tim	15	16	14	7
Tom	17	11	9	8
Jon	12	12	13	6
Fred	10	18	15	9

7. One group of participants had a normal night's sleep, a second group was sleep deprived for 24 hours, and a third group was sleep deprived for 48 hours. Each group was given a task to measure the ability to maintain sustained attention on an audio vigilance task. The participants listened to sound pulses. Occasionally, a pulse was shorter than the usual duration. The participants' job was to detect these shorter-than-normal pulses. The data below represent the correct detections. Did sleep deprivation affect task performance? What is the specific pattern of differences among the three groups?

Normal Sleep	24 Hour Deprivation	48 Hour Deprivation
85	60	60
83	58	48
76	76	38
64	52	47
75	63	50

8. Two different teaching methods were used with students of superior, average or poor mathematical ability. The data below represent final exam performance. Did mathematical ability impact performance? Did teaching method impact performance?

Ability	Method 1	Method 2
Superior	39, 48, 44, 41, 42	49, 47, 43, 47, 48
Average	43, 40, 42, 36, 35	38, 45, 42, 46, 44
Poor	30, 29, 37, 33, 36	37, 34, 40, 41, 33

9. Registered Democrats and registered Republicans were questioned about their support for oil drilling in a wildlife area. Here are the results:

	Support Proposition?	
	Yes	**No**
Democrat	17	40
Republican	37	29

a. Was support for the proposition associated with party affiliation?

b. Did significantly more people vote "No" than "Yes"?

The *ESC* User's Manual: Part II
Annotated Screen Captures from the CD-ROM

Basic Skills

Workbook: Basic Skills.xls
Worksheet: Intro

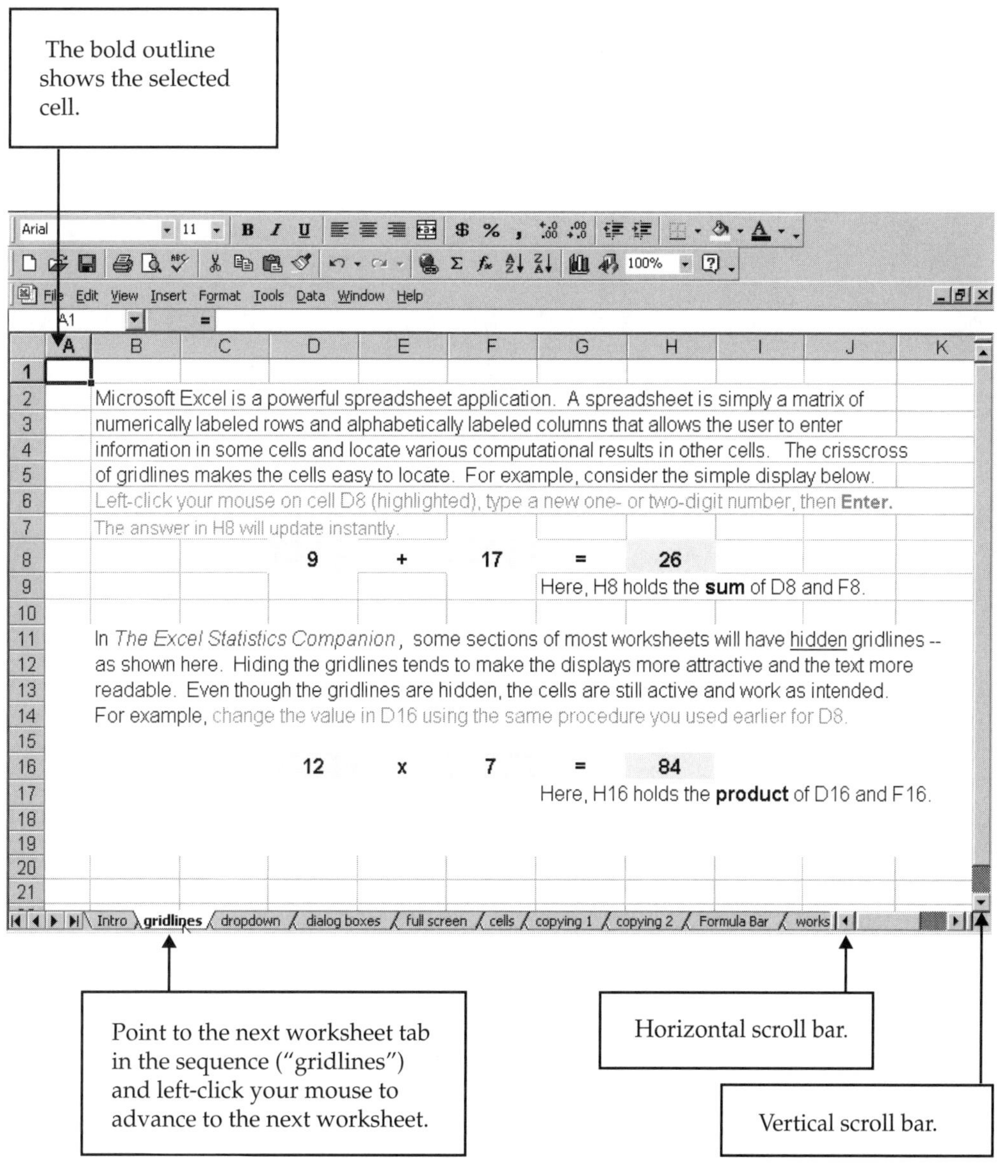

The bold outline shows the selected cell.
Microsoft Excel is a powerful spreadsheet application. A spreadsheet is simply a matrix of numerically labeled rows and alphabetically labeled columns that allows the user to enter information in some cells and locate various computational results in other cells. The crisscross of gridlines makes the cells easy to locate. For example, consider the simple display below.
Left-click your mouse on cell D8 (highlighted), type a new one- or two-digit number, then Enter.
The answer in H8 will update instantly.
9 + 17 = 26
Here, H8 holds the sum of D8 and F8.
In The Excel Statistics Companion, some sections of most worksheets will have hidden gridlines -- as shown here. Hiding the gridlines tends to make the displays more attractive and the text more readable. Even though the gridlines are hidden, the cells are still active and work as intended.
For example, change the value in D16 using the same procedure you used earlier for D8.
12 x 7 = 84
Here, H16 holds the product of D16 and F16.
Intro
gridlines
dropdown
dialog boxes
full screen
cells
copying 1
copying 2
Formula Bar
Point to the next worksheet tab in the sequence ("gridlines") and left-click your mouse to advance to the next worksheet.
Horizontal scroll bar.
Vertical scroll bar.

Workbook: Basic Skills.xls
Worksheet: gridlines

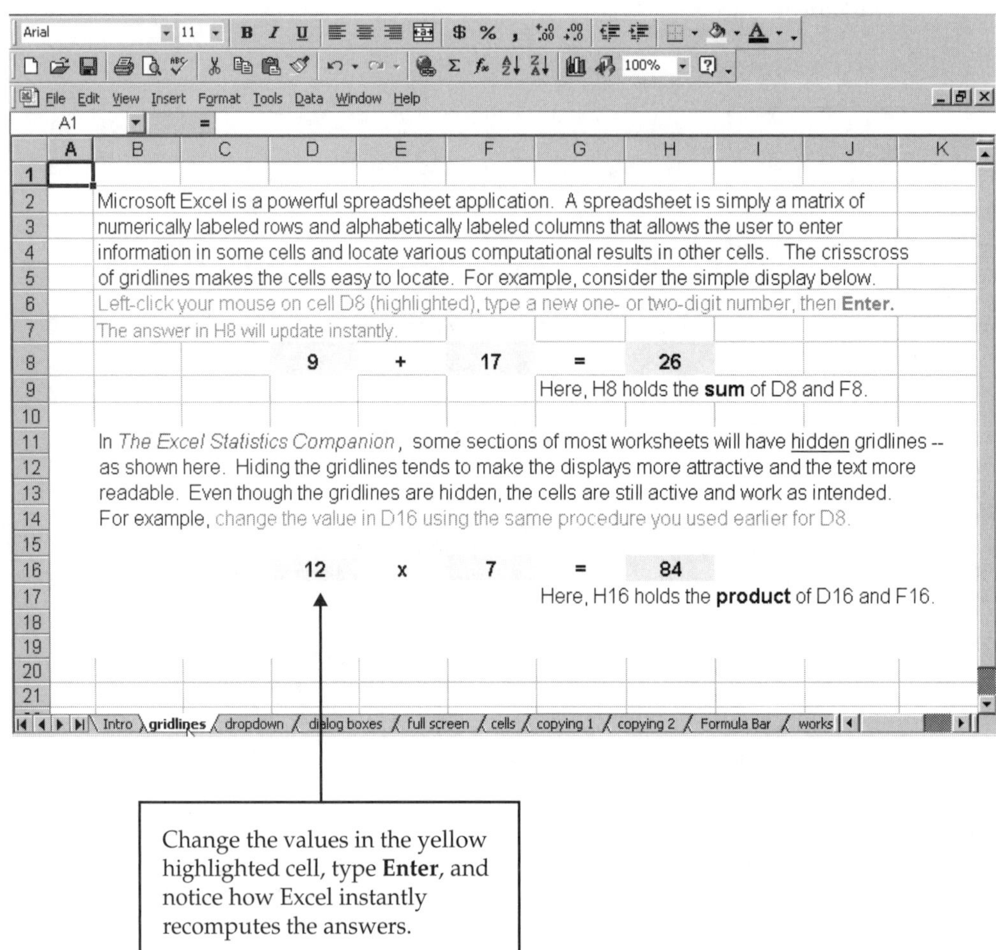
Microsoft Excel is a powerful spreadsheet application. A spreadsheet is simply a matrix of numerically labeled rows and alphabetically labeled columns that allows the user to enter information in some cells and locate various computational results in other cells. The crisscross of gridlines makes the cells easy to locate. For example, consider the simple display below.
Left-click your mouse on cell D8 (highlighted), type a new one- or two-digit number, then Enter.
The answer in H8 will update instantly.
9 + 17 = 26
Here, H8 holds the sum of D8 and F8.
In The Excel Statistics Companion, some sections of most worksheets will have hidden gridlines -- as shown here. Hiding the gridlines tends to make the displays more attractive and the text more readable. Even though the gridlines are hidden, the cells are still active and work as intended.
For example, change the value in D16 using the same procedure you used earlier for D8.
12 x 7 = 84
Here, H16 holds the product of D16 and F16.
Intro
gridlines
dropdown
dialog boxes
full screen
cells
copying 1
copying 2
Formula Bar
works
Change the values in the yellow highlighted cell, type Enter, and notice how Excel instantly recomputes the answers.

Workbook: Basic Skills.xls
Worksheet: dropdown

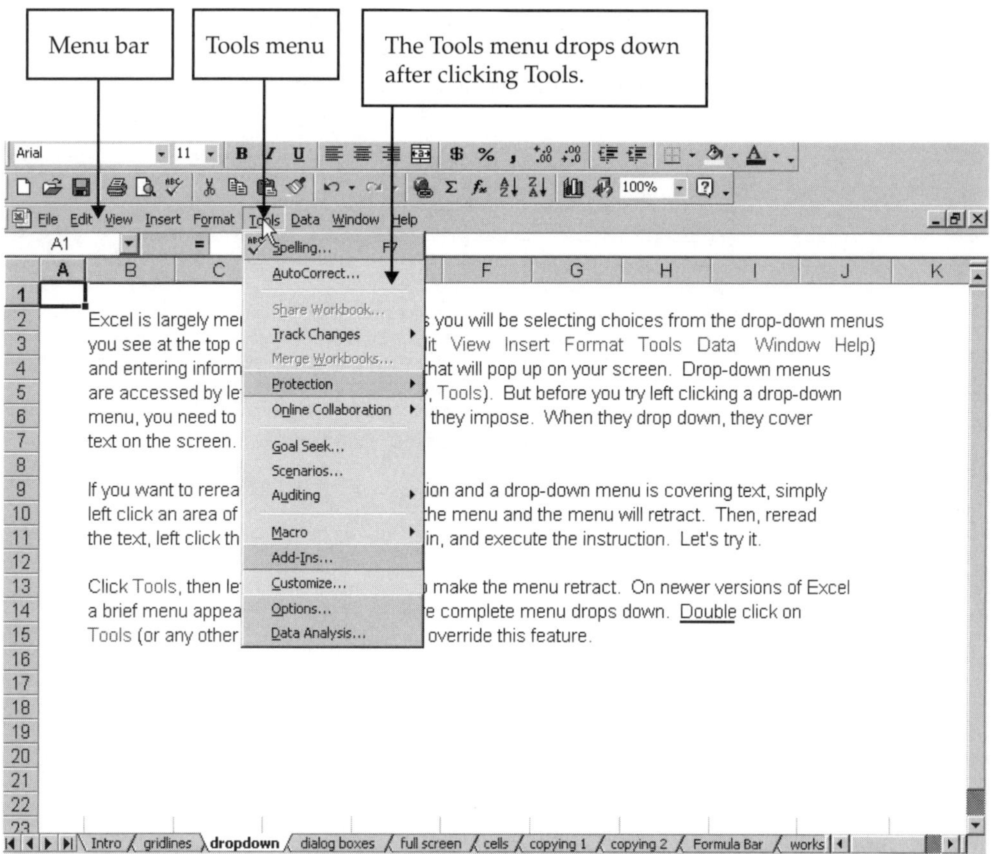
Menu bar
Tools menu
The Tools menu drops down after clicking Tools.
File Edit View Insert Format Tools Data Window Help
Spelling... F7
AutoCorrect...
Share Workbook...
Track Changes
Merge Workbooks...
Protection
Online Collaboration
Goal Seek...
Scenarios...
Auditing
Macro
Add-Ins...
Customize...
Options...
Data Analysis...
Intro gridlines dropdown dialog boxes full screen cells copying 1 copying 2 Formula Bar works

Workbook: Basic Skills.xls
Worksheet: dialog boxes

This image shows the dialog box that appears after selecting Spelling from the Tools menu. If a spell-check box appears inviting you to change text, click the Cancel button and the "continue" box will appear as shown below. The mouse pointer is positioned on the title bar of the box.

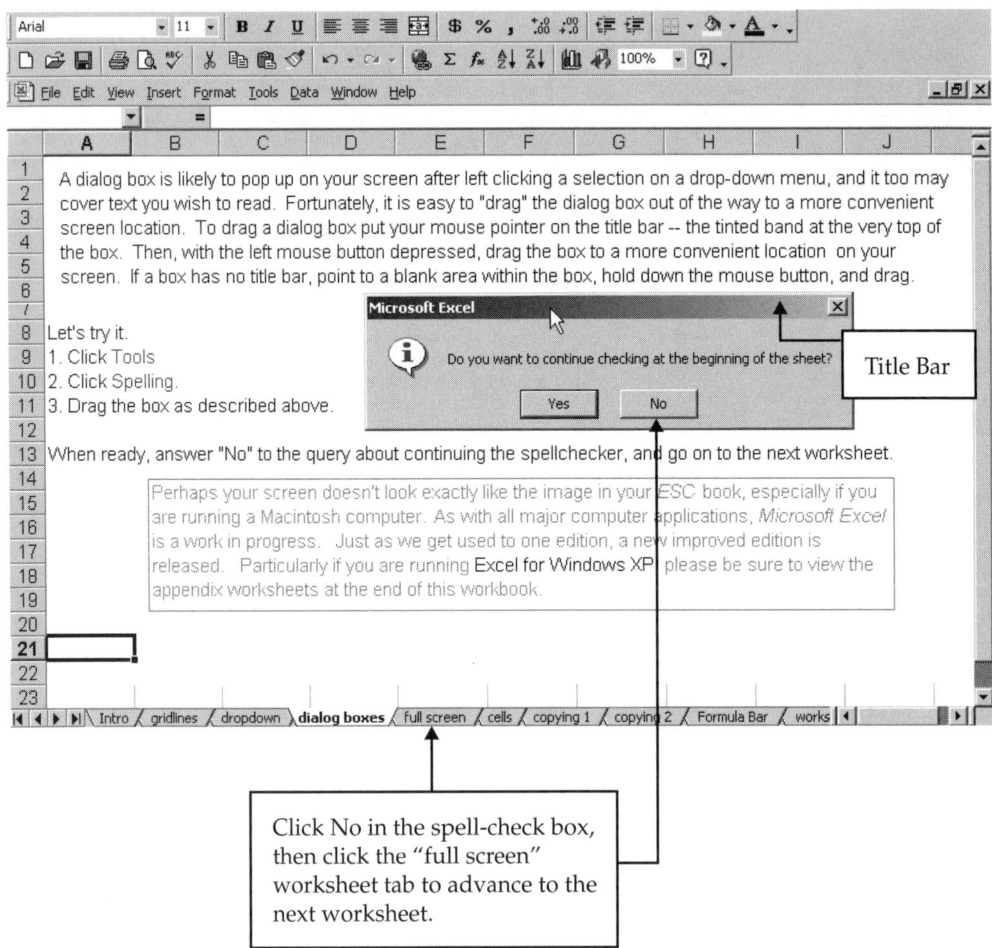
A dialog box is likely to pop up on your screen after left clicking a selection on a drop-down menu, and it too may cover text you wish to read. Fortunately, it is easy to "drag" the dialog box out of the way to a more convenient screen location. To drag a dialog box put your mouse pointer on the title bar -- the tinted band at the very top of the box. Then, with the left mouse button depressed, drag the box to a more convenient location on your screen. If a box has no title bar, point to a blank area within the box, hold down the mouse button, and drag.
Let's try it.
1. Click Tools
2. Click Spelling.
3. Drag the box as described above.
Microsoft Excel
Do you want to continue checking at the beginning of the sheet?
Yes
No
Title Bar
When ready, answer "No" to the query about continuing the spellchecker, and go on to the next worksheet.
Perhaps your screen doesn't look exactly like the image in your ESC book, especially if you are running a Macintosh computer. As with all major computer applications, Microsoft Excel is a work in progress. Just as we get used to one edition, a new improved edition is released. Particularly if you are running Excel for Windows XP please be sure to view the appendix worksheets at the end of this workbook.
Intro
gridlines
dropdown
dialog boxes
full screen
cells
copying 1
copying 2
Formula Bar
Click No in the spell-check box, then click the "full screen" worksheet tab to advance to the next worksheet.

Workbook: Basic Skills.xls
Worksheet: full screen (a)

This image shows the "full screen" worksheet with the View drop-down menu visible. The mouse pointer is resting on the Full Screen menu choice.

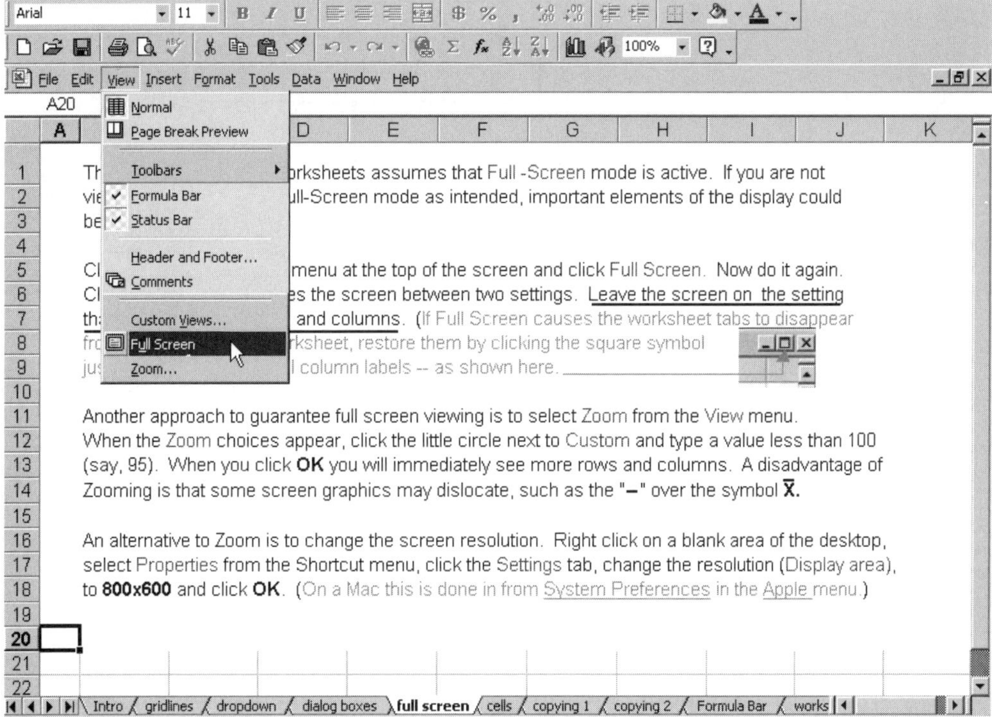
File Edit View Insert Format Tools Data Window Help
Normal
Page Break Preview
Toolbars
Formula Bar
Status Bar
Header and Footer...
Comments
Custom Views...
Full Screen
Zoom...
rksheets assumes that Full -Screen mode is active. If you are not
ll-Screen mode as intended, important elements of the display could
menu at the top of the screen and click Full Screen. Now do it again.
s the screen between two settings. Leave the screen on the setting
and columns. (If Full Screen causes the worksheet tabs to disappear
rksheet, restore them by clicking the square symbol
l column labels -- as shown here.
Another approach to guarantee full screen viewing is to select Zoom from the View menu.
When the Zoom choices appear, click the little circle next to Custom and type a value less than 100
(say, 95). When you click OK you will immediately see more rows and columns. A disadvantage of
Zooming is that some screen graphics may dislocate, such as the "–" over the symbol X̄.
An alternative to Zoom is to change the screen resolution. Right click on a blank area of the desktop,
select Properties from the Shortcut menu, click the Settings tab, change the resolution (Display area),
to 800x600 and click OK. (On a Mac this is done in from System Preferences in the Apple menu.)
Intro gridlines dropdown dialog boxes full screen cells copying 1 copying 2 Formula Bar works

Each time you click Full Screen the view will toggle between screen settings. Leave the setting on the view that exposes the most rows and columns. Be aware, however, that the screen that exposes the most rows and columns of the Excel worksheet may also hide the maximize, minimize, and close buttons for the active window that normally appear in the upper right corner. If such a screen view is hindering your desire to minimize or close a window, click View – Full Screen again, and the buttons will come into view.

Workbook: Basic Skills.xls
Worksheet: full screen (b)

This screen shows the first step for using the zoom feature, which is to click on Zoom from the View menu.

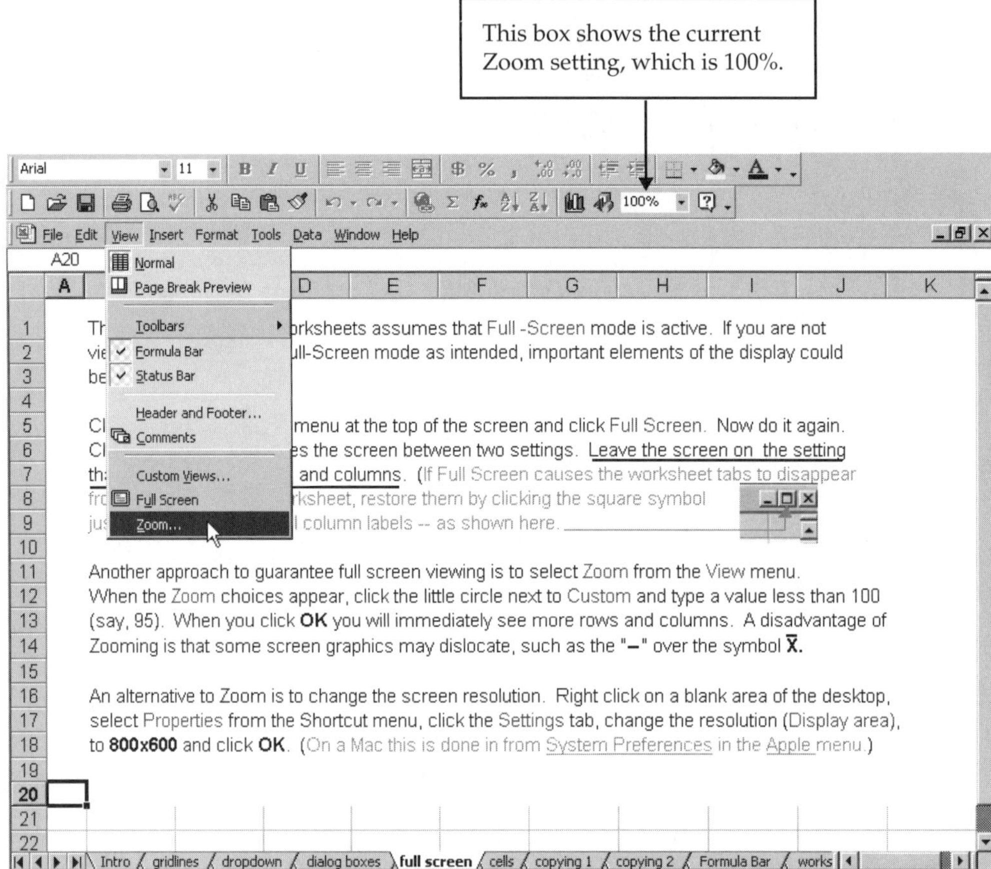
This box shows the current Zoom setting, which is 100%.
Arial
11
100%
File Edit View Insert Format Tools Data Window Help
A20
Normal
Page Break Preview
Toolbars
Formula Bar
Status Bar
Header and Footer...
Comments
Custom Views...
Full Screen
Zoom...
orksheets assumes that Full -Screen mode is active. If you are not
ull-Screen mode as intended, important elements of the display could
menu at the top of the screen and click Full Screen. Now do it again.
es the screen between two settings. Leave the screen on the setting
and columns. (If Full Screen causes the worksheet tabs to disappear
rksheet, restore them by clicking the square symbol
l column labels -- as shown here.
Another approach to guarantee full screen viewing is to select Zoom from the View menu.
When the Zoom choices appear, click the little circle next to Custom and type a value less than 100
(say, 95). When you click OK you will immediately see more rows and columns. A disadvantage of
Zooming is that some screen graphics may dislocate, such as the "–" over the symbol X̄.
An alternative to Zoom is to change the screen resolution. Right click on a blank area of the desktop,
select Properties from the Shortcut menu, click the Settings tab, change the resolution (Display area),
to 800x600 and click OK. (On a Mac this is done in from System Preferences in the Apple menu.)
Intro / gridlines / dropdown / dialog boxes / full screen / cells / copying 1 / copying 2 / Formula Bar / works

An alternative to the Full Screen command, changing the Zoom setting from 100% to a lower number such as 95%, ensures that you will see the entire screen display as intended. The screen image does, however, become smaller with each increment below 100%. So, changing the Zoom setting to less than 100% will, if taken to the extreme, make some screen elements too small for comfortable viewing.

Workbook: Basic Skills.xls
Worksheet: full screen (c)

The Zoom dialog box allows you to select an array of pre-selected screen sizes from 25% to 200%, but for our purposes it is best to enter a value in the Custom field (95% or thereabouts) as shown.

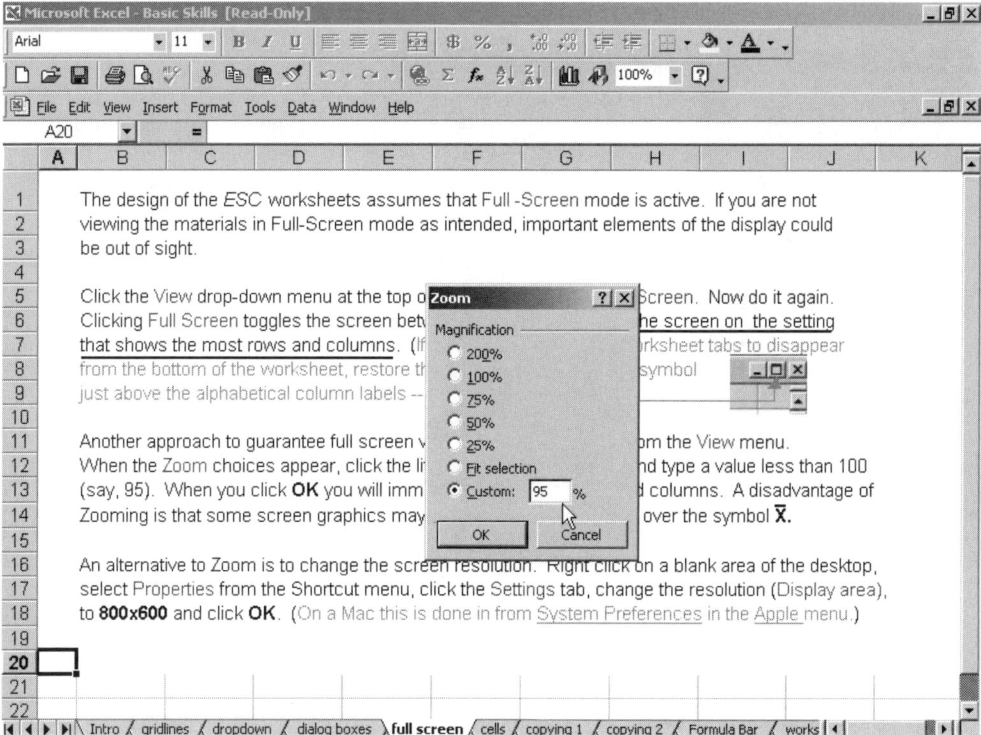
Microsoft Excel - Basic Skills [Read-Only]
Arial
11
100%
File Edit View Insert Format Tools Data Window Help
A20
The design of the ESC worksheets assumes that Full -Screen mode is active. If you are not
viewing the materials in Full-Screen mode as intended, important elements of the display could
be out of sight.
Click the View drop-down menu at the top o
Screen. Now do it again.
Clicking Full Screen toggles the screen betv
he screen on the setting
that shows the most rows and columns. (If
rksheet tabs to disappear
from the bottom of the worksheet, restore th
symbol
just above the alphabetical column labels --
Another approach to guarantee full screen v
om the View menu.
When the Zoom choices appear, click the li
nd type a value less than 100
(say, 95). When you click OK you will imm
d columns. A disadvantage of
Zooming is that some screen graphics may
over the symbol X.
Zoom
Magnification
200%
100%
75%
50%
25%
Fit selection
Custom: 95 %
OK
Cancel
An alternative to Zoom is to change the scre
n a blank area of the desktop,
select Properties from the Shortcut menu, click the Settings tab, change the resolution (Display area),
to 800x600 and click OK. (On a Mac this is done in from System Preferences in the Apple menu.)
Intro gridlines dropdown dialog boxes full screen cells copying 1 copying 2 Formula Bar works

> The Zoom feature contains several preset Zoom values from 25% to 200%, but you will likely have the best result entering your own value in the Custom field.

Workbook: Basic Skills.xls
Worksheet: full screen (d)

This is the box that appears when you click Options from the Tools drop-down menu. The mouse pointer is resting on the View tab, and the window shows the selected viewing options. Clicking other tabs (Edit, General, etc.) will give you access to other options, but they are of no concern to us at this time.

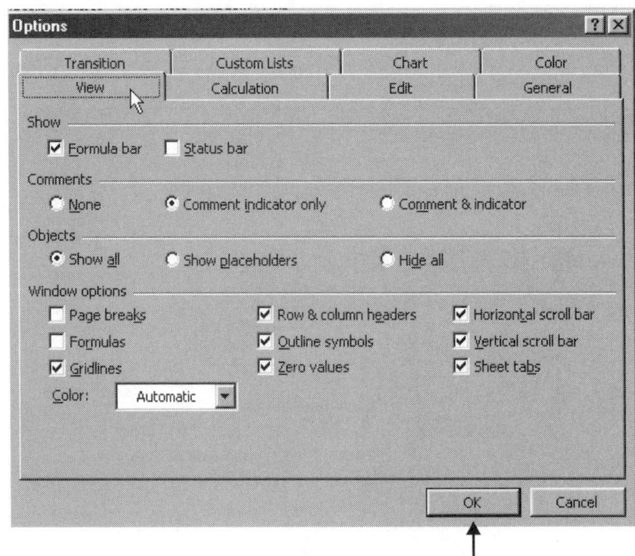
Options
Transition
Custom Lists
Chart
Color
View
Calculation
Edit
General
Show
Formula bar
Status bar
Comments
None
Comment indicator only
Comment & indicator
Objects
Show all
Show placeholders
Hide all
Window options
Page breaks
Formulas
Gridlines
Color:
Automatic
Row & column headers
Outline symbols
Zero values
Horizontal scroll bar
Vertical scroll bar
Sheet tabs
OK
Cancel

The View options you see checked here are, with the possible exception of Gridlines, important to select before running *The Excel Statistics Companion*. On a few worksheets, Gridlines is deselected. The rest of the work-sheets do show the gridlines, which facilitates locating specific cells on the worksheet.

Once you have checked the View features that you wish to be incorporated into your screen display, click **OK**.

Workbook: Basic Skills.xls
Worksheet: cells

This is what your screen should look like after having selected cells A14 to A17.

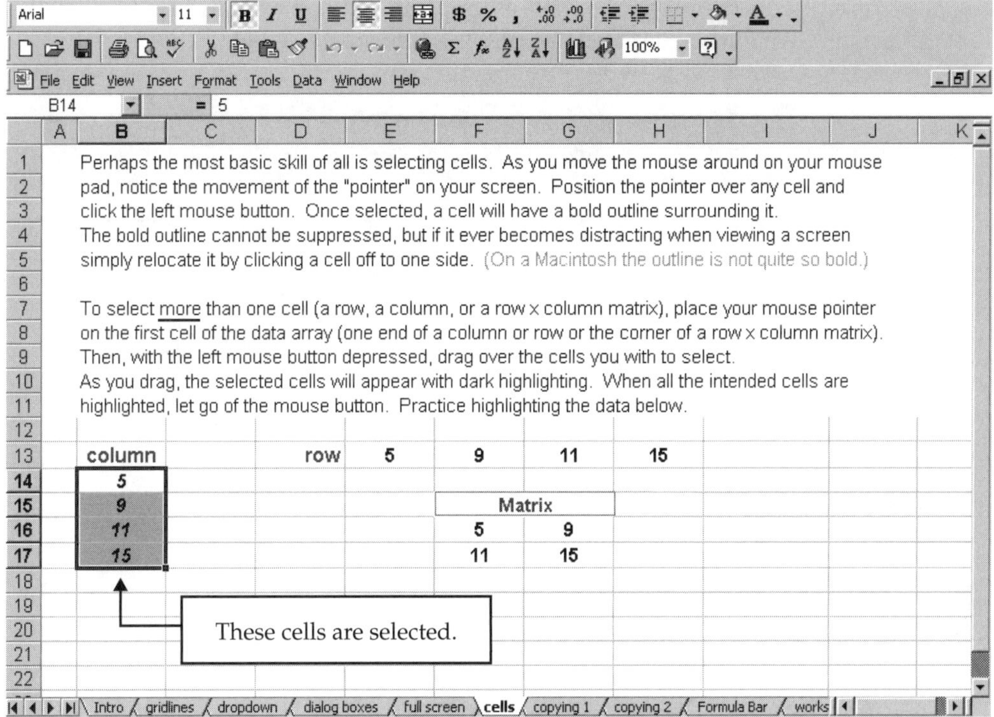

Perhaps the most basic skill of all is selecting cells. As you move the mouse around on your mouse pad, notice the movement of the "pointer" on your screen. Position the pointer over any cell and click the left mouse button. Once selected, a cell will have a bold outline surrounding it.
The bold outline cannot be suppressed, but if it ever becomes distracting when viewing a screen simply relocate it by clicking a cell off to one side. (On a Macintosh the outline is not quite so bold.)
To select more than one cell (a row, a column, or a row x column matrix), place your mouse pointer on the first cell of the data array (one end of a column or row or the corner of a row x column matrix).
Then, with the left mouse button depressed, drag over the cells you with to select.
As you drag, the selected cells will appear with dark highlighting. When all the intended cells are highlighted, let go of the mouse button. Practice highlighting the data below.
column
row 5 9 11 15
5
9
11
15
Matrix
5 9
11 15
These cells are selected.

If your drag-to-highlight operation is somewhat off the mark either by including unwanted cells or failing to include intended cells, just click in any empty cell on the worksheet and the highlighting will disappear. Then try again.

Workbook: Basic Skills.xls
Worksheet: copying 1 (a)

Once you point and click on cell H3, which contains "5," you will see a bold border surrounding the cell. This confirms that the cell is "selected." If you continue to hold the mouse pointer over the selected cell and right-click, the shortcut edit menu (shown below) appears. With the mouse pointer on the Copy menu option, left-click to copy the contents of cell H3.

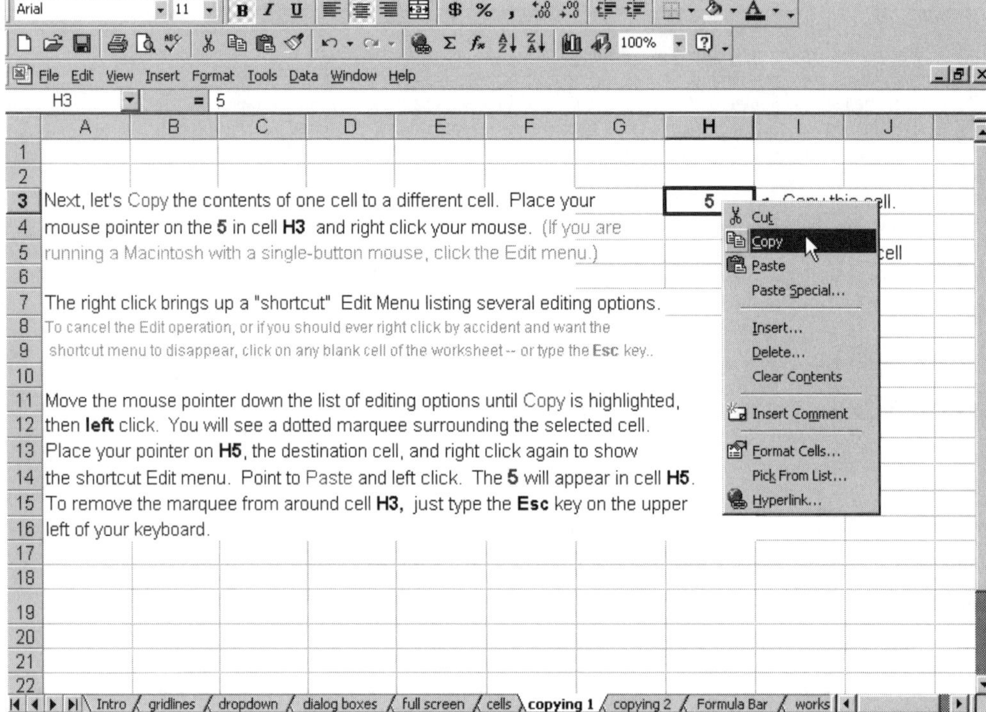
File Edit View Insert Format Tools Data Window Help
H3 = 5
Next, let's Copy the contents of one cell to a different cell. Place your
mouse pointer on the 5 in cell H3 and right click your mouse. (If you are
running a Macintosh with a single-button mouse, click the Edit menu.)
The right click brings up a "shortcut" Edit Menu listing several editing options.
To cancel the Edit operation, or if you should ever right click by accident and want the
shortcut menu to disappear, click on any blank cell of the worksheet -- or type the Esc key..
Move the mouse pointer down the list of editing options until Copy is highlighted,
then left click. You will see a dotted marquee surrounding the selected cell.
Place your pointer on H5, the destination cell, and right click again to show
the shortcut Edit menu. Point to Paste and left click. The 5 will appear in cell H5.
To remove the marquee from around cell H3, just type the Esc key on the upper
left of your keyboard.
Cut
Copy
Paste
Paste Special...
Insert...
Delete...
Clear Contents
Insert Comment
Format Cells...
Pick From List...
Hyperlink...
Intro gridlines dropdown dialog boxes full screen cells copying 1 copying 2 Formula Bar works

The Copy operation places the contents of the copied cells into an area of the computer's memory – a "buffer." The information will stay in the buffer until displaced by a subsequent Copy operation. The Paste command does not, therefore, empty the buffer when it pastes the copied cells. The buffer remains intact until the next Cut or Copy replaces the former contents.

Workbook: Basic Skills.xls
Worksheet: copying 1 (b)

Now point to and click cell H5. While holding the mouse pointer over cell H5, right-click and the shortcut menu will reappear. This time, click Paste from the menu, and the "5" you just copied from cell H3 will be pasted to cell H5.

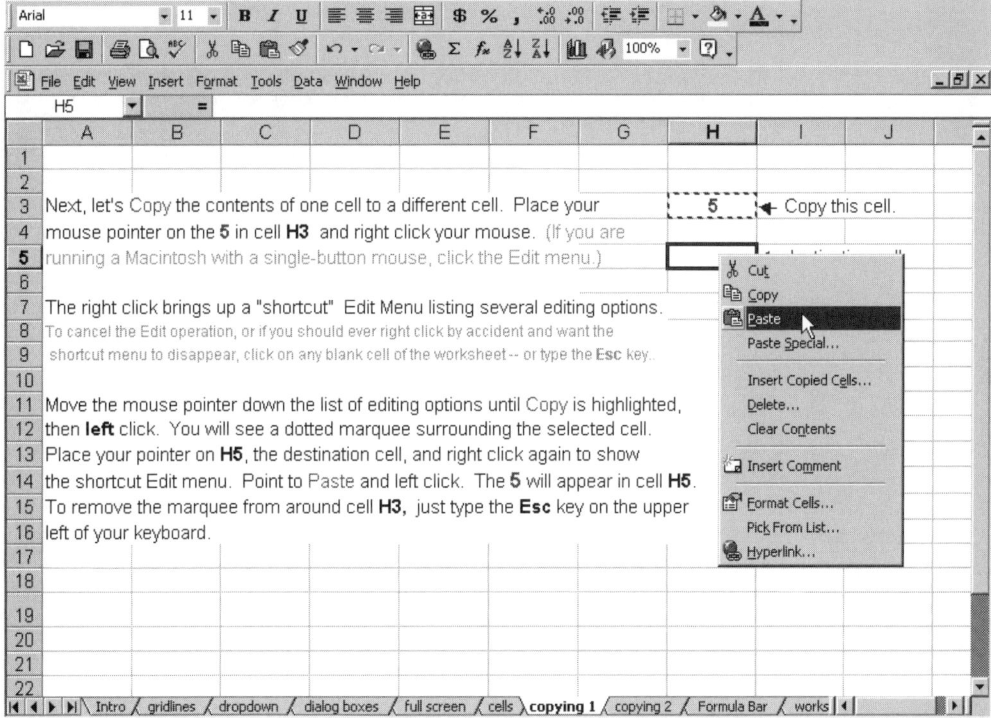
Next, let's Copy the contents of one cell to a different cell. Place your
mouse pointer on the 5 in cell H3 and right click your mouse. (If you are
running a Macintosh with a single-button mouse, click the Edit menu.)
The right click brings up a "shortcut" Edit Menu listing several editing options.
To cancel the Edit operation, or if you should ever right click by accident and want the
shortcut menu to disappear, click on any blank cell of the worksheet -- or type the Esc key.
Move the mouse pointer down the list of editing options until Copy is highlighted,
then left click. You will see a dotted marquee surrounding the selected cell.
Place your pointer on H5, the destination cell, and right click again to show
the shortcut Edit menu. Point to Paste and left click. The 5 will appear in cell H5.
To remove the marquee from around cell H3, just type the Esc key on the upper
left of your keyboard.
5
Copy this cell.
Cut
Copy
Paste
Paste Special...
Insert Copied Cells...
Delete...
Clear Contents
Insert Comment
Format Cells...
Pick From List...
Hyperlink...
Intro
gridlines
dropdown
dialog boxes
full screen
cells
copying 1
copying 2
Formula Bar
works

> The dotted marquee will surround the selected cell as soon as the Copy command is executed. Thus, the dotted marquee shows you the specific cell (or cells) that you will be pasting when you execute the Paste command. If you make an error, a single left-click in the Formula Bar will cancel the operation and rid the display of the dotted marquee. At that point you have the option of starting over.

Workbook: Basic Skills.xls
Worksheet: copying 2

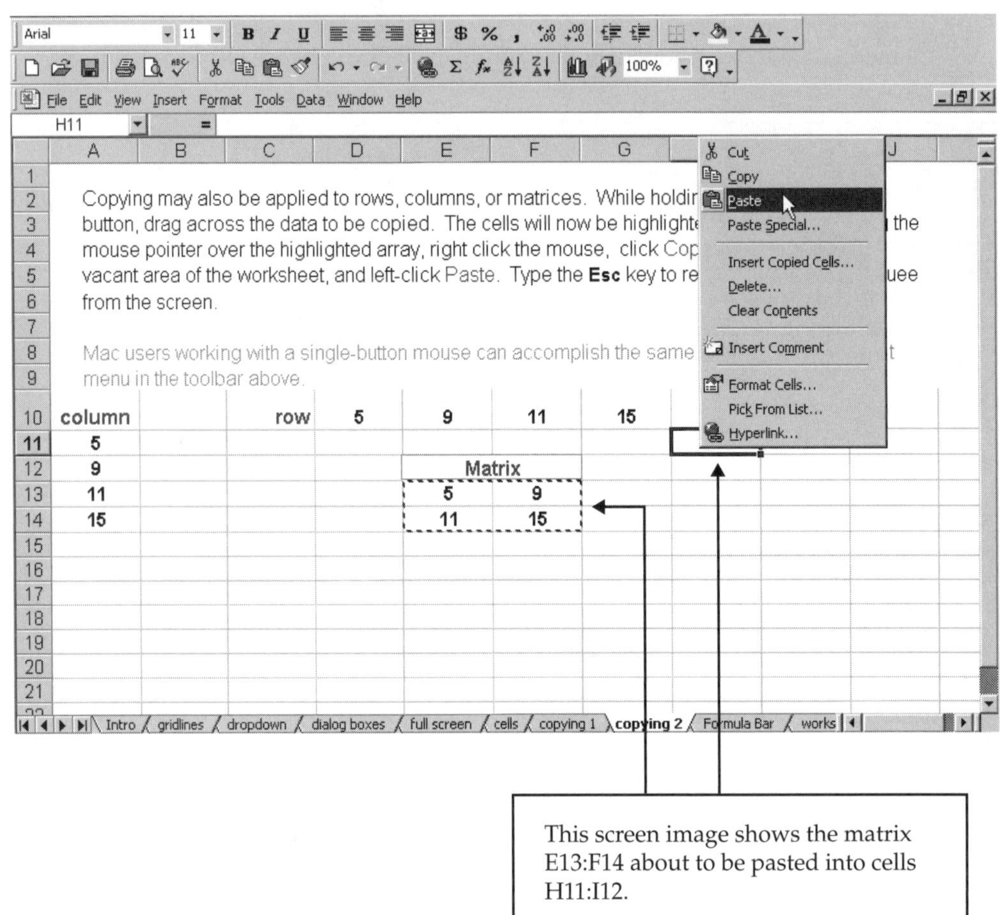
Copying may also be applied to rows, columns, or matrices. While holdir
button, drag across the data to be copied. The cells will now be highlight
mouse pointer over the highlighted array, right click the mouse, click Cop
vacant area of the worksheet, and left-click Paste. Type the Esc key to re
from the screen.
Mac users working with a single-button mouse can accomplish the same
menu in the toolbar above.
column
row
Matrix
Cut
Copy
Paste
Paste Special...
Insert Copied Cells...
Delete...
Clear Contents
Insert Comment
Format Cells...
Pick From List...
Hyperlink...
Intro
gridlines
dropdown
dialog boxes
full screen
cells
copying 1
copying 2
Formula Bar

This screen image shows the matrix E13:F14 about to be pasted into cells H11:I12.

Workbook: Basic Skills.xls
Worksheet: Formula Bar

In the View menu (bottom of page), clicking on Formula Bar causes a check mark to appear in the menu and the Formula Bar to be displayed on your screen. The contents of selected cells appear in the Formula Bar. Here you see cell A10 selected, so the text in cell A10 appears in the Formula Bar.

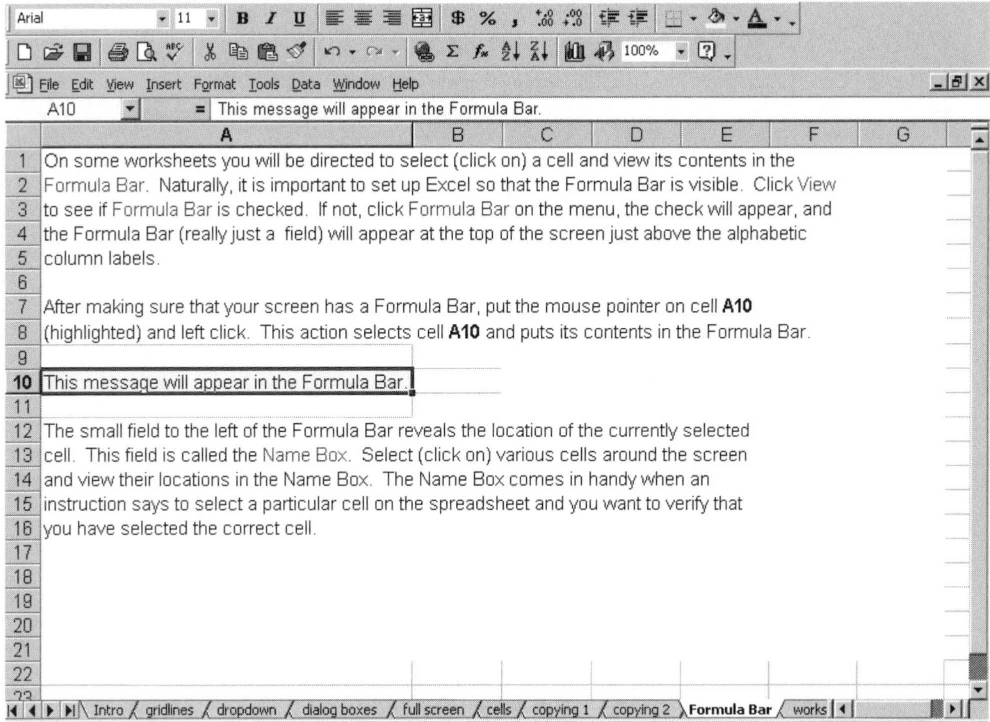
File Edit View Insert Format Tools Data Window Help
A10
This message will appear in the Formula Bar.
On some worksheets you will be directed to select (click on) a cell and view its contents in the Formula Bar. Naturally, it is important to set up Excel so that the Formula Bar is visible. Click View to see if Formula Bar is checked. If not, click Formula Bar on the menu, the check will appear, and the Formula Bar (really just a field) will appear at the top of the screen just above the alphabetic column labels.
After making sure that your screen has a Formula Bar, put the mouse pointer on cell A10 (highlighted) and left click. This action selects cell A10 and puts its contents in the Formula Bar.
This message will appear in the Formula Bar.
The small field to the left of the Formula Bar reveals the location of the currently selected cell. This field is called the Name Box. Select (click on) various cells around the screen and view their locations in the Name Box. The Name Box comes in handy when an instruction says to select a particular cell on the spreadsheet and you want to verify that you have selected the correct cell.
Intro gridlines dropdown dialog boxes full screen cells copying 1 copying 2 Formula Bar works

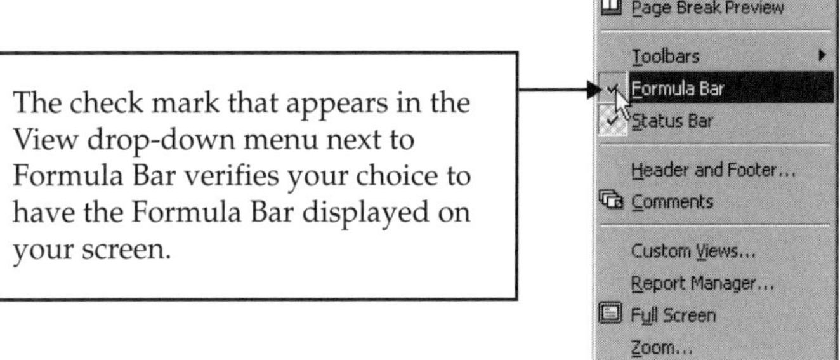
The check mark that appears in the View drop-down menu next to Formula Bar verifies your choice to have the Formula Bar displayed on your screen.
View
Normal
Page Break Preview
Toolbars
Formula Bar
Status Bar
Header and Footer...
Comments
Custom Views...
Report Manager...
Full Screen
Zoom...

Workbook: Basic Skills.xls
Worksheet: worksheets (a)

Only a small part of the spreadsheet is visible on the screen at any time. Scrolling down and right provides access to otherwise hidden rows and columns.

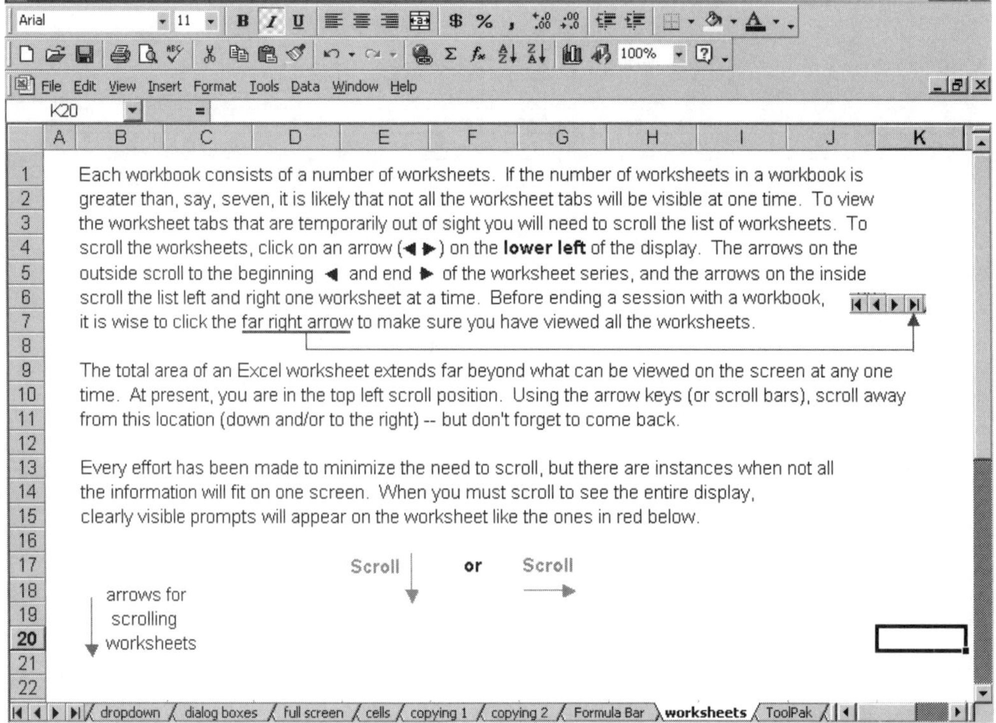
K20
Each workbook consists of a number of worksheets. If the number of worksheets in a workbook is greater than, say, seven, it is likely that not all the worksheet tabs will be visible at one time. To view the worksheet tabs that are temporarily out of sight you will need to scroll the list of worksheets. To scroll the worksheets, click on an arrow (◀ ▶) on the **lower left** of the display. The arrows on the outside scroll to the beginning ◀ and end ▶ of the worksheet series, and the arrows on the inside scroll the list left and right one worksheet at a time. Before ending a session with a workbook, it is wise to click the far right arrow to make sure you have viewed all the worksheets.
The total area of an Excel worksheet extends far beyond what can be viewed on the screen at any one time. At present, you are in the top left scroll position. Using the arrow keys (or scroll bars), scroll away from this location (down and/or to the right) -- but don't forget to come back.
Every effort has been made to minimize the need to scroll, but there are instances when not all the information will fit on one screen. When you must scroll to see the entire display, clearly visible prompts will appear on the worksheet like the ones in red below.
Scroll
or
Scroll
arrows for scrolling worksheets
dropdown
dialog boxes
full screen
cells
copying 1
copying 2
Formula Bar
worksheets
ToolPak

Workbook: Basic Skills
Worksheet: worksheets (b)

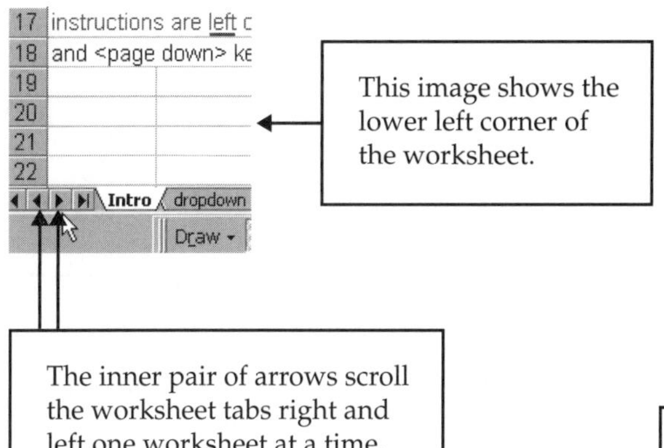
17 instructions are left c
18 and <page down> ke
19
20
21
22
Intro
dropdown
Draw
This image shows the lower left corner of the worksheet.

The inner pair of arrows scroll the worksheet tabs right and left one worksheet at a time.

Some workbooks contain many more worksheets than will display at any one time as tabs on the bottom of the screen. To make sure that you have viewed all the worksheets in a workbook, it is a good idea to scroll the worksheet tabs to the end of the list before closing your session.

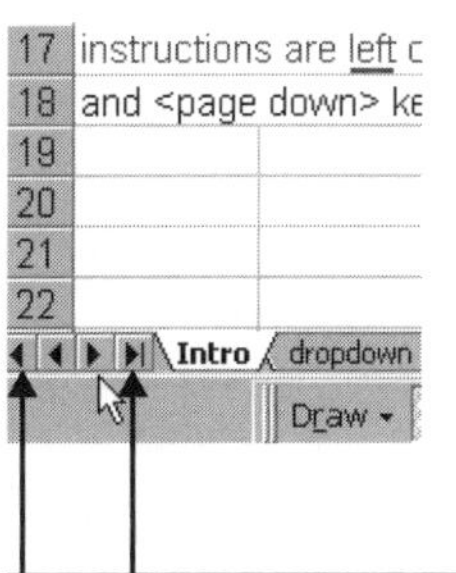
17 instructions are left c
18 and <page down> ke
19
20
21
22
Intro
dropdown
Draw

The outer arrows scroll the tabs to the beginning and end of the workbook.

Workbook: Basic Skills.xls
Worksheet: ToolPak

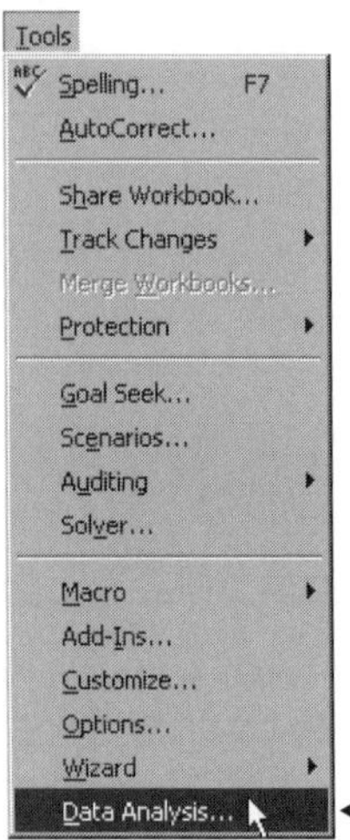
Tools
Spelling... F7
AutoCorrect...
Share Workbook...
Track Changes
Merge Workbooks...
Protection
Goal Seek...
Scenarios...
Auditing
Solver...
Macro
Add-Ins...
Customize...
Options...
Wizard
Data Analysis...

If the Data Analysis ToolPak is installed on your computer, you will see Data Analysis on the Tools menu. The Data Analysis menu option may appear at the bottom of the list as it does here. More current versions of Excel "learn" which functions are regularly used and put them more toward the top of the list.

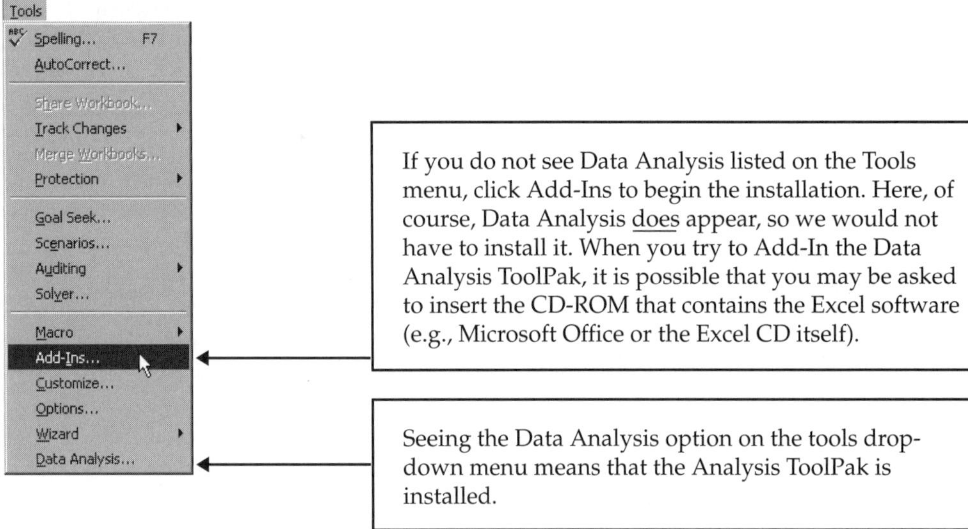
Tools
Spelling... F7
AutoCorrect...
Share Workbook...
Track Changes
Merge Workbooks...
Protection
Goal Seek...
Scenarios...
Auditing
Solver...
Macro
Add-Ins...
Customize...
Options...
Wizard
Data Analysis...

If you do not see Data Analysis listed on the Tools menu, click Add-Ins to begin the installation. Here, of course, Data Analysis does appear, so we would not have to install it. When you try to Add-In the Data Analysis ToolPak, it is possible that you may be asked to insert the CD-ROM that contains the Excel software (e.g., Microsoft Office or the Excel CD itself).

Seeing the Data Analysis option on the tools drop-down menu means that the Analysis ToolPak is installed.

Workbook: Basic Skills.xls
Worksheet: ToolPak

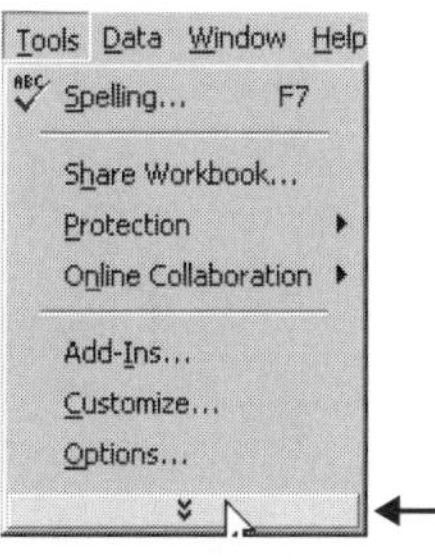
Tools Data Window Help
Spelling... F7
Share Workbook...
Protection
Online Collaboration
Add-Ins...
Customize...
Options...

In later versions of Excel you may not immediately see all the Tools menu options. Let your pointer linger over the "more" bar and more choices will appear, including Add-Ins. A double-click on Tools will cause the entire menu to be displayed without the delay.

Check this box.

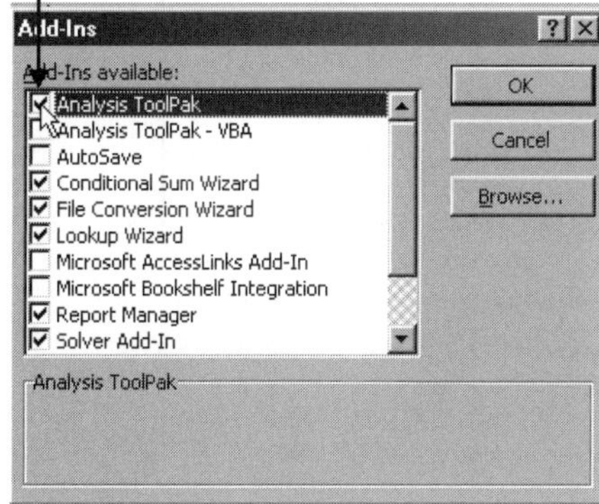
Add-Ins
Add-Ins available:
Analysis ToolPak
Analysis ToolPak - VBA
AutoSave
Conditional Sum Wizard
File Conversion Wizard
Lookup Wizard
Microsoft AccessLinks Add-In
Microsoft Bookshelf Integration
Report Manager
Solver Add-In
OK
Cancel
Browse...
Analysis ToolPak

Once you click Add-Ins from the Tools menu, the last step is to click the box next to Analysis ToolPak and click **OK**. In later versions of Excel, the Analysis ToolPak check box may not be first on the list of Add-Ins.

Worksheet: Basic Skills.xls
Workbook: Formula

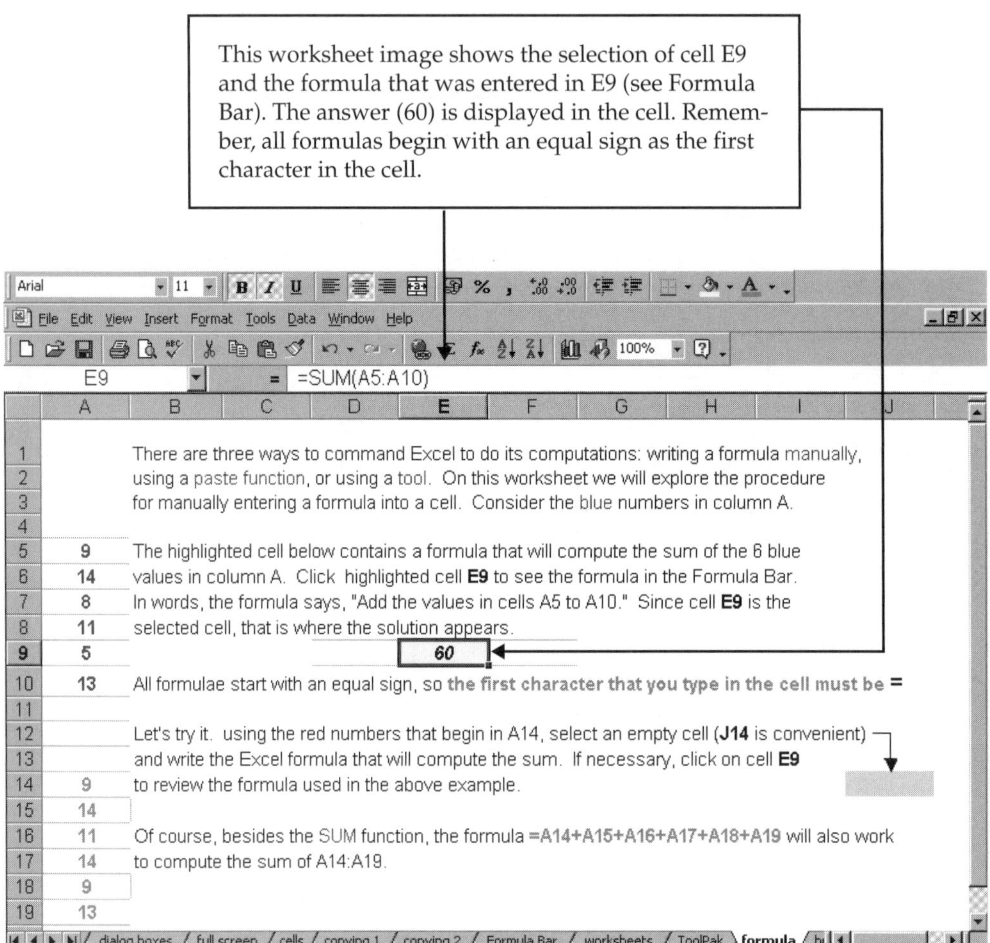
This worksheet image shows the selection of cell E9 and the formula that was entered in E9 (see Formula Bar). The answer (60) is displayed in the cell. Remember, all formulas begin with an equal sign as the first character in the cell.
E9
=SUM(A5:A10)
There are three ways to command Excel to do its computations: writing a formula manually, using a paste function, or using a tool. On this worksheet we will explore the procedure for manually entering a formula into a cell. Consider the blue numbers in column A.
The highlighted cell below contains a formula that will compute the sum of the 6 blue values in column A. Click highlighted cell E9 to see the formula in the Formula Bar. In words, the formula says, "Add the values in cells A5 to A10." Since cell E9 is the selected cell, that is where the solution appears.
60
All formulae start with an equal sign, so the first character that you type in the cell must be =
Let's try it. using the red numbers that begin in A14, select an empty cell (J14 is convenient) and write the Excel formula that will compute the sum. If necessary, click on cell E9 to review the formula used in the above example.
Of course, besides the SUM function, the formula =A14+A15+A16+A17+A18+A19 will also work to compute the sum of A14:A19.
9
14
8
11
5
13
9
14
11
14
9
13
dialog boxes
full screen
cells
copying 1
copying 2
Formula Bar
worksheets
ToolPak
formula

Worksheet: Basic Skills.xls
Workbook: buttons

These images show some Excel operations that may be accessed by clicking buttons on the toolbar.

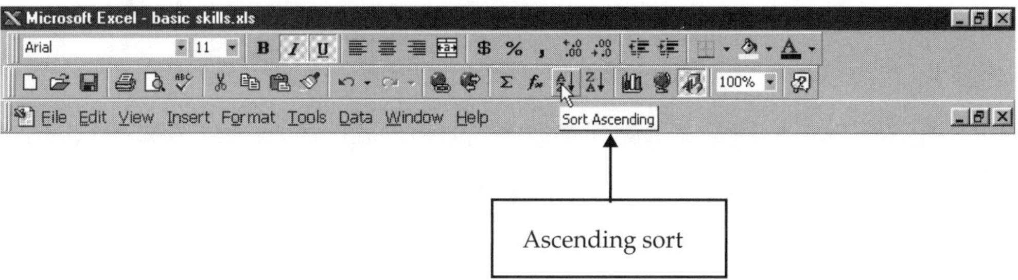
Microsoft Excel - basic skills.xls
Arial
11
File Edit View Insert Format Tools Data Window Help
100%
Sort Ascending
Ascending sort

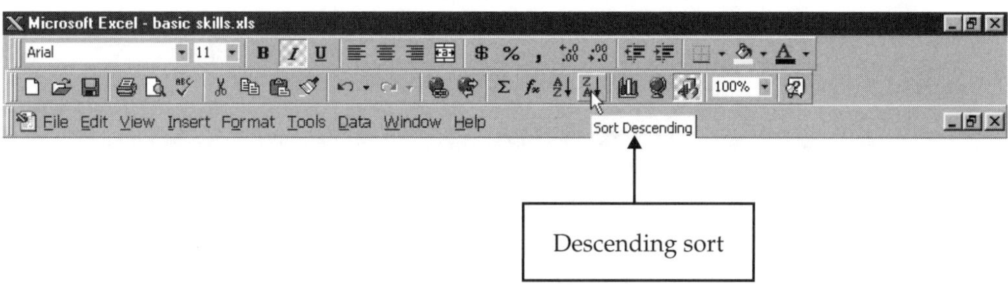
Microsoft Excel - basic skills.xls
Arial
11
File Edit View Insert Format Tools Data Window Help
100%
Sort Descending
Descending sort

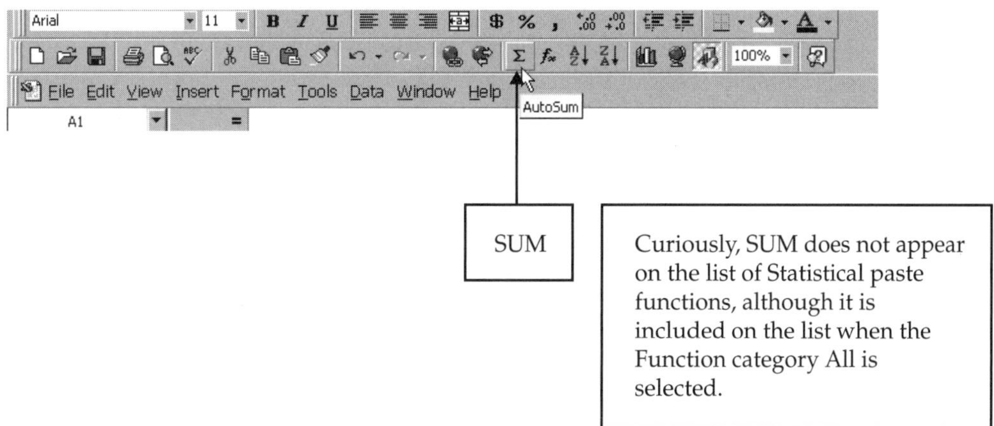
Arial
11
File Edit View Insert Format Tools Data Window Help
100%
AutoSum
A1
=
SUM
Curiously, SUM does not appear on the list of Statistical paste functions, although it is included on the list when the Function category All is selected.

Workbook: Basic Skills.xls
Worksheet: more buttons

If you make a procedural error and must revert back to an earlier screen state, all you have to do is click the undo button. The computer stores many previous keyboard actions, and each click of the undo button reverses those actions one at a time. If the button "grays out," it means you have reached the beginning of the operation sequence, and no further backtracking is possible.

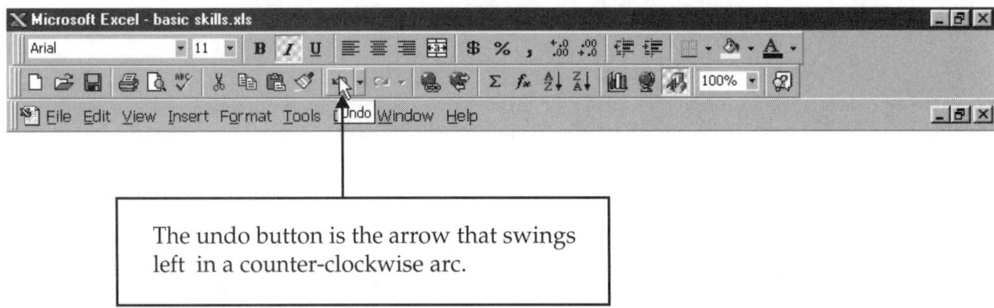
Microsoft Excel - basic skills.xls
Arial
11
100%
File Edit View Insert Format Tools
Undo
Window Help
The undo button is the arrow that swings left in a counter-clockwise arc.

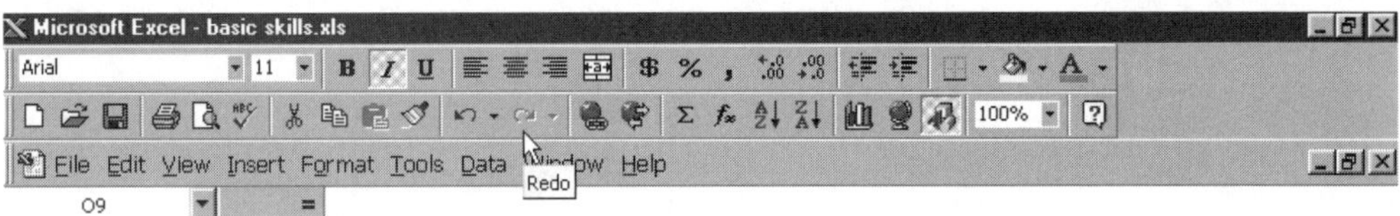
Microsoft Excel - basic skills.xls
Arial
11
100%
File Edit View Insert Format Tools Data
Help
Redo
O9

After you undo an operation, it is an easy matter to redo it by clicking the redo button. It is the arrow that swings to the right in a clockwise arc. If the button is "grayed out," it means there is no action in memory to be "redone."

Workbook: Basic Skills.xls
Worksheet: functions (a)

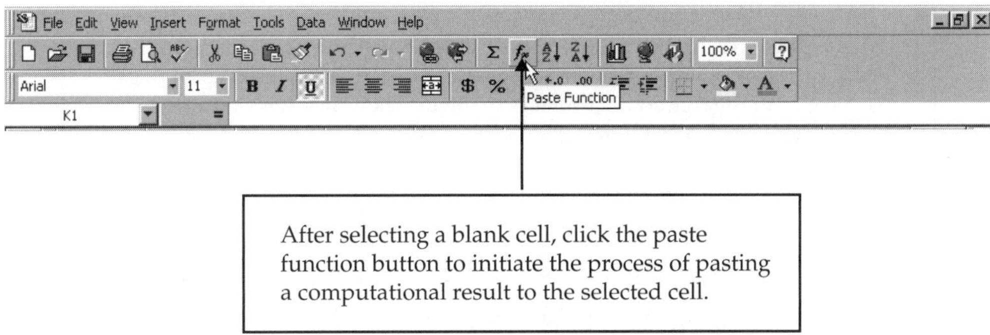
File Edit View Insert Format Tools Data Window Help
Arial
11
100%
Paste Function
K1
=
After selecting a blank cell, click the paste function button to initiate the process of pasting a computational result to the selected cell.

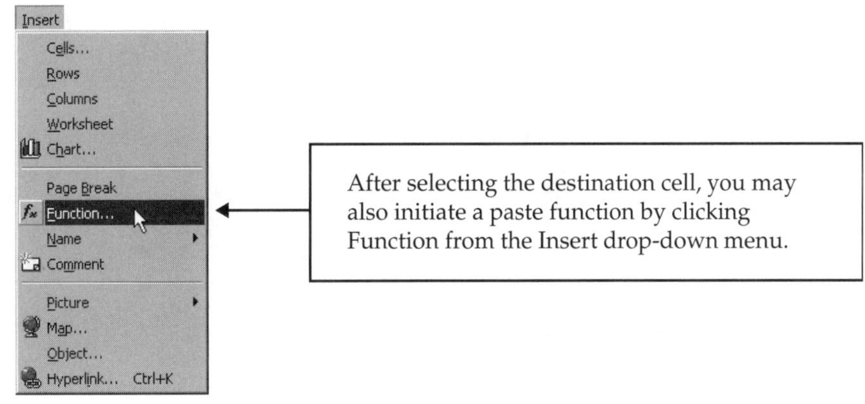
Insert
Cells...
Rows
Columns
Worksheet
Chart...
Page Break
Function...
Name
Comment
Picture
Map...
Object...
Hyperlink... Ctrl+K
After selecting the destination cell, you may also initiate a paste function by clicking Function from the Insert drop-down menu.

Workbook: Basic Skills.xls
Worksheet: functions (b)

There are two lists in the Paste Function dialog box. Click Statistics from the left (Function category) menu and a statistic (AVERAGE, in the present instance) from the right (Function name) menu. Then click **OK**. In future sessions with Excel, use the scroll bar as needed to reveal the remaining statistical functions.

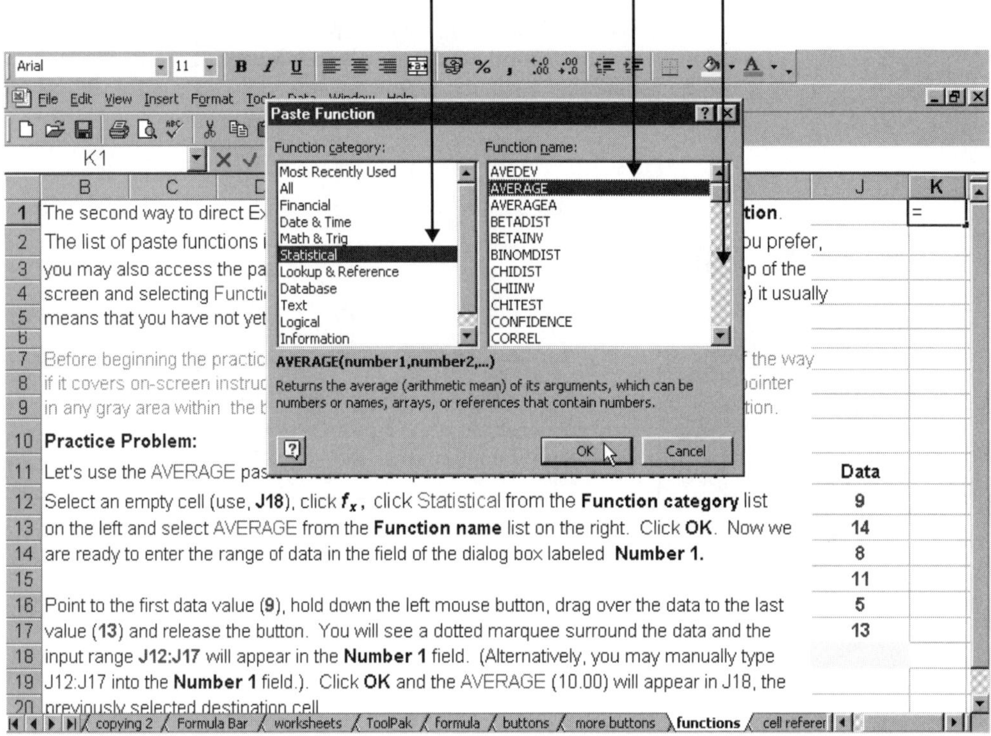
Paste Function
Function category:
Most Recently Used
All
Financial
Date & Time
Math & Trig
Statistical
Lookup & Reference
Database
Text
Logical
Information
Function name:
AVEDEV
AVERAGE
AVERAGEA
BETADIST
BETAINV
BINOMDIST
CHIDIST
CHIINV
CHITEST
CONFIDENCE
CORREL
AVERAGE(number1,number2,...)
Returns the average (arithmetic mean) of its arguments, which can be numbers or names, arrays, or references that contain numbers.
OK
Cancel
K1
Practice Problem:
Data
9
14
8
11
5
13
Select an empty cell (use, J18), click fx, click Statistical from the Function category list
on the left and select AVERAGE from the Function name list on the right. Click OK. Now we
are ready to enter the range of data in the field of the dialog box labeled Number 1.
Point to the first data value (9), hold down the left mouse button, drag over the data to the last
value (13) and release the button. You will see a dotted marquee surround the data and the
input range J12:J17 will appear in the Number 1 field. (Alternatively, you may manually type
J12:J17 into the Number 1 field.). Click OK and the AVERAGE (10.00) will appear in J18, the
copying 2
Formula Bar
worksheets
ToolPak
formula
buttons
more buttons
functions

Depending on the version of Excel you are using, the dialog box that comes up after clicking f_x may or may not look exactly like the one pictured above. Basically, however, the various versions of this Excel dialog ask for the same information: select a category (to which you will respond Statistical) and scroll to and select a function from the list. See the Windows XP version of this dialog at the end of this chapter.

Workbook: Basic Skills.xls
Worksheet: functions (c)

Click this tiny spreadsheet icon, hold down a left mouse click, and drag over the data to select the Input Range for your data.

The last step is to fill in the dialog box for the function. In the Number 1 field, as shown, enter the range of data to which the paste function will apply – J12:J17. Click **OK** to paste the result to the selected cell (J18). Notice that the paste function result for AVERAGE (here, 10) appears in the box even before clicking **OK**.

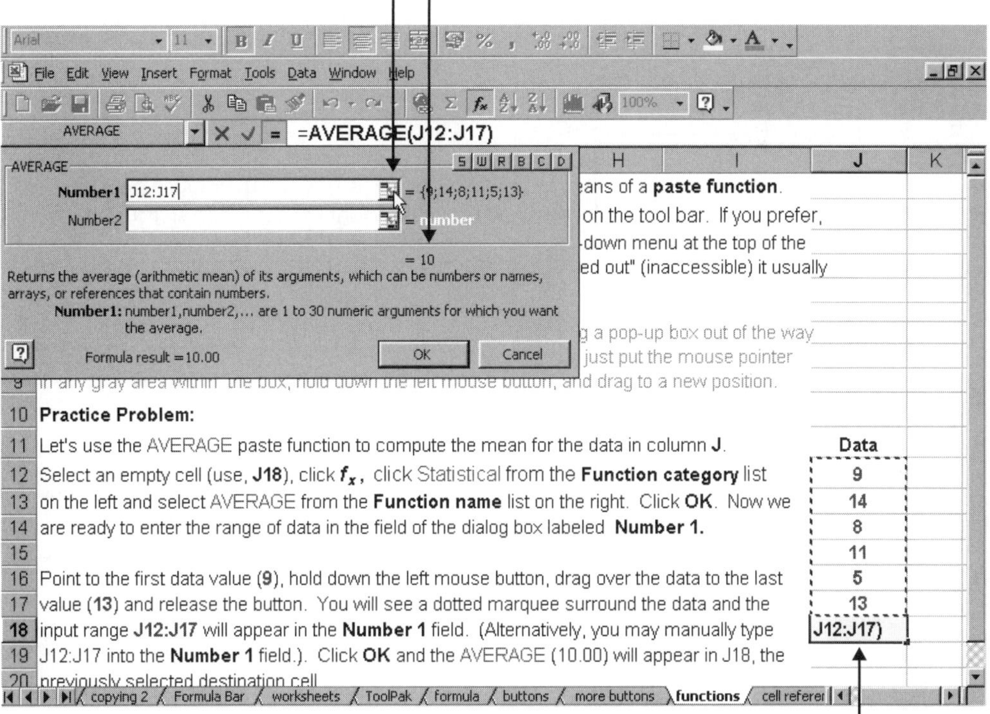
File Edit View Insert Format Tools Data Window Help
AVERAGE
=AVERAGE(J12:J17)
AVERAGE
Number1 J12:J17
= {9;14;8;11;5;13}
Number2
= number
= 10
Returns the average (arithmetic mean) of its arguments, which can be numbers or names, arrays, or references that contain numbers.
Number1: number1,number2,... are 1 to 30 numeric arguments for which you want the average.
Formula result =10.00
OK
Cancel
10 Practice Problem:
11 Let's use the AVERAGE paste function to compute the mean for the data in column J.
12 Select an empty cell (use, J18), click fx, click Statistical from the Function category list
13 on the left and select AVERAGE from the Function name list on the right. Click OK. Now we
14 are ready to enter the range of data in the field of the dialog box labeled Number 1.
16 Point to the first data value (9), hold down the left mouse button, drag over the data to the last
17 value (13) and release the button. You will see a dotted marquee surround the data and the
18 input range J12:J17 will appear in the Number 1 field. (Alternatively, you may manually type
19 J12:J17 into the Number 1 field.). Click OK and the AVERAGE (10.00) will appear in J18, the
Data
9
14
8
11
5
13
J12:J17)
copying 2 / Formula Bar / worksheets / ToolPak / formula / buttons / more buttons / functions / cell referen

The range of numbers on which the paste function will operate will appear in the selected cell. This information also appears in the Formula Bar. If the cell is too small, not all the formula contents will fit in the cell, but this will not affect Excel's computation.

Workbook: Basic Skills.xls
Worksheet: cell references

Basic Skills [Read-Only]

	A	B
1	Data	X - $\bar{X}$
2	9	=a2-a8
3	14	
4	8	
5	11	
6	5	
7	13	
8	10.00	

This image shows the formula in cell B2. Notice that Excel does not require that cell references be typed using uppercase letters. Excel will automatically change lowercase entries to uppercase.

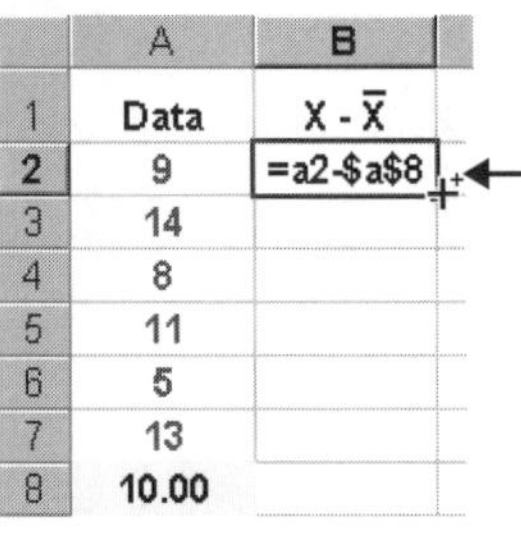

	A	B
1	Data	X - $\bar{X}$
2	9	=a2-a8
3	14	
4	8	
5	11	
6	5	
7	13	
8	10.00	

The fill handle appears as a plus sign on a PC (and a square on a Macintosh) when the mouse pointer rests on the lower right corner of the selected cell.

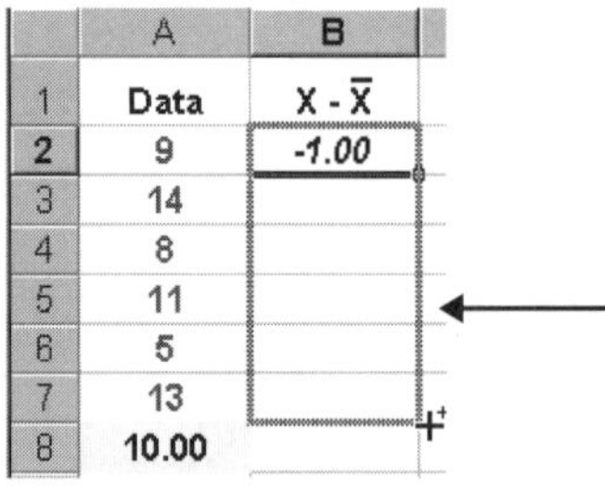

	A	B
1	Data	X - $\bar{X}$
2	9	-1.00
3	14	
4	8	
5	11	
6	5	
7	13	
8	10.00	

Dragging down to row 7 produces a border around the cells that will receive the copied formula.

	A	B
1	Data	X - $\bar{X}$
2	9	-1.00
3	14	4.00
4	8	-2.00
5	11	1.00
6	5	-5.00
7	13	3.00
8	10.00	

After releasing the mouse button the display will look like this. Click in any empty cell to remove the highlighting from column B.

Workbook: Basic Skills.xls
Worksheet: view dialog

When working with the Excel Statistics Companion, it is often helpful to see what inputs were used to arrive at a particular paste-function result. Formula values and cell references, while visible in the Formula Bar, are more easily understood when seen in the form of a dialog box. Click on the cell that displays the paste-function result and click f_x on the toolbar. The dialog box will appear on the screen as shown below. Click the Cancel or OK button to close the dialog box.

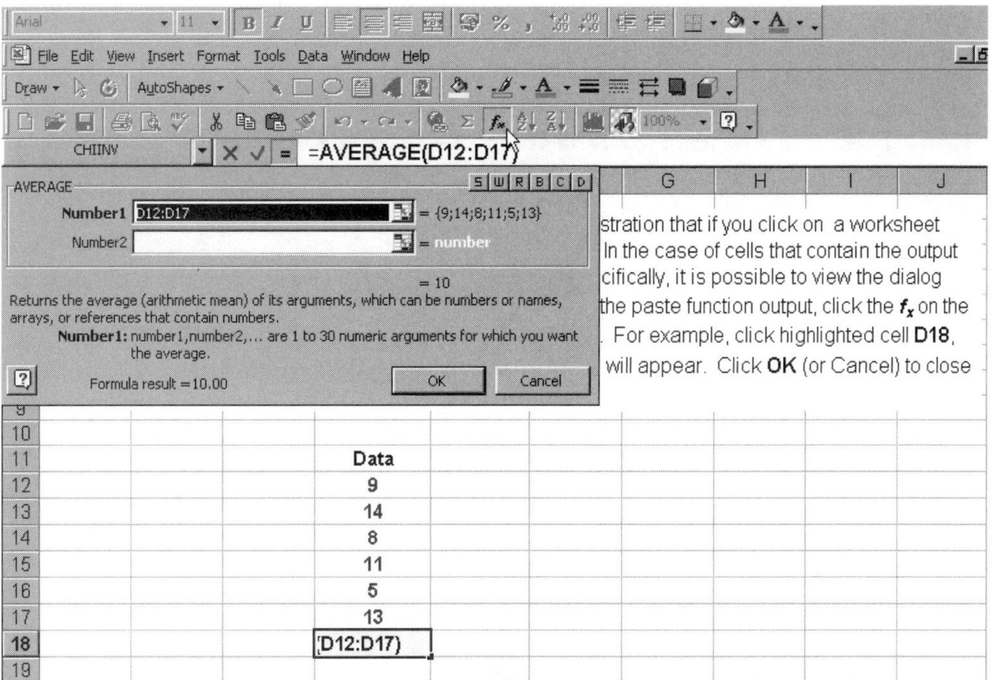
File Edit View Insert Format Tools Data Window Help
CHIINV
=AVERAGE(D12:D17)
AVERAGE
Number1 D12:D17 = {9;14;8;11;5;13}
Number2 = number
= 10
Returns the average (arithmetic mean) of its arguments, which can be numbers or names, arrays, or references that contain numbers.
Number1: number1,number2,... are 1 to 30 numeric arguments for which you want the average.
Formula result =10.00
OK
Cancel
stration that if you click on a worksheet
In the case of cells that contain the output
cifically, it is possible to view the dialog
the paste function output, click the f_x on the
For example, click highlighted cell D18,
will appear. Click OK (or Cancel) to close
Data
9
14
8
11
5
13
D12:D17)

Workbook: Basic Skills.xls
Worksheet: error example

The "error example" worksheet shows what happens when Excel tries to put information in a cell that is too small to hold the value. The ##### error message appears. One remedy is to widen the column, which also increases the width of the cells in that column. In the current example, widening the column allows the data to replace the error message in the destination cell. The procedure for widening is captured in the following images.

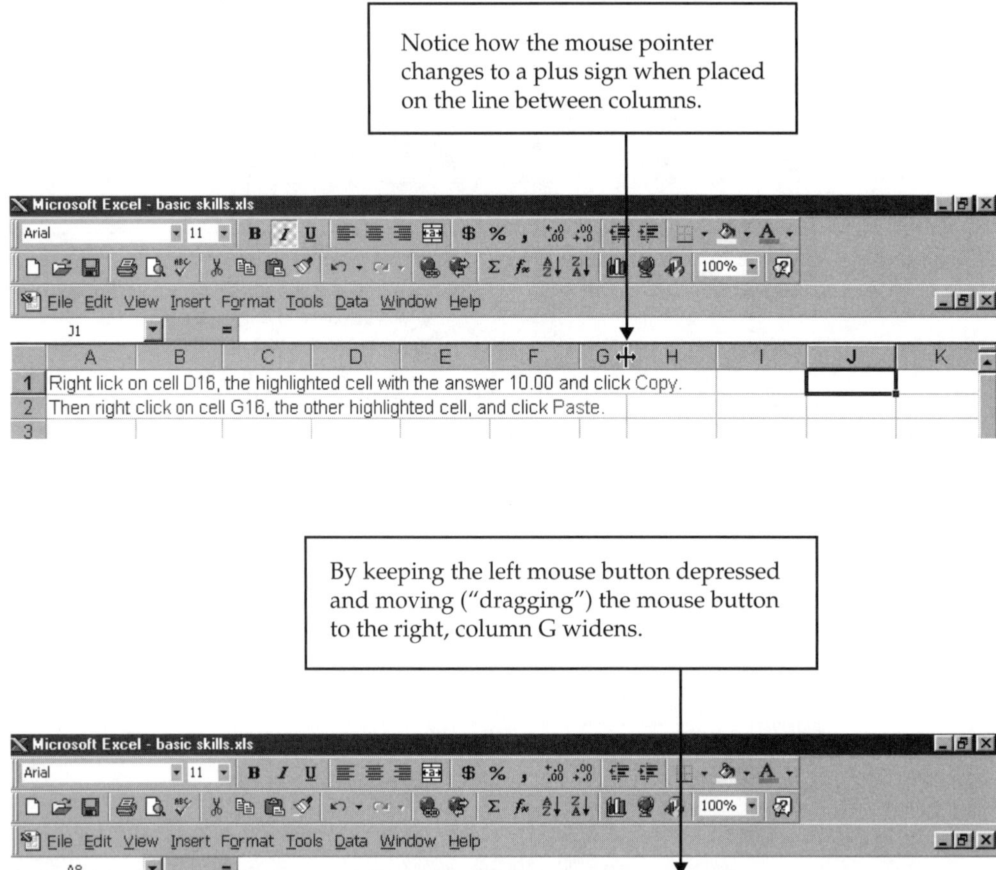
Notice how the mouse pointer changes to a plus sign when placed on the line between columns.
Microsoft Excel - basic skills.xls
Right lick on cell D16, the highlighted cell with the answer 10.00 and click Copy.
Then right click on cell G16, the other highlighted cell, and click Paste.
By keeping the left mouse button depressed and moving ("dragging") the mouse button to the right, column G widens.
Microsoft Excel - basic skills.xls
Right lick on cell D16, the highlighted cell with the answer 10.00 and click Copy.
Then right click on cell G16, the other highlighted cell, and click Paste.

Workbook: Basic Skills.xls
Worksheet: copy & paste special

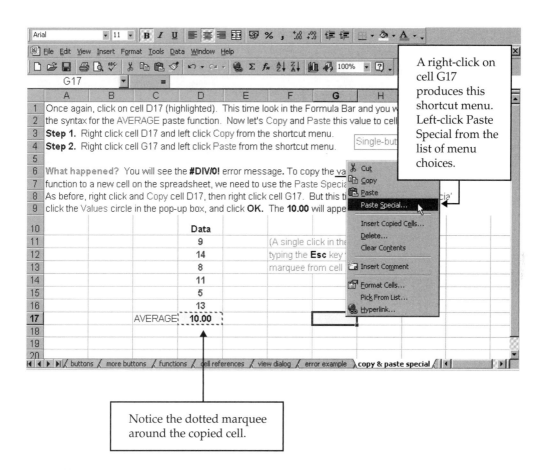

A right-click on cell G17 produces this shortcut menu. Left-click Paste Special from the list of menu choices.

Notice the dotted marquee around the copied cell.

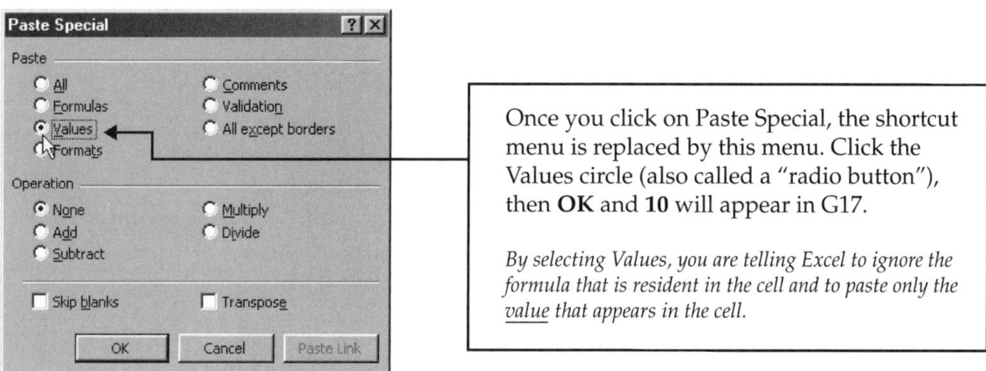
Paste Special
Paste
All
Formulas
Values
Formats
Comments
Validation
All except borders
Operation
None
Add
Subtract
Multiply
Divide
Skip blanks
Transpose
OK
Cancel
Paste Link

Once you click on Paste Special, the shortcut menu is replaced by this menu. Click the Values circle (also called a "radio button"), then **OK** and **10** will appear in G17.

By selecting Values, you are telling Excel to ignore the formula that is resident in the cell and to paste only the <u>*value*</u> *that appears in the cell.*

Workbook: Basic Skills.xls
Worksheet: indexing

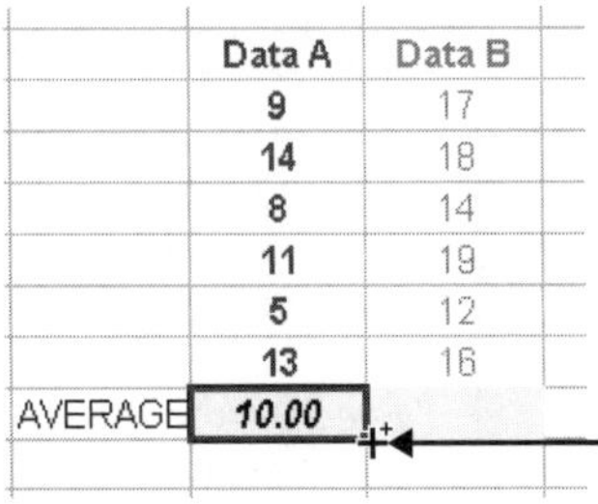

	Data A	Data B
	9	17
	14	18
	8	14
	11	19
	5	12
	13	16
AVERAGE	*10.00*	

Cell D17 holds an AVERAGE. You may drag to copy ("fill") the formula to cell E17 and thereby produce an AVERAGE for Data B. The key is positioning the mouse on the lower right of the cell until the pointer changes to the plus sign (or □ on the Macintosh). Once you see the plus sign, hold down the left mouse button, drag one cell to the right, and release the mouse button.

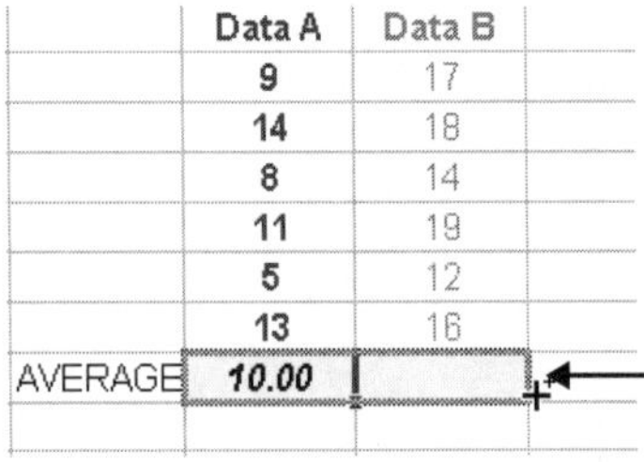

	Data A	Data B
	9	17
	14	18
	8	14
	11	19
	5	12
	13	16
AVERAGE	*10.00*	

This is what the display will look like after the drag operation – but before you release the left mouse button. A gray border surrounds the affected cells.

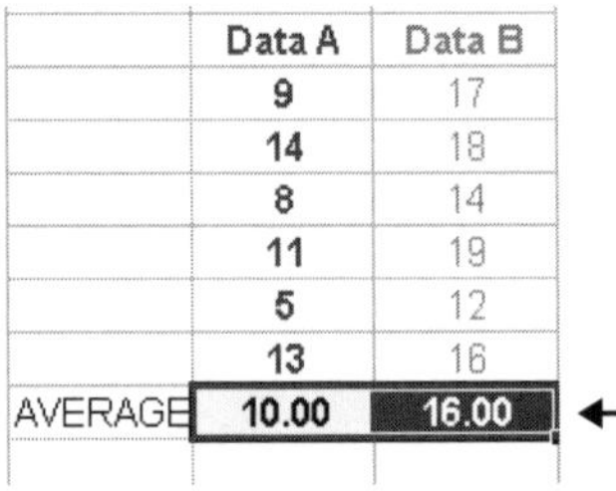

	Data A	Data B
	9	17
	14	18
	8	14
	11	19
	5	12
	13	16
AVERAGE	10.00	16.00

When you release the left mouse button the AVERAGE of Data set B will appear in cell E17. Excel "knows" that you want the AVERAGE of the Data B column even though you dragged the formula **AVERAGE(D11:D16)** from column A. This is called "indexing." You will see the formula **AVERAGE(E11:E16)** in the Formula Bar when cell E17 is selected.

Workbook: Basic Skills.xls
Worksheet: tools

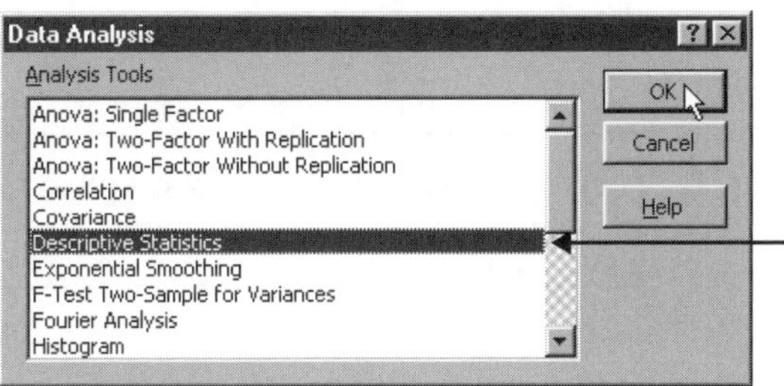
Data Analysis
Analysis Tools
OK
Cancel
Help
Anova: Single Factor
Anova: Two-Factor With Replication
Anova: Two-Factor Without Replication
Correlation
Covariance
Descriptive Statistics
Exponential Smoothing
F-Test Two-Sample for Variances
Fourier Analysis
Histogram

This box pops up when you click Data Analysis from the Tools drop-down menu. The instruction on the worksheet asks for you to click Descriptive Statistics from the list of tools.

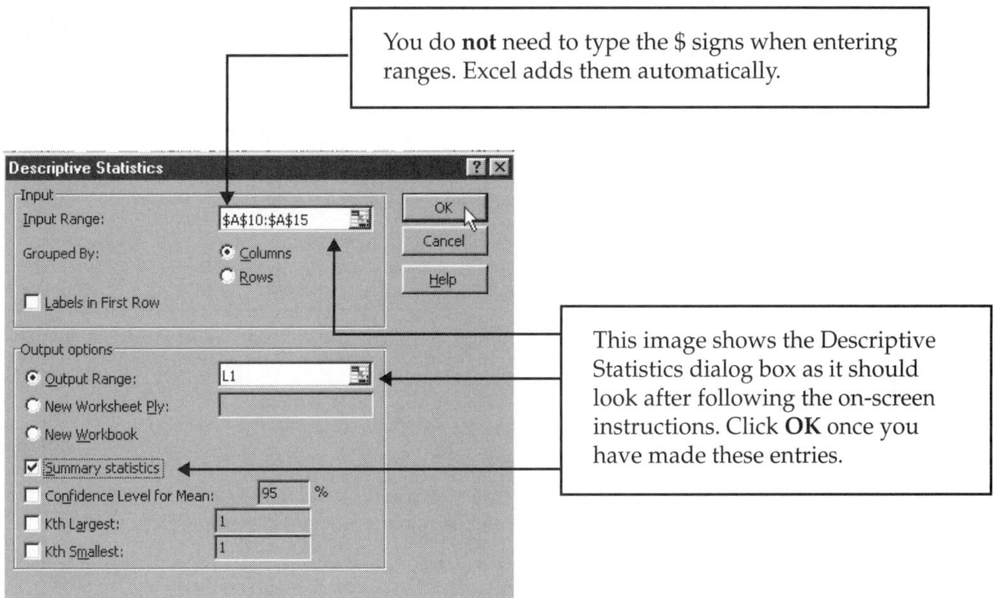
You do **not** need to type the $ signs when entering ranges. Excel adds them automatically.
Descriptive Statistics
Input
Input Range:
$A$10:$A$15
Grouped By:
Columns
Rows
Labels in First Row
OK
Cancel
Help
Output options
Output Range:
L1
New Worksheet Ply:
New Workbook
Summary statistics
Confidence Level for Mean:
95
%
Kth Largest:
1
Kth Smallest:
1
This image shows the Descriptive Statistics dialog box as it should look after following the on-screen instructions. Click **OK** once you have made these entries.

Workbook: Basic Skills.xls
Worksheet: col. Width

Widening columns is sometimes necessary to have a proper view of an output table.

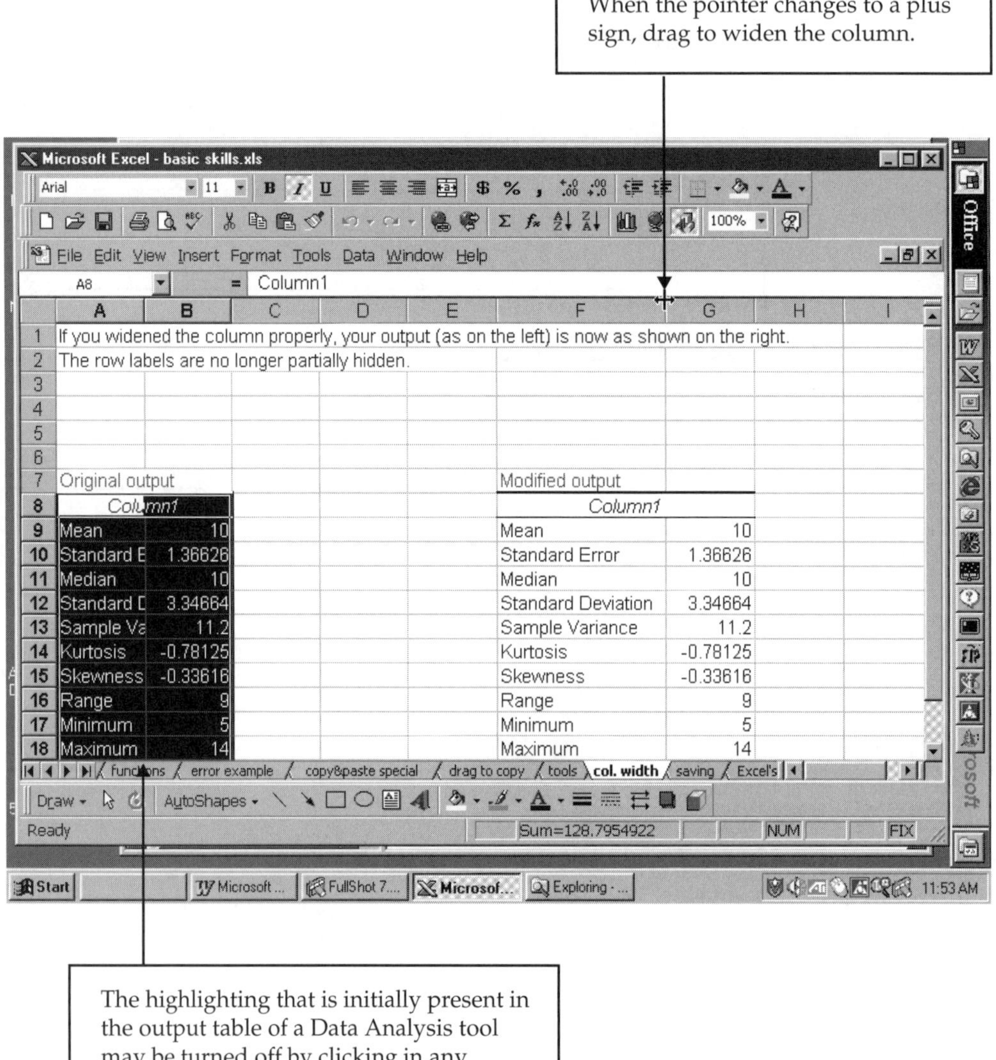
When the pointer changes to a plus sign, drag to widen the column.
Microsoft Excel - basic skills.xls
A8 = Column1
If you widened the column properly, your output (as on the left) is now as shown on the right.
The row labels are no longer partially hidden.
Original output
Modified output
Column1
Mean 10
Standard E 1.36626
Median 10
Standard D 3.34664
Sample Va 11.2
Kurtosis -0.78125
Skewness -0.33616
Range 9
Minimum 5
Maximum 14
Mean 10
Standard Error 1.36626
Median 10
Standard Deviation 3.34664
Sample Variance 11.2
Kurtosis -0.78125
Skewness -0.33616
Range 9
Minimum 5
Maximum 14
functions / error example / copy&paste special / drag to copy / tools / col. width / saving / Excel's
Ready
Sum=128.7954922
The highlighting that is initially present in the output table of a Data Analysis tool may be turned off by clicking in any empty cell of the worksheet.

Workbook: Basic Skills.xls
Worksheet: saving

If you wish to save any work you have completed in an Excel workbook, save it using the Save As option from the File menu. You will, of course, need to tell Excel where to save the file (the Save in field) and enter a file name (the File name field).

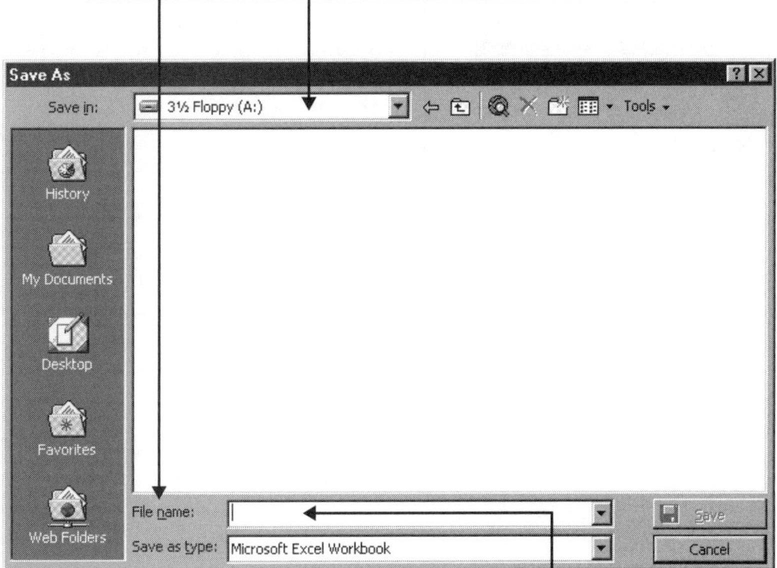
Save As
Save in:
3½ Floppy (A:)
Tools
History
My Documents
Desktop
Favorites
Web Folders
File name:
Save as type:
Microsoft Excel Workbook
Save
Cancel

Before clicking **OK**, you must enter a file name in the File name field

The CD-ROM that contains your Excel software cannot be modified with a save operation, so it is impossible to corrupt a file unintentionally on your ESC CD-ROM. Using Save As from the File menu, save a file on which you are working to your hard drive, floppy, zip disk – or another CD-ROM if you have the hardware on your computer to burn a CD.

Workbook: Basic Skills.xls
Worksheet: Help

The Paste Function dialog box has two question marks that you may click to access help.

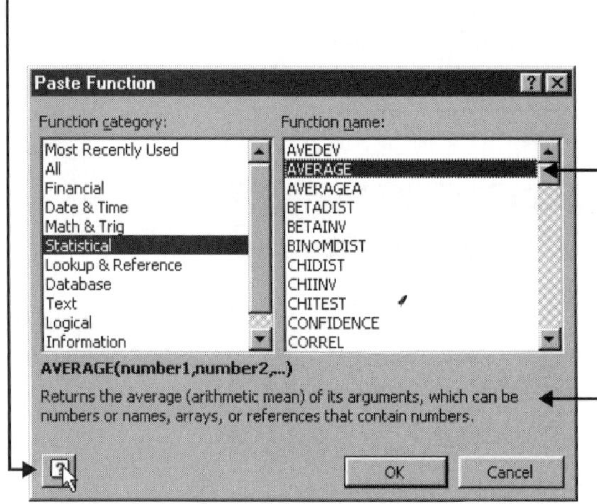
Paste Function
Function category:
Function name:
Most Recently Used
All
Financial
Date & Time
Math & Trig
Statistical
Lookup & Reference
Database
Text
Logical
Information
AVEDEV
AVERAGE
AVERAGEA
BETADIST
BETAINV
BINOMDIST
CHIDIST
CHIINV
CHITEST
CONFIDENCE
CORREL
AVERAGE(number1,number2,...)
Returns the average (arithmetic mean) of its arguments, which can be numbers or names, arrays, or references that contain numbers.
OK
Cancel

One click on a Function name will highlight it and show a brief explanation of the function at the bottom of the box. Two clicks (or **OK** after highlighting the Function name) will open the dialog box for that function.

Here is Excel's explanation for the AVERAGE paste function.

When using a Data Analysis tool, the question mark for help is here.

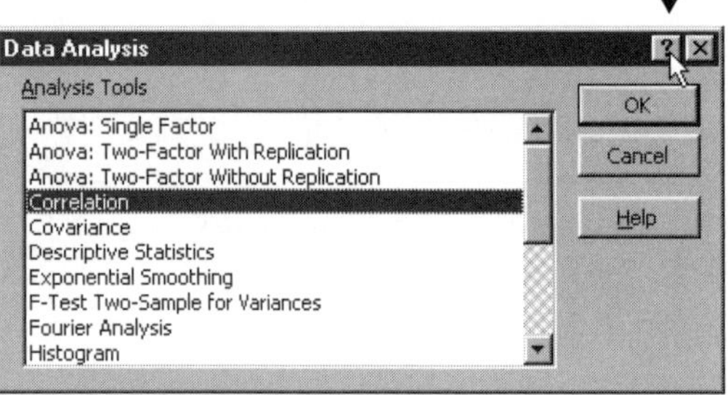
Data Analysis
Analysis Tools
Anova: Single Factor
Anova: Two-Factor With Replication
Anova: Two-Factor Without Replication
Correlation
Covariance
Descriptive Statistics
Exponential Smoothing
F-Test Two-Sample for Variances
Fourier Analysis
Histogram
OK
Cancel
Help

Workbook: Basic Skills.xls
Worksheet: Help

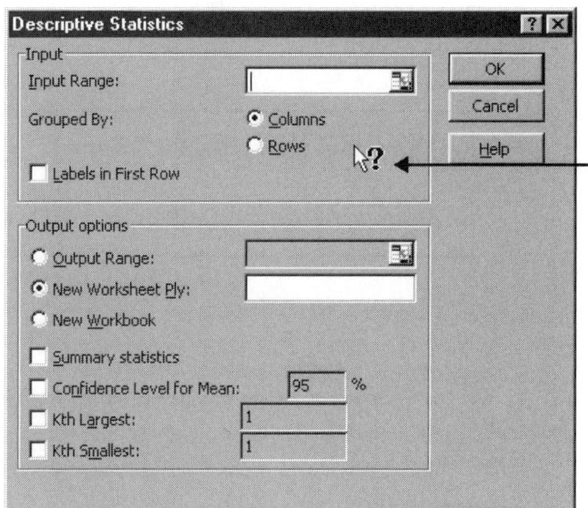
Descriptive Statistics
Input
Input Range:
Grouped By:
Columns
Rows
Labels in First Row
OK
Cancel
Help
Output options
Output Range:
New Worksheet Ply:
New Workbook
Summary statistics
Confidence Level for Mean:
95
%
Kth Largest:
1
Kth Smallest:
1

After clicking the question mark button, the question mark becomes bold and moves along with the mouse pointer. The next step is to left-click. A box will pop up with a general description of the tool along with a link to specific instructions that relate to each query in the dialog box.

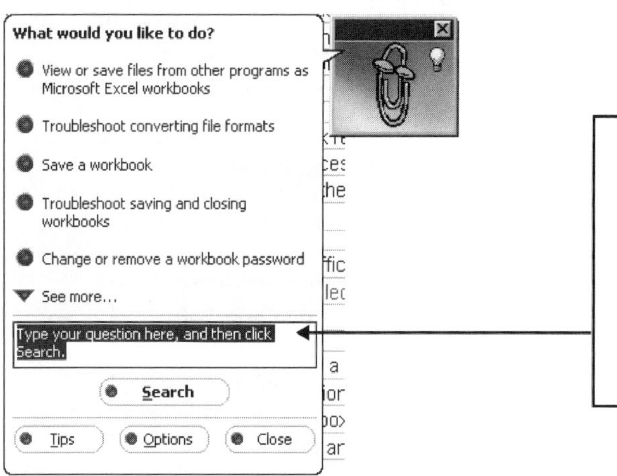
What would you like to do?
View or save files from other programs as Microsoft Excel workbooks
Troubleshoot converting file formats
Save a workbook
Troubleshoot saving and closing workbooks
Change or remove a workbook password
See more...
Type your question here, and then click Search.
Search
Tips
Options
Close

This is Excel's office assistant, which is accessed by clicking the question mark at the top right of your screen or the Help menu on the menu bar. Your assistant might look a little different than mine. Type in your question where shown and Excel will do its best to help.

Workbook: Basic Skills.xls
Worksheet: opening (a)

Chances are you will be using the auto-loading feature of the CD-ROM with its handy click-and-load menu links. But if you wish to load files manually…

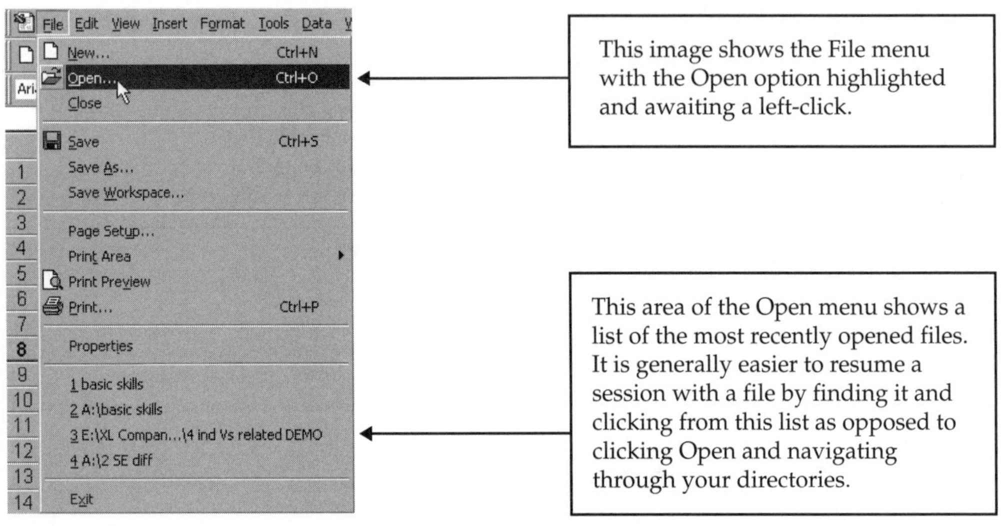
File Edit View Insert Format Tools Data
New… Ctrl+N
Open… Ctrl+O
Close
Save Ctrl+S
Save As…
Save Workspace…
Page Setup…
Print Area
Print Preview
Print… Ctrl+P
Properties
1 basic skills
2 A:\basic skills
3 E:\XL Compan…\4 ind Vs related DEMO
4 A:\2 SE diff
Exit
This image shows the File menu with the Open option highlighted and awaiting a left-click.
This area of the Open menu shows a list of the most recently opened files. It is generally easier to resume a session with a file by finding it and clicking from this list as opposed to clicking Open and navigating through your directories.

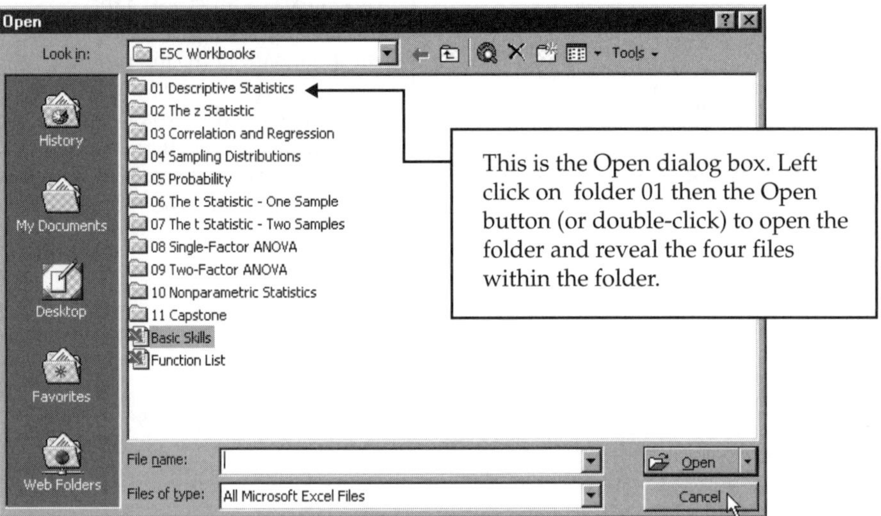
Open
Look in: ESC Workbooks
Tools
01 Descriptive Statistics
02 The z Statistic
03 Correlation and Regression
04 Sampling Distributions
05 Probability
06 The t Statistic - One Sample
07 The t Statistic - Two Samples
08 Single-Factor ANOVA
09 Two-Factor ANOVA
10 Nonparametric Statistics
11 Capstone
Basic Skills
Function List
History
My Documents
Desktop
Favorites
Web Folders
File name:
Files of type: All Microsoft Excel Files
Open
Cancel
This is the Open dialog box. Left click on folder 01 then the Open button (or double-click) to open the folder and reveal the four files within the folder.

Workbook: Basic Skills.xls
Worksheet: opening (b)

This screen shows the five Excel files in the Descriptive Statistics folder with folder 1-1 highlighted and ready to open with a click of the open button (lower right of window).

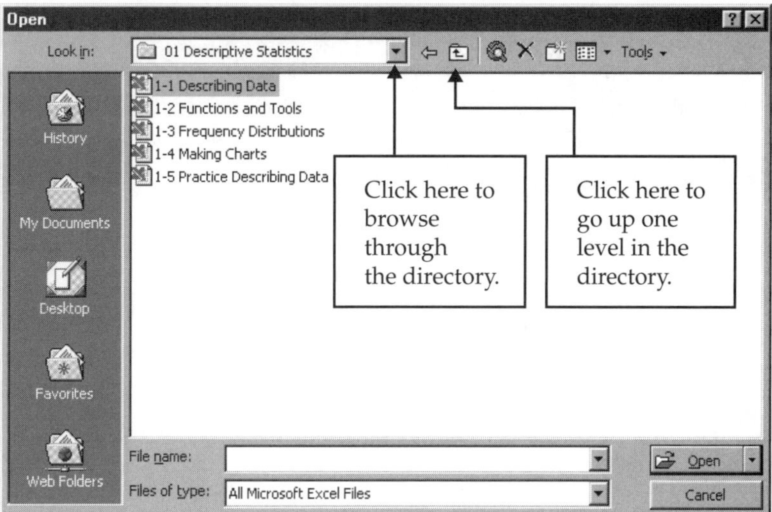
Open
Look in:
01 Descriptive Statistics
Tools
History
My Documents
Desktop
Favorites
Web Folders
1-1 Describing Data
1-2 Functions and Tools
1-3 Frequency Distributions
1-4 Making Charts
1-5 Practice Describing Data
Click here to browse through the directory.
Click here to go up one level in the directory.
File name:
Files of type:
All Microsoft Excel Files
Open
Cancel

As mentioned earlier, most users prefer to use the auto-loading feature of the *ESC* CD-ROM. After inserting the CD-ROM, a user interface displays a menu listing (and briefly describes) all the *ESC* workbooks. Simply click on a workbook title and the file will load automatically.

If you have installed *ESC* on the hard drive ("fixed disk") of your PC, you may use the procedures described above to navigate through folders and subfolders to locate the folder that holds the *ESC* files. Then, simply click on the "Start" file in the ESC folder to run the user interface and view the handy menu.

Workbook: Basic Skills.xls
Worksheet: opening (c)

After opening the Describing Data file, the first worksheet in the workbook appears on the screen. You will need to click Close on the File menu (shown below) to resume your session with the basic skills workbook.

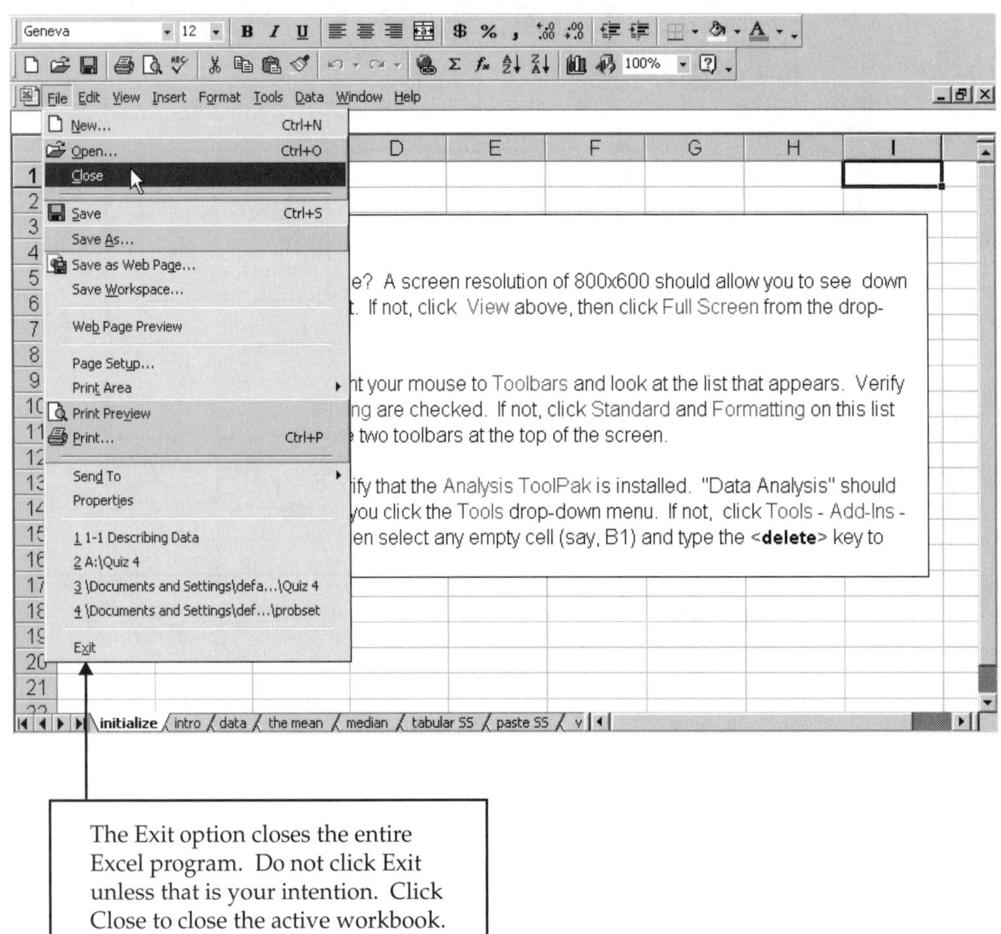
File Edit View Insert Format Tools Data Window Help
New... Ctrl+N
Open... Ctrl+O
Close
Save Ctrl+S
Save As...
Save as Web Page...
Save Workspace...
Web Page Preview
Page Setup...
Print Area
Print Preview
Print... Ctrl+P
Send To
Properties
1 1-1 Describing Data
2 A:\Quiz 4
3 \Documents and Settings\defa...\Quiz 4
4 \Documents and Settings\def...\probset
Exit
initialize intro data the mean median tabular SS paste SS
The Exit option closes the entire Excel program. Do not click Exit unless that is your intention. Click Close to close the active workbook.

Workbook: Basic Skills.xls
Worksheet: XP Toolbar

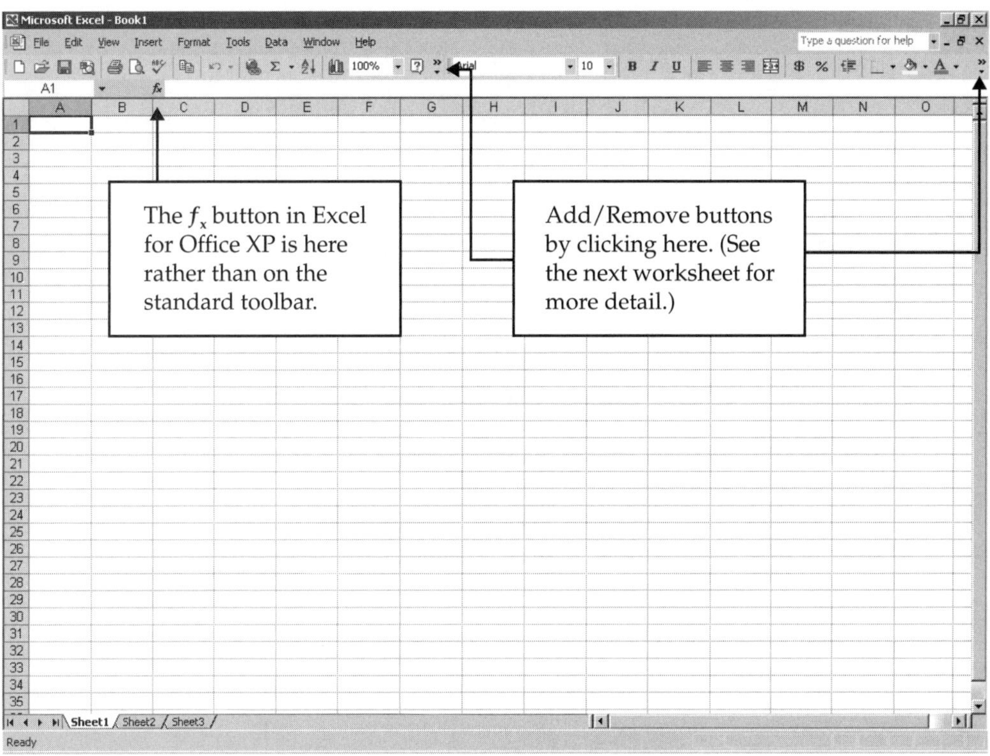
Microsoft Excel - Book1
File Edit View Insert Format Tools Data Window Help
Type a question for help
The f_x button in Excel for Office XP is here rather than on the standard toolbar.
Add/Remove buttons by clicking here. (See the next worksheet for more detail.)
Sheet1 Sheet2 Sheet3
Ready

Workbook: Basic Skills.xls
Worksheet: XP Buttons

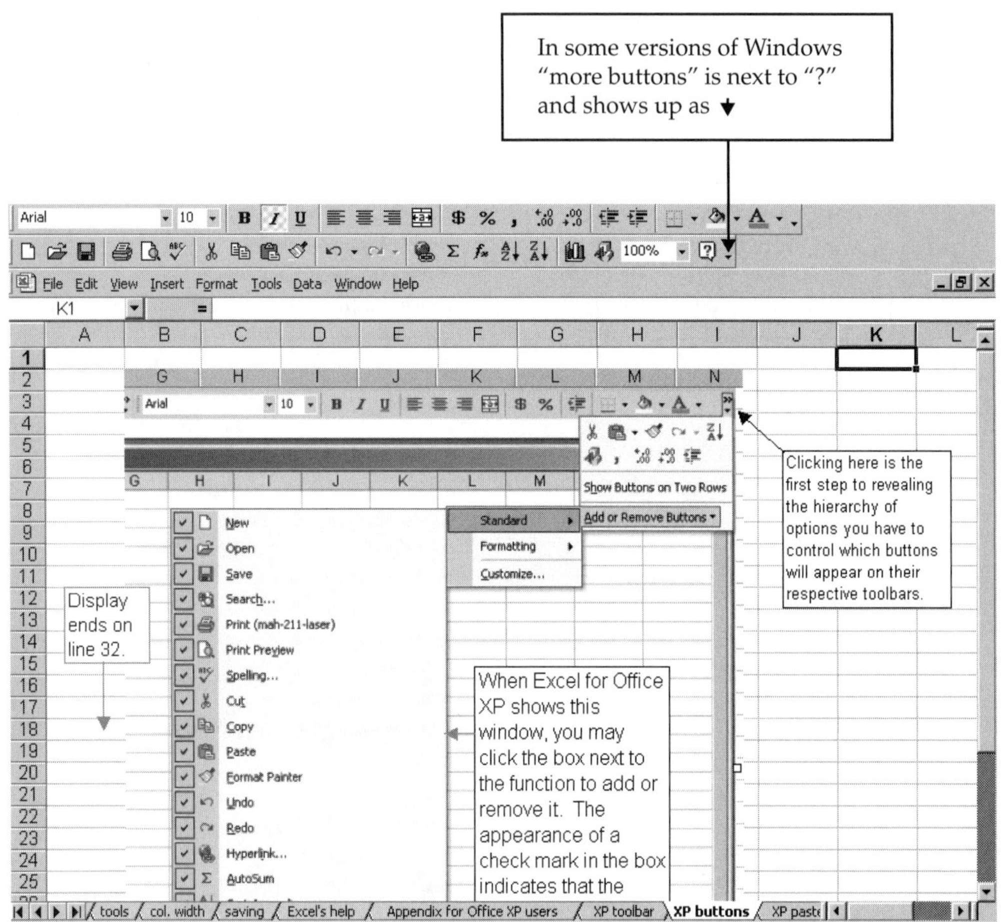
In some versions of Windows "more buttons" is next to "?" and shows up as ↓
Clicking here is the first step to revealing the hierarchy of options you have to control which buttons will appear on their respective toolbars.
Display ends on line 32.
When Excel for Office XP shows this window, you may click the box next to the function to add or remove it. The appearance of a check mark in the box indicates that the
Show Buttons on Two Rows
Add or Remove Buttons
Standard
Formatting
Customize...
New
Open
Save
Search...
Print (mah-211-laser)
Print Preview
Spelling...
Cut
Copy
Paste
Format Painter
Undo
Redo
Hyperlink...
AutoSum
File Edit View Insert Format Tools Data Window Help
tools col. width saving Excel's help Appendix for Office XP users XP toolbar XP buttons XP paste

Workbook: Basic Skills.xls
Worksheet: XP Paste Function

The Insert Function dialog box pops up after clicking the f_x to the left of the Formula Bar or clicking Function from the Insert drop-down menu. This dialog box is different in appearance compared to earlier versions of Excel, but the same procedures are followed. Select Statistical from the list of categories and select a function from the list that appears.

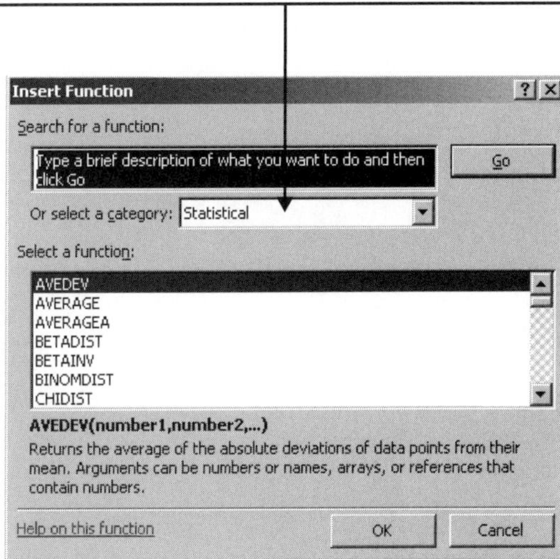
Insert Function
Search for a function:
Type a brief description of what you want to do and then click Go
Go
Or select a category: Statistical
Select a function:
AVEDEV
AVERAGE
AVERAGEA
BETADIST
BETAINV
BINOMDIST
CHIDIST
AVEDEV(number1,number2,...)
Returns the average of the absolute deviations of data points from their mean. Arguments can be numbers or names, arrays, or references that contain numbers.
Help on this function
OK
Cancel

CHAPTER 1-1

Describing Data

Folder: 01 Descriptive Statistics
Workbook: Describing Data.xls
Worksheet: data

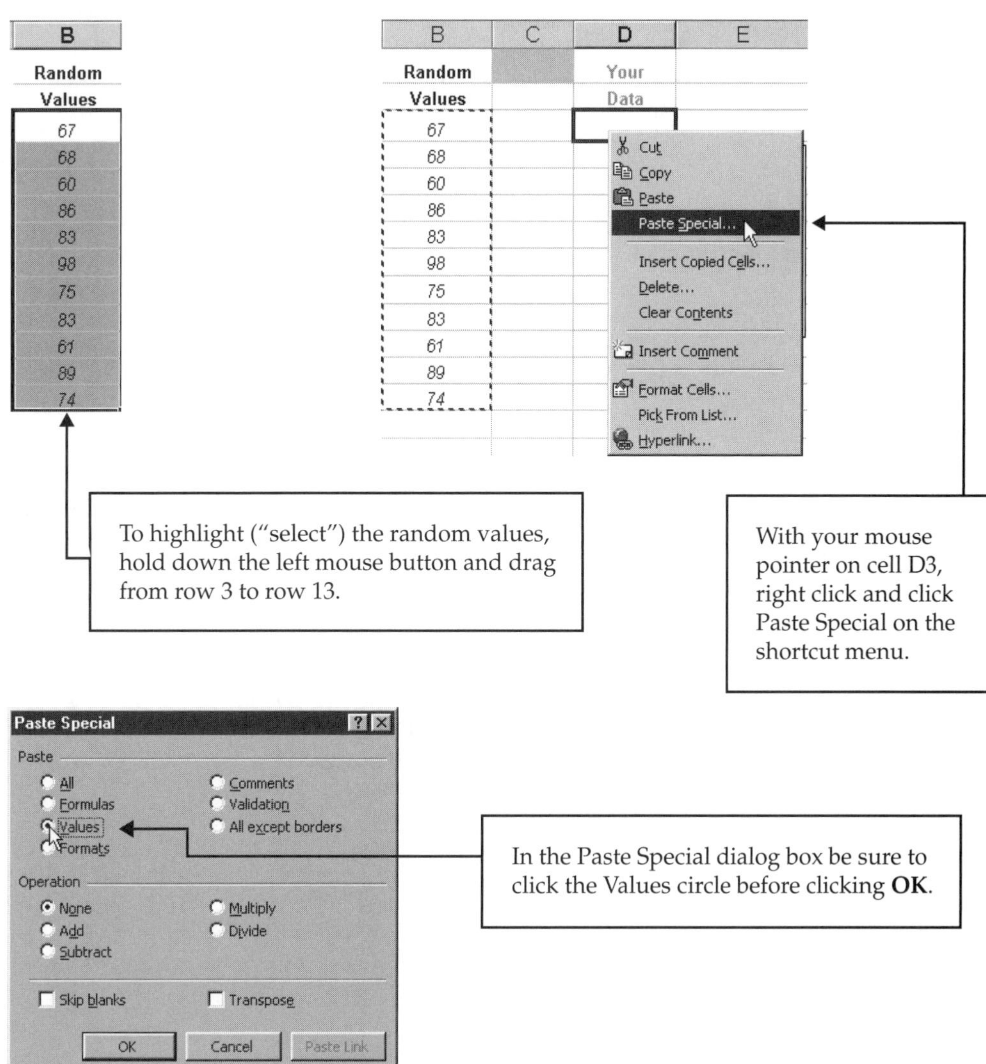
B
Random Values
67
68
60
86
83
98
75
83
61
89
74
B
C
D
E
Random Values
Your Data
Cut
Copy
Paste
Paste Special...
Insert Copied Cells...
Delete...
Clear Contents
Insert Comment
Format Cells...
Pick From List...
Hyperlink...
To highlight ("select") the random values, hold down the left mouse button and drag from row 3 to row 13.
With your mouse pointer on cell D3, right click and click Paste Special on the shortcut menu.
Paste Special
Paste
All
Formulas
Values
Formats
Comments
Validation
All except borders
Operation
None
Add
Subtract
Multiply
Divide
Skip blanks
Transpose
OK
Cancel
Paste Link
In the Paste Special dialog box be sure to click the Values circle before clicking OK.

Folder: 01 Descriptive Statistics
Workbook: Describing Data.xls
Worksheet: the mean

C	D
	Your Data
	67
	68
	60
	86
	83
	98
	75
	83
	61
	89
	74
SUM=	
N =	11

The workbook has been set up to forward your data automatically to "the mean" worksheet. The values that appear on your screen will, of course, be different from the ones shown here.

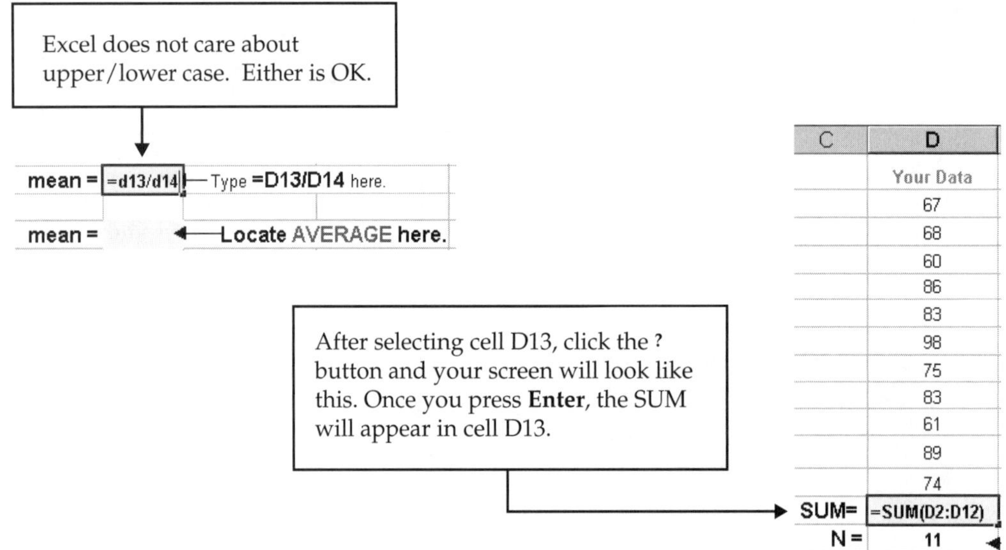
Excel does not care about upper/lower case. Either is OK.
mean = =d13/d14
Type =D13/D14 here.
mean =
Locate AVERAGE here.
C
D
Your Data
67
68
60
86
83
98
75
83
61
89
74
SUM= =SUM(D2:D12)
N = 11
After selecting cell D13, click the ? button and your screen will look like this. Once you press **Enter**, the SUM will appear in cell D13.

Folder 01: Descriptive Statistics
Workbook: Describing Data.xls
Worksheet: the mean

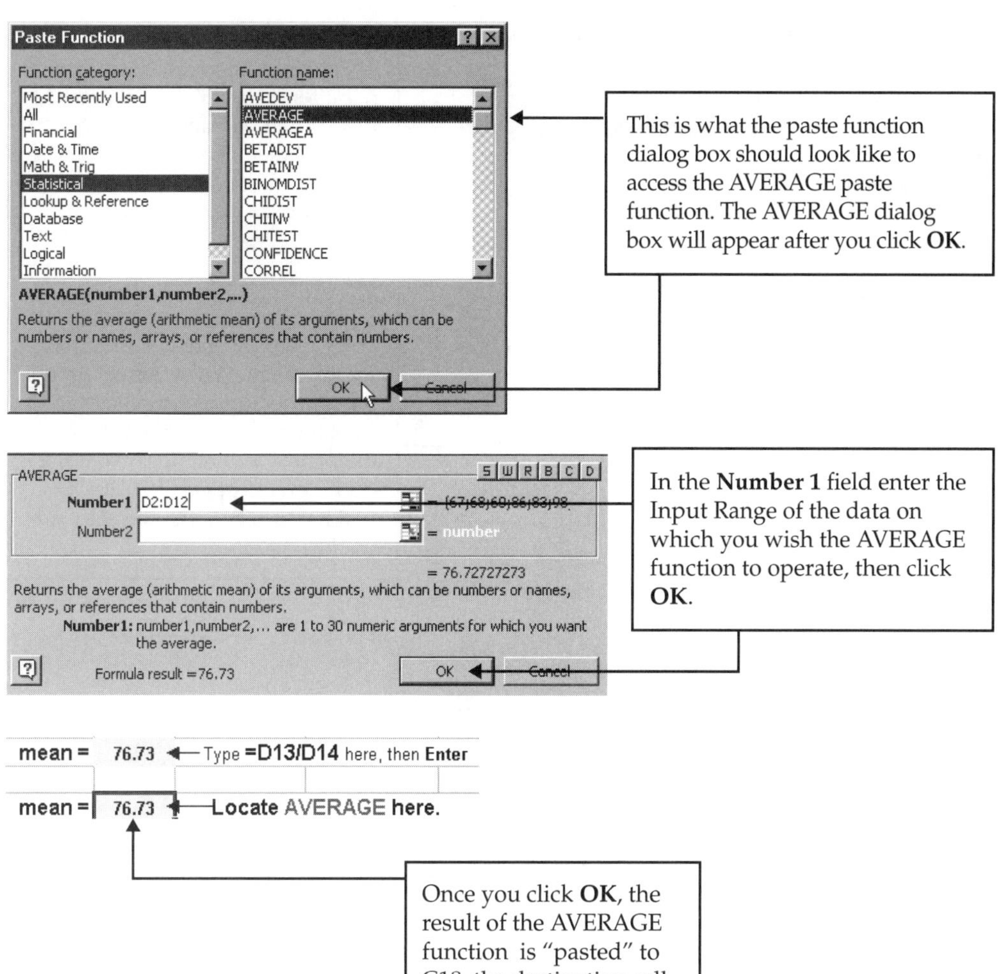
Paste Function
Function category:
Function name:
Most Recently Used
All
Financial
Date & Time
Math & Trig
Statistical
Lookup & Reference
Database
Text
Logical
Information
AVEDEV
AVERAGE
AVERAGEA
BETADIST
BETAINV
BINOMDIST
CHIDIST
CHIINV
CHITEST
CONFIDENCE
CORREL
AVERAGE(number1,number2,...)
Returns the average (arithmetic mean) of its arguments, which can be numbers or names, arrays, or references that contain numbers.
OK
Cancel
This is what the paste function dialog box should look like to access the AVERAGE paste function. The AVERAGE dialog box will appear after you click OK.
AVERAGE
Number1 D2:D12
Number2
= number
= 76.72727273
Returns the average (arithmetic mean) of its arguments, which can be numbers or names, arrays, or references that contain numbers.
Number1: number1,number2,... are 1 to 30 numeric arguments for which you want the average.
Formula result =76.73
OK
Cancel
In the Number 1 field enter the Input Range of the data on which you wish the AVERAGE function to operate, then click OK.
mean = 76.73 Type =D13/D14 here, then Enter
mean = 76.73 Locate AVERAGE here.

Once you click **OK**, the result of the AVERAGE function is "pasted" to C18, the destination cell.

Folder: 01 Descriptive Statistics
Workbook: Describing Data.xls
Worksheet: median

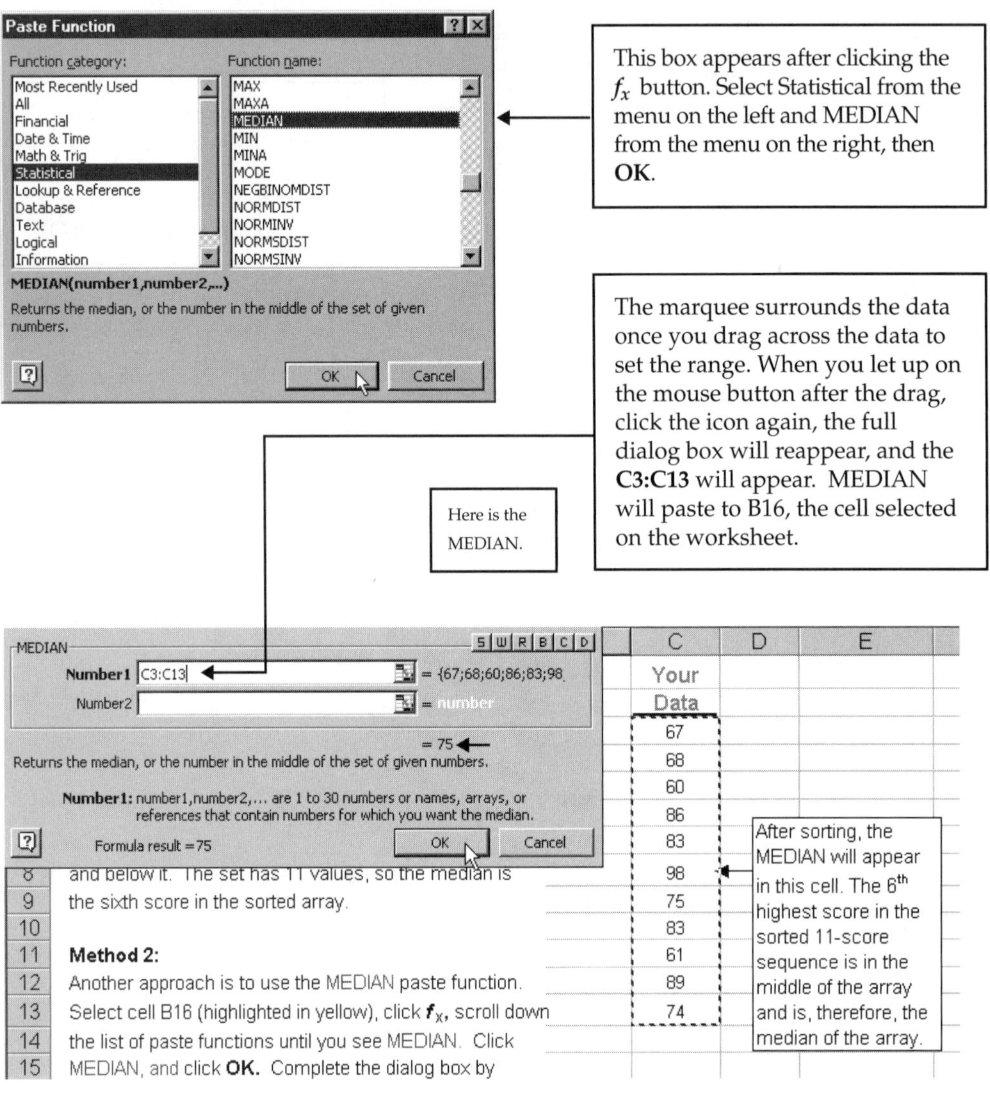
Paste Function
Function category:
Most Recently Used
All
Financial
Date & Time
Math & Trig
Statistical
Lookup & Reference
Database
Text
Logical
Information
Function name:
MAX
MAXA
MEDIAN
MIN
MINA
MODE
NEGBINOMDIST
NORMDIST
NORMINV
NORMSDIST
NORMSINV
MEDIAN(number1,number2,...)
Returns the median, or the number in the middle of the set of given numbers.
OK
Cancel
This box appears after clicking the f_x button. Select Statistical from the menu on the left and MEDIAN from the menu on the right, then **OK**.
The marquee surrounds the data once you drag across the data to set the range. When you let up on the mouse button after the drag, click the icon again, the full dialog box will reappear, and the **C3:C13** will appear. MEDIAN will paste to B16, the cell selected on the worksheet.
Here is the MEDIAN.
MEDIAN
Number1 C3:C13 = {67;68;60;86;83;98
Number2 = number
= 75
Returns the median, or the number in the middle of the set of given numbers.
Number1: number1,number2,... are 1 to 30 numbers or names, arrays, or references that contain numbers for which you want the median.
Formula result =75
OK
Cancel
C
D
E
Your Data
67
68
60
86
83
98
75
83
61
89
74
After sorting, the MEDIAN will appear in this cell. The 6th highest score in the sorted 11-score sequence is in the middle of the array and is, therefore, the median of the array.
8 and below it. The set has 11 values, so the median is
9 the sixth score in the sorted array.
10
11 Method 2:
12 Another approach is to use the MEDIAN paste function.
13 Select cell B16 (highlighted in yellow), click f_x, scroll down
14 the list of paste functions until you see MEDIAN. Click
15 MEDIAN, and click OK. Complete the dialog box by

Folder: 01 Descriptive Statistics
Workbook: Describing Data.xls
Worksheet: tabular SS

Keep in mind that the data in column G are randomly selected values. They will undoubtedly produce answers different from the ones on your screen.

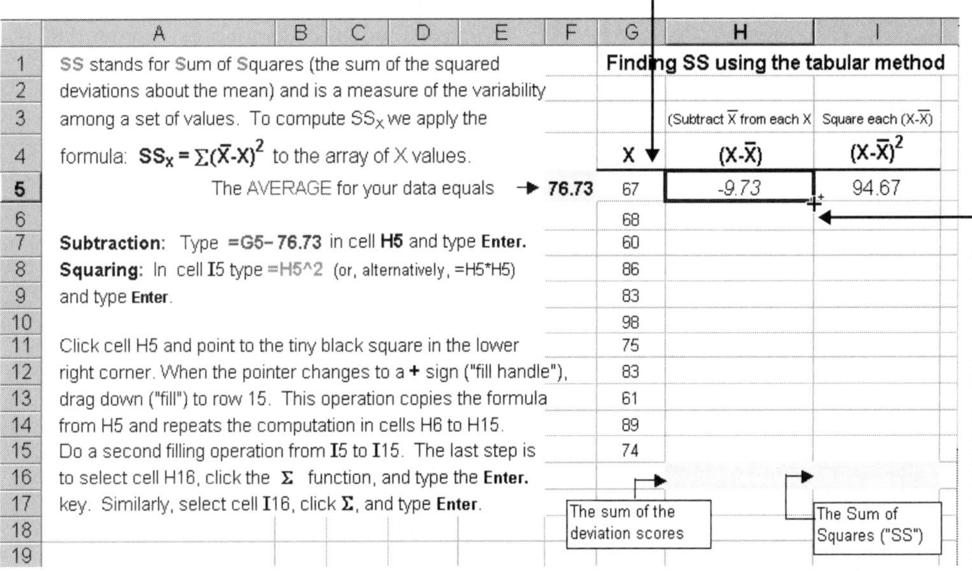

SS stands for Sum of Squares (the sum of the squared deviations about the mean) and is a measure of the variability among a set of values. To compute SSx we apply the formula: SSx = Σ(X̄-X)² to the array of X values.
Finding SS using the tabular method
(Subtract X̄ from each X
Square each (X-X̄)
X
(X-X̄)
(X-X̄)²
The AVERAGE for your data equals 76.73
67
-9.73
94.67
68
60
86
83
98
75
83
61
89
74
Subtraction: Type =G5-76.73 in cell H5 and type Enter.
Squaring: In cell I5 type =H5^2 (or, alternatively, =H5*H5) and type Enter.
Click cell H5 and point to the tiny black square in the lower right corner. When the pointer changes to a + sign ("fill handle"), drag down ("fill") to row 15. This operation copies the formula from H5 and repeats the computation in cells H6 to H15.
Do a second filling operation from I5 to I15. The last step is to select cell H16, click the Σ function, and type the Enter. key. Similarly, select cell I16, click Σ, and type Enter.
The sum of the deviation scores
The Sum of Squares ("SS")

After entering the formula in cell C5, put the pointer on the lower right corner. When it changes to a plus sign, (a square on a Macintosh) drag down to line 15. Repeat for cell I5. This will fill both columns with the deviation scores (col. H) and the squares of those deviation scores (col. I).

Folder: 01 Descriptive Statistics
Workbook: Describing Data.xls
Worksheet: tabular SS

F	G	H	I
	Finding SS using the tabular method		
ility			
		(Subtract $\overline{X}$ from each X	Square each $(X-\overline{X})$
	X	$(X-\overline{X})$	$(X-\overline{X})^2$
→ **76.73**	67	-9.73	94.67
	68	-8.73	76.21
.	60	-16.73	279.89
	86	9.27	85.93
	83	6.27	39.31
	98	21.27	452.41
	75	-1.73	2.99
ıdle"),	83	6.27	39.31
ıula	61	-15.73	247.43
	89	12.27	150.55
is	74	-2.73	7.45
·.		-0.03	**1476.18**

The sum of the deviation scores

The Sum of Squares ("SS")

This image shows the table filled in following the fill operation. The fill operation copies the formula to the other cells. The highlighted cell shows the SUM (Σ button) for the data above. Your answer in col. **I** will be different because your data will be different. But no matter what your data are, the sum of the deviation scores should be zero – or considering rounding error, very close to zero.

Notice how the Excel formulae and the capacity to drag them here and there enable us to follow hand calculation methods with a minimum of work. The advantage to viewing the hand calculation methods is that they convey substantial information about the statistic. Here, for example, it is easy to see that the Sum of Squares ("SS") statistic is the sum of the squared deviations of each data value from the mean of all the data values. So we can view the process as defined mathematically without the tedium of hand calculations!

Folder: 01 Descriptive Statistics
Workbook: Describing Data.xls
Worksheet: paste SS

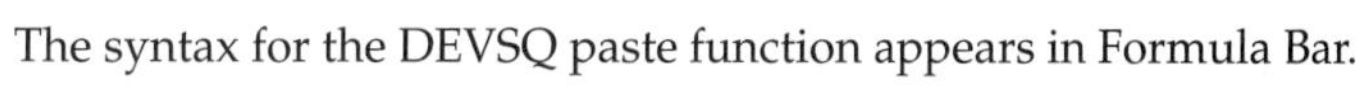
The syntax for the DEVSQ paste function appears in Formula Bar.

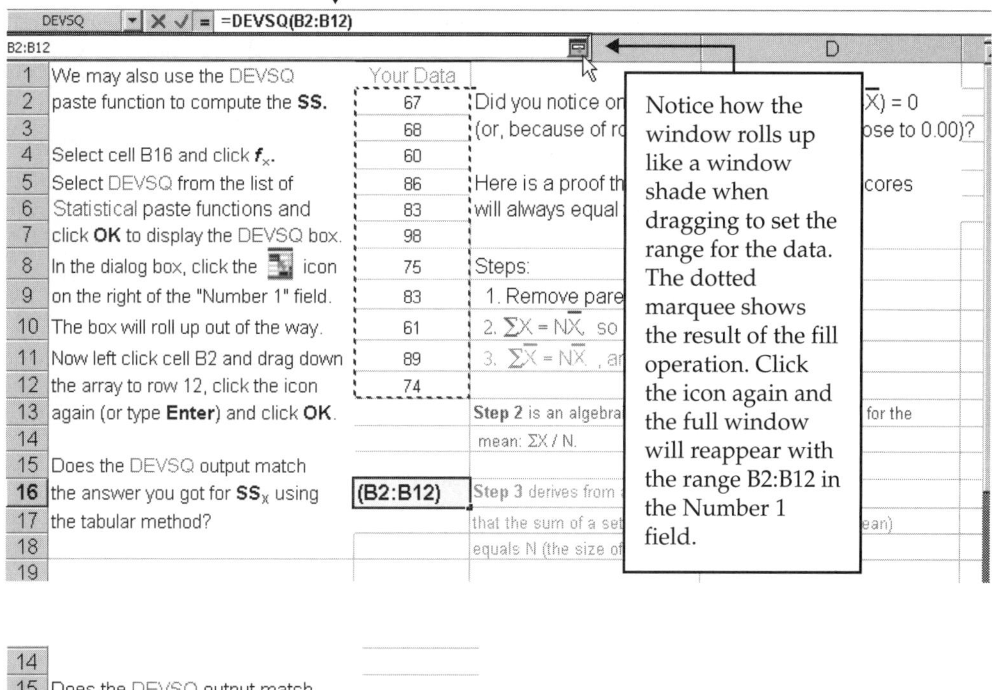
DEVSQ
=DEVSQ(B2:B12)
B2:B12
D
We may also use the DEVSQ paste function to compute the SS.
Select cell B16 and click fx.
Select DEVSQ from the list of Statistical paste functions and click OK to display the DEVSQ box.
In the dialog box, click the icon on the right of the "Number 1" field.
The box will roll up out of the way.
Now left click cell B2 and drag down the array to row 12, click the icon again (or type Enter) and click OK.
Does the DEVSQ output match the answer you got for SSX using the tabular method?
Your Data
67
68
60
86
83
98
75
83
61
89
74
(B2:B12)
Notice how the window rolls up like a window shade when dragging to set the range for the data. The dotted marquee shows the result of the fill operation. Click the icon again and the full window will reappear with the range B2:B12 in the Number 1 field.

14		
15	Does the DEVSQ output match	
16	the answer you got for SS_X using	*1476.18*
17	the tabular method?	

Once you click **OK** in the Paste Function dialog box, the answer to the DEVSQ function will paste to the highlighted destination cell.

Folder: 01 Descriptive Statistics
Workbook: Describing Data.xls
Worksheet: variance and SD

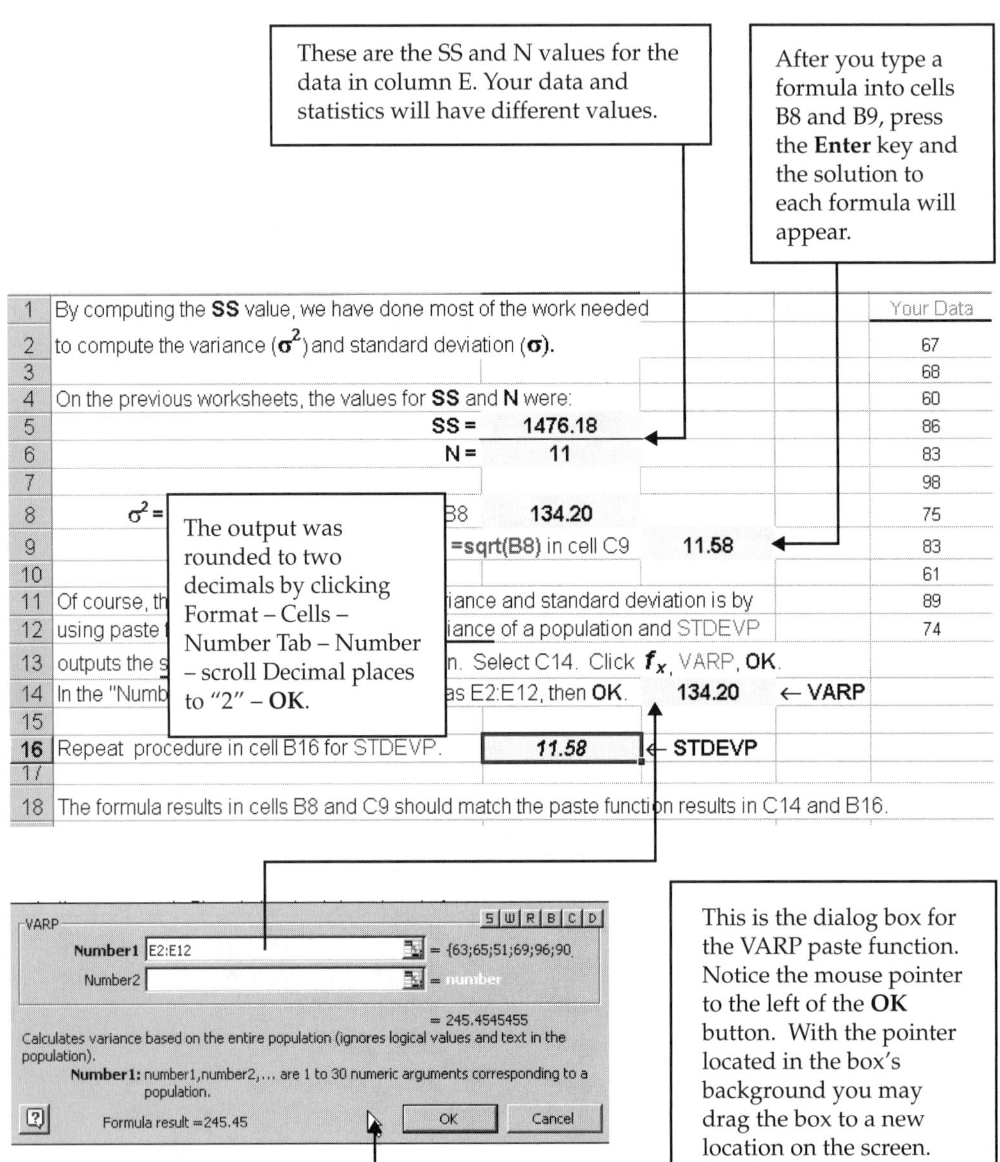

These are the SS and N values for the data in column E. Your data and statistics will have different values.
After you type a formula into cells B8 and B9, press the **Enter** key and the solution to each formula will appear.
1 By computing the **SS** value, we have done most of the work needed
2 to compute the variance (σ²) and standard deviation (σ).
4 On the previous worksheets, the values for **SS** and **N** were:
5 SS = 1476.18
6 N = 11
8 σ² = B8 134.20
9 =sqrt(B8) in cell C9 11.58
11 Of course, th iance and standard deviation is by
12 using paste iance of a population and STDEVP
13 outputs the n. Select C14. Click fx, VARP, OK.
14 In the "Numb as E2:E12, then OK. 134.20 ← VARP
16 Repeat procedure in cell B16 for STDEVP. 11.58 ← STDEVP
18 The formula results in cells B8 and C9 should match the paste function results in C14 and B16.
Your Data
67
68
60
86
83
98
75
83
61
89
74
The output was rounded to two decimals by clicking Format – Cells – Number Tab – Number – scroll Decimal places to "2" – OK.
VARP
Number1 E2:E12 = {63;65;51;69;96;90
Number2 = number
= 245.4545455
Calculates variance based on the entire population (ignores logical values and text in the population).
Number1: number1,number2,... are 1 to 30 numeric arguments corresponding to a population.
Formula result =245.45
OK
Cancel
This is the dialog box for the VARP paste function. Notice the mouse pointer to the left of the OK button. With the pointer located in the box's background you may drag the box to a new location on the screen.

CHAPTER 1-2

Functions and Tools

Folder: 01 Descriptive Statistics
Workbook: Functions and Tools.xls
Worksheet: rank and percentile

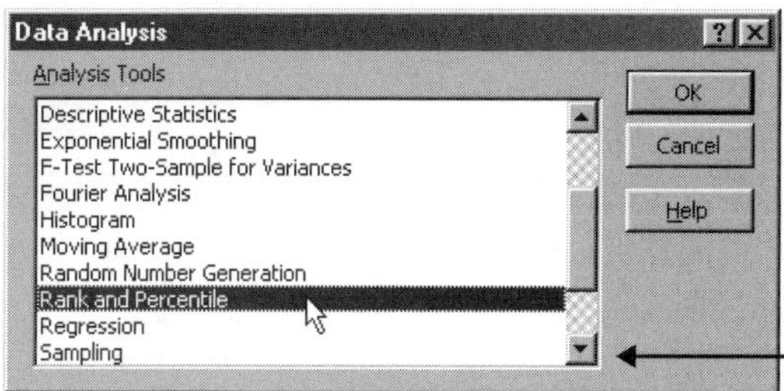

Data Analysis
Analysis Tools
Descriptive Statistics
Exponential Smoothing
F-Test Two-Sample for Variances
Fourier Analysis
Histogram
Moving Average
Random Number Generation
Rank and Percentile
Regression
Sampling
OK
Cancel
Help

Once you click Data Analysis on the Tools menu, scroll this list to find the Rank and Percentile tool, then Click **OK**.

The Rank and Percentile dialog box appears after you click the sequence Tools – Data Analysis – Rank and Percentile.

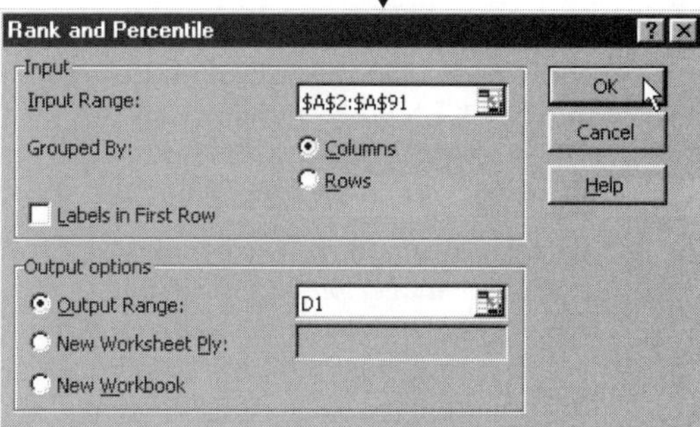

Rank and Percentile
Input
Input Range:
$A$2:$A$91
Grouped By:
Columns
Rows
Labels in First Row
Output options
Output Range:
D1
New Worksheet Ply:
New Workbook
OK
Cancel
Help

This is what the Rank and Percentile dialog box should look like once you have entered the required information. Excel automatically includes the $ signs in the syntax if you use the drag technique to set the Input Range. You do not need to type the $ signs if you are typing in the information manually. The last step is to click **OK**.

The Rank and Percentile output table will initially appear highlighted on the spreadsheet. Click on any empty cell to remove highlighting.

Folder: 01 Descriptive Statistics
Workbook: Functions and Tools.xls
Worksheet: pasteEX

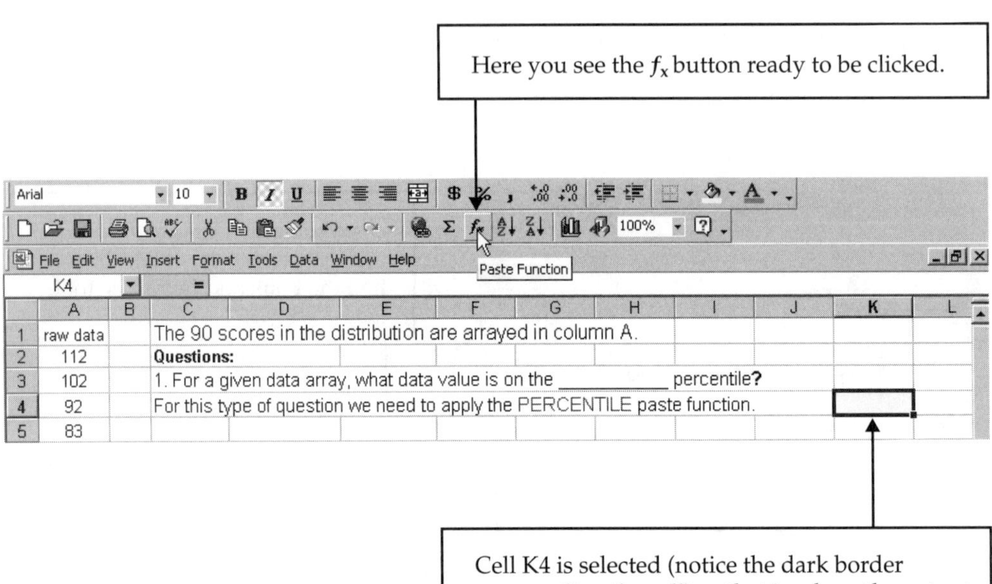
Here you see the f_x button ready to be clicked.
Paste Function
K4
raw data
The 90 scores in the distribution are arrayed in column A.
Questions:
1. For a given data array, what data value is on the ________ percentile?
For this type of question we need to apply the PERCENTILE paste function.
Cell K4 is selected (notice the dark border surrounding the cell) so that is where the output of the paste function will appear.

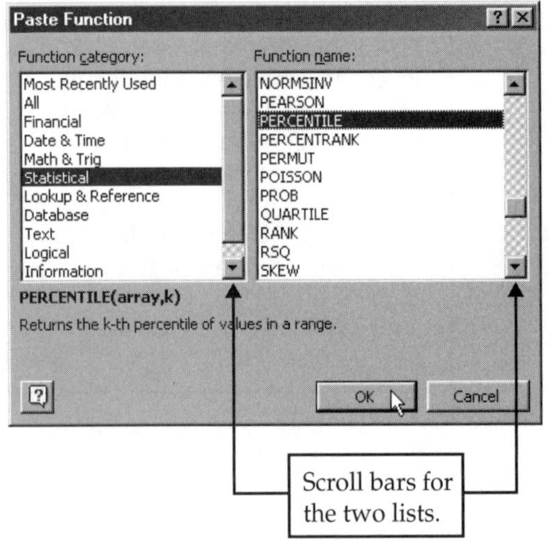
Paste Function
Function category:
Function name:
PERCENTILE(array,k)
Returns the k-th percentile of values in a range.
OK
Cancel
Scroll bars for the two lists.

This is the Paste Function dialog box showing Statistical selected on the left and PERCENTILE on the right. Click **OK** to show the dialog box for the PERCENTILE paste function.

If your Paste Function screen differs from this image, keep in mind that you have to make two menu selections. One will be called the Function category and the other will be called the Function name.

Folder: 01 Descriptive Statistics
Workbook: Functions and Tools.xls
Worksheet: pasteEX

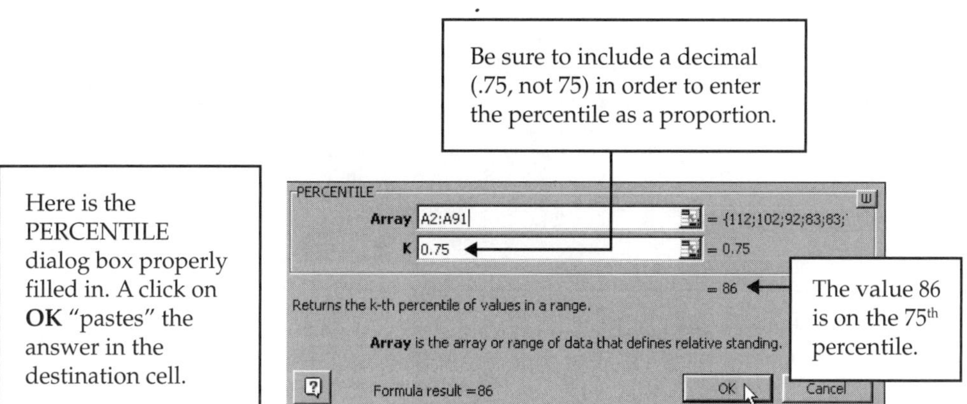
Be sure to include a decimal (.75, not 75) in order to enter the percentile as a proportion.
Here is the PERCENTILE dialog box properly filled in. A click on **OK** "pastes" the answer in the destination cell.
PERCENTILE
Array A2:A91 = {112;102;92;83;83;
K 0.75 = 0.75
= 86
Returns the k-th percentile of values in a range.
Array is the array or range of data that defines relative standing.
Formula result =86
OK
Cancel
The value 86 is on the 75th percentile.

The reverse process, finding a percentile given a data value, is shown below using the PERCENTRANK paste function.

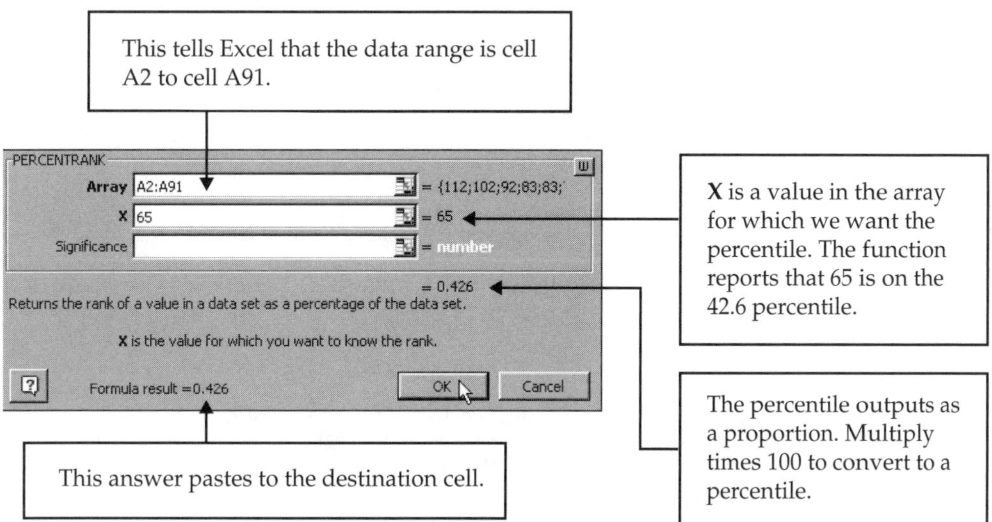
This tells Excel that the data range is cell A2 to cell A91.
PERCENTRANK
Array A2:A91 = {112;102;92;83;83;
X 65 = 65
Significance = number
= 0.426
Returns the rank of a value in a data set as a percentage of the data set.
X is the value for which you want to know the rank.
Formula result =0.426
OK
Cancel
X is a value in the array for which we want the percentile. The function reports that 65 is on the 42.6 percentile.
The percentile outputs as a proportion. Multiply times 100 to convert to a percentile.
This answer pastes to the destination cell.

Folder: 01 Descriptive Statistics
Workbook: Functions and Tools.xls
Worksheet: descriptive

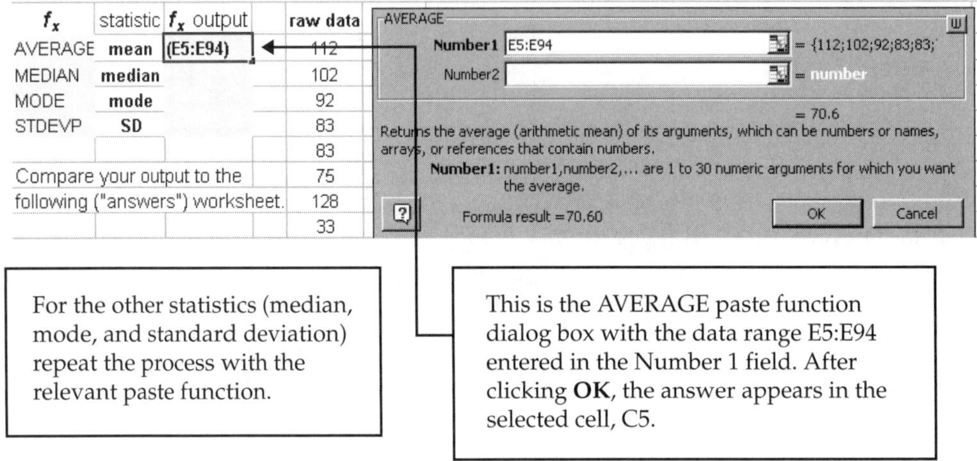

For the other statistics (median, mode, and standard deviation) repeat the process with the relevant paste function.
This is the AVERAGE paste function dialog box with the data range E5:E94 entered in the Number 1 field. After clicking **OK**, the answer appears in the selected cell, C5.
AVERAGE
Number1 E5:E94
Number2
= 70.6
Returns the average (arithmetic mean) of its arguments, which can be numbers or names, arrays, or references that contain numbers.
Number1: number1,number2,... are 1 to 30 numeric arguments for which you want the average.
Formula result =70.60
OK
Cancel

After using paste functions to compute values for the statistics on the left, the worksheet introduces an alternative method: the Descriptive Statistics tool.

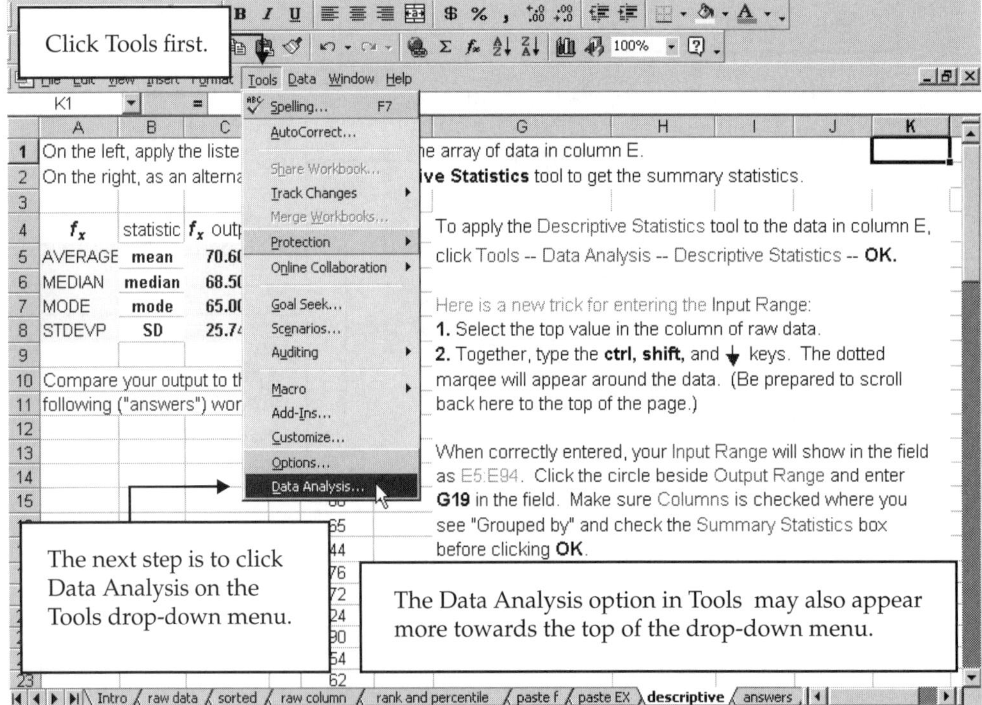

Click Tools first.
The next step is to click Data Analysis on the Tools drop-down menu.
The Data Analysis option in Tools may also appear more towards the top of the drop-down menu.
To apply the Descriptive Statistics tool to the data in column E, click Tools -- Data Analysis -- Descriptive Statistics -- OK.
Here is a new trick for entering the Input Range:
1. Select the top value in the column of raw data.
2. Together, type the ctrl, shift, and ↓ keys. The dotted marqee will appear around the data. (Be prepared to scroll back here to the top of the page.)
When correctly entered, your Input Range will show in the field as E5:E94. Click the circle beside Output Range and enter G19 in the field. Make sure Columns is checked where you see "Grouped by" and check the Summary Statistics box before clicking OK.

Folder: 01 Descriptive Statistics
Workbook: Functions and Tools.xls
Worksheet: descriptive

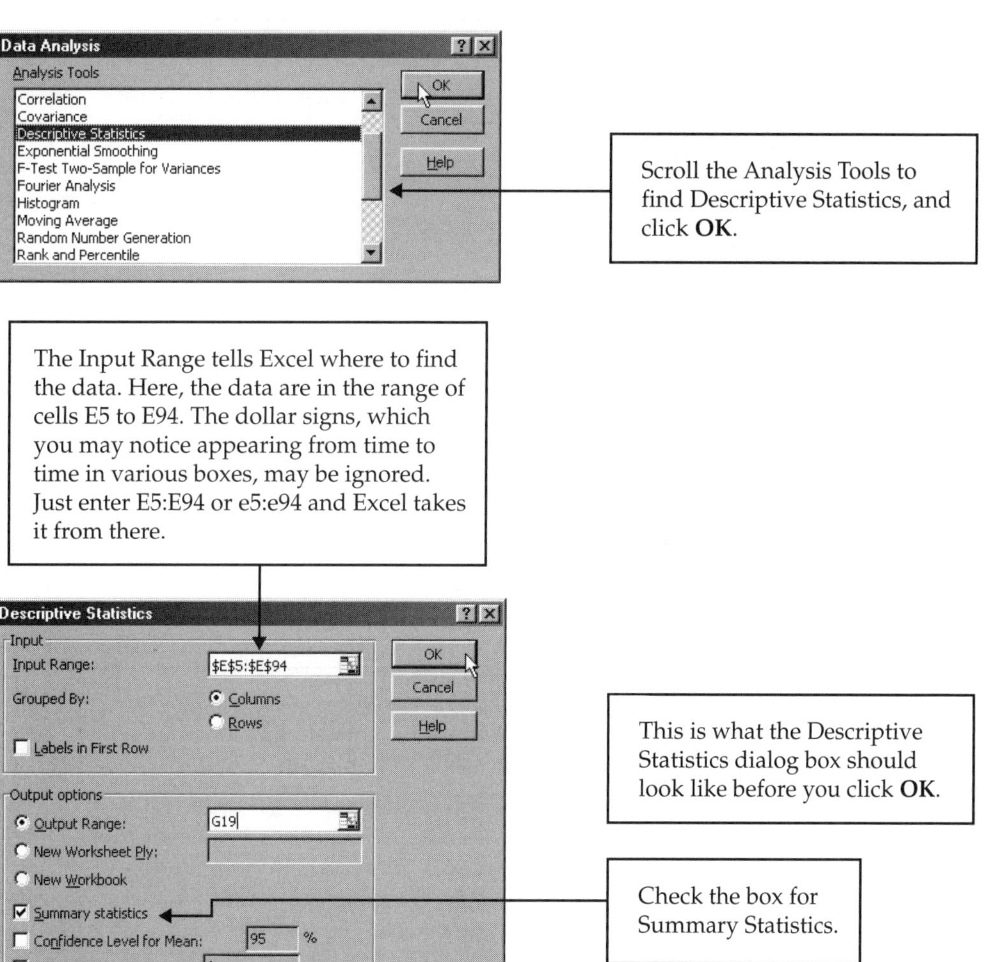
Data Analysis
Analysis Tools
Correlation
Covariance
Descriptive Statistics
Exponential Smoothing
F-Test Two-Sample for Variances
Fourier Analysis
Histogram
Moving Average
Random Number Generation
Rank and Percentile
OK
Cancel
Help
Scroll the Analysis Tools to find Descriptive Statistics, and click **OK**.
The Input Range tells Excel where to find the data. Here, the data are in the range of cells E5 to E94. The dollar signs, which you may notice appearing from time to time in various boxes, may be ignored. Just enter E5:E94 or e5:e94 and Excel takes it from there.
Descriptive Statistics
Input
Input Range:
$E$5:$E$94
Grouped By:
Columns
Rows
Labels in First Row
Output options
Output Range:
G19
New Worksheet Ply:
New Workbook
Summary statistics
Confidence Level for Mean:
95
%
Kth Largest:
1
Kth Smallest:
1
This is what the Descriptive Statistics dialog box should look like before you click **OK**.
Check the box for Summary Statistics.

Folder 01: Descriptive Statistics
Workbook: Functions and Tools.xls
Worksheet: descriptive

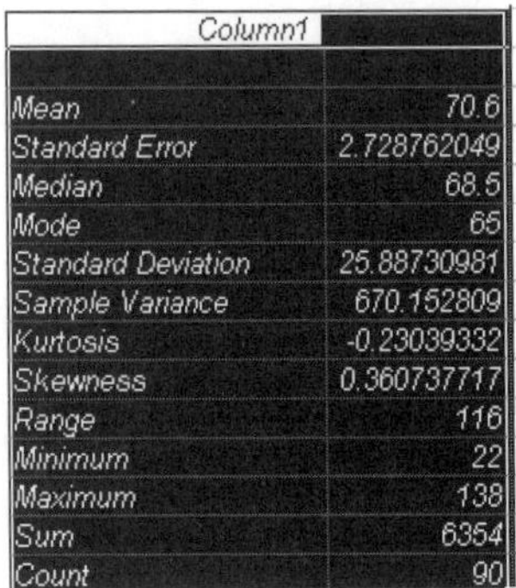

Column1	
Mean	70.6
Standard Error	2.728762049
Median	68.5
Mode	65
Standard Deviation	25.88730981
Sample Variance	670.152809
Kurtosis	-0.23039332
Skewness	0.360737717
Range	116
Minimum	22
Maximum	138
Sum	6354
Count	90

Initially, Excel displays the output table with highlighting.

In practice, it is likely you will have to widen the destination column to read the statistic labels. Here, for your convenience, column G has already been widened to allow the table to display properly.

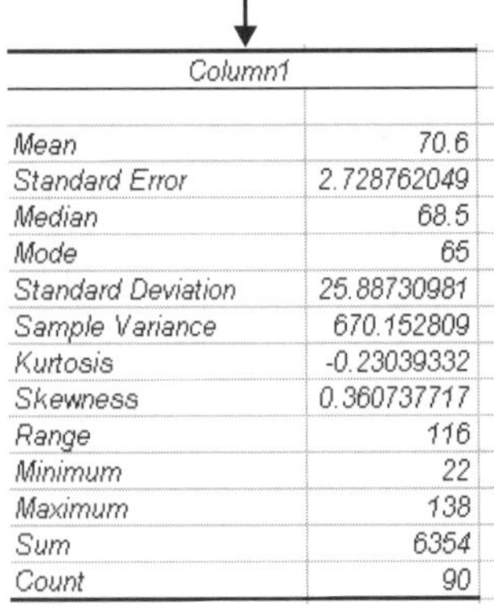

Column1	
Mean	70.6
Standard Error	2.728762049
Median	68.5
Mode	65
Standard Deviation	25.88730981
Sample Variance	670.152809
Kurtosis	-0.23039332
Skewness	0.360737717
Range	116
Minimum	22
Maximum	138
Sum	6354
Count	90

Clicking anywhere in the worksheet causes the highlighting to disappear so the table looks like this.

Check to see how closely these values match the values computed by the paste functions.

CHAPTER 1-3

Frequency Distributions

Folder: 01 Descriptive Statistics
Workbook: Frequency Distributions.xls
Worksheet: make ungrouped

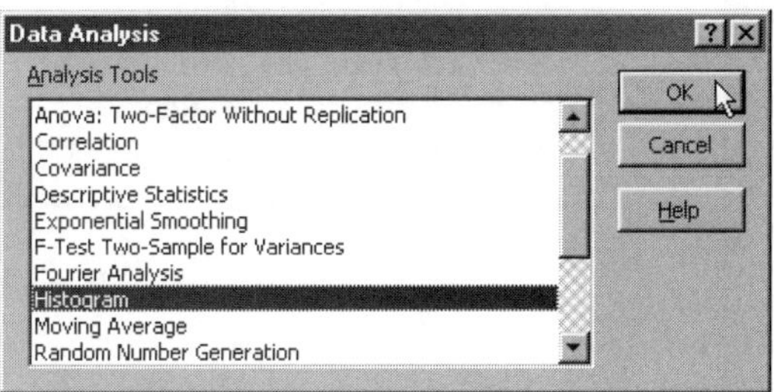
Data Analysis
Analysis Tools
Anova: Two-Factor Without Replication
Correlation
Covariance
Descriptive Statistics
Exponential Smoothing
F-Test Two-Sample for Variances
Fourier Analysis
Histogram
Moving Average
Random Number Generation
OK
Cancel
Help

After clicking Data Analysis on the Tools drop-down menu, scroll the list of Tools to Histogram, click it to highlight, then click **OK**.

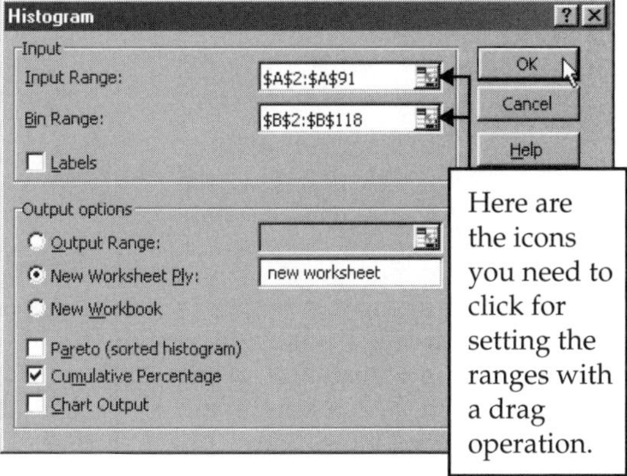
Histogram
Input
Input Range:
$A$2:$A$91
Bin Range:
$B$2:$B$118
Labels
OK
Cancel
Help
Output options
Output Range:
New Worksheet Ply:
new worksheet
New Workbook
Pareto (sorted histogram)
Cumulative Percentage
Chart Output
Here are the icons you need to click for setting the ranges with a drag operation.

If you enter the Input Range and Bin ranges manually, you will not need to type the $ signs. Excel adds $$ when you set ranges using the drag method, which is to click the icon, drag the dotted marquee over the range, and click the icon again. Recall that the box will roll up like a window shade when you first click the icon. You may have to look around the screen a bit to spot the icon for the final click.

Folder: 01 Descriptive Statistics
Workbook: Frequency Distributions.xls
Worksheets: make grouped /edit table

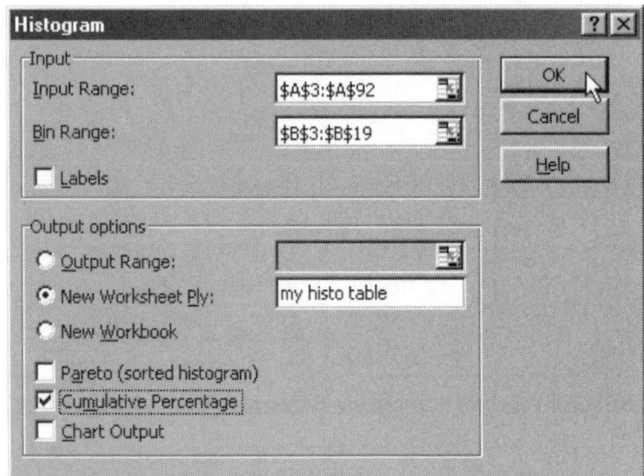
Histogram
Input
Input Range:
$A$3:$A$92
Bin Range:
$B$3:$B$19
Labels
OK
Cancel
Help
Output options
Output Range:
New Worksheet Ply:
my histo table
New Workbook
Pareto (sorted histogram)
Cumulative Percentage
Chart Output

Enter the information in the fields as shown and click **OK**. The Histogram tool will then output a grouped frequency distribution.

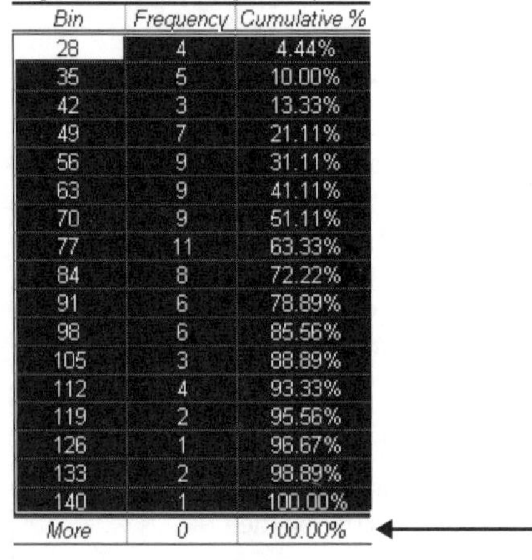

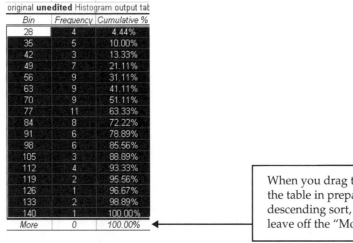

original **unedited** Histogram output tab

Bin	*Frequency*	*Cumulative %*
28	4	4.44%
35	5	10.00%
42	3	13.33%
49	7	21.11%
56	9	31.11%
63	9	41.11%
70	9	51.11%
77	11	63.33%
84	8	72.22%
91	6	78.89%
98	6	85.56%
105	3	88.89%
112	4	93.33%
119	2	95.56%
126	1	96.67%
133	2	98.89%
140	1	100.00%
More	*0*	*100.00%*

When you drag to highlight the table in preparation for the descending sort, be careful to leave off the "More" row.

CHAPTER 1-4

Making Charts

Folder: 01 Descriptive Statistics
Workbook: Making Charts.xls
Worksheet: make chart

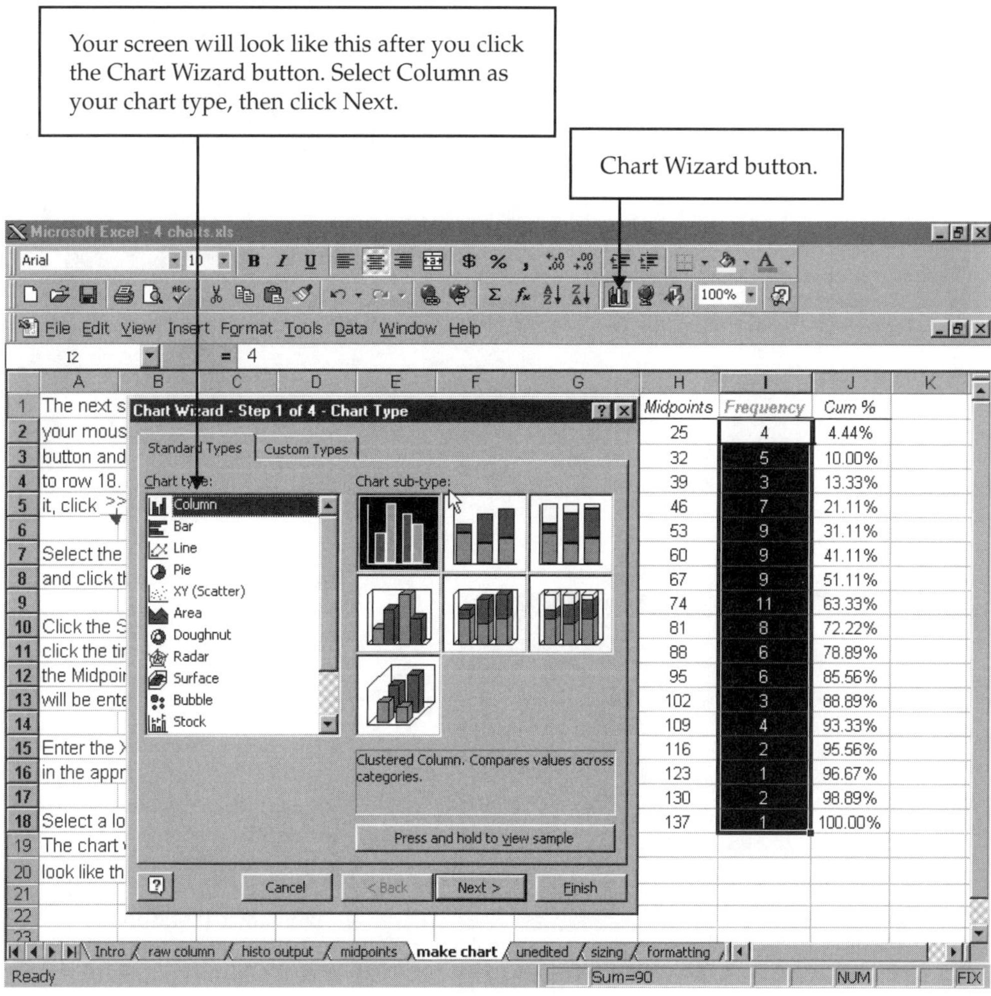

Your screen will look like this after you click the Chart Wizard button. Select Column as your chart type, then click Next.
Chart Wizard button.
Microsoft Excel - 4 charts.xls
File Edit View Insert Format Tools Data Window Help
Chart Wizard - Step 1 of 4 - Chart Type
Standard Types
Custom Types
Chart type:
Column
Bar
Line
Pie
XY (Scatter)
Area
Doughnut
Radar
Surface
Bubble
Stock
Chart sub-type:
Clustered Column. Compares values across categories.
Press and hold to view sample
Cancel
< Back
Next >
Finish
Midpoints
Frequency
Cum %
25 4 4.44%
32 5 10.00%
39 3 13.33%
46 7 21.11%
53 9 31.11%
60 9 41.11%
67 9 51.11%
74 11 63.33%
81 8 72.22%
88 6 78.89%
95 6 85.56%
102 3 88.89%
109 4 93.33%
116 2 95.56%
123 1 96.67%
130 2 98.89%
137 1 100.00%
Intro
raw column
histo output
midpoints
make chart
unedited
sizing
formatting
Ready
Sum=90
NUM
FIX

Folder: 01 Descriptive Statistics
Workbook: Making Charts.xls
Worksheet: make chart

Clicking Next on the step 1 dialog box brings up this box. Click on the Series tab and the screen shown below will come into view.

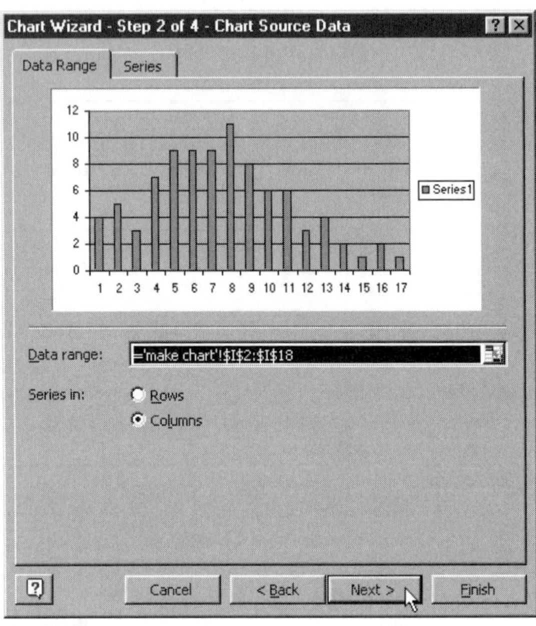
Chart Wizard - Step 2 of 4 - Chart Source Data
Data Range
Series
Series1
Data range:
='make chart'!$I$2:$I$18
Series in:
Rows
Columns
Cancel
< Back
Next >
Finish

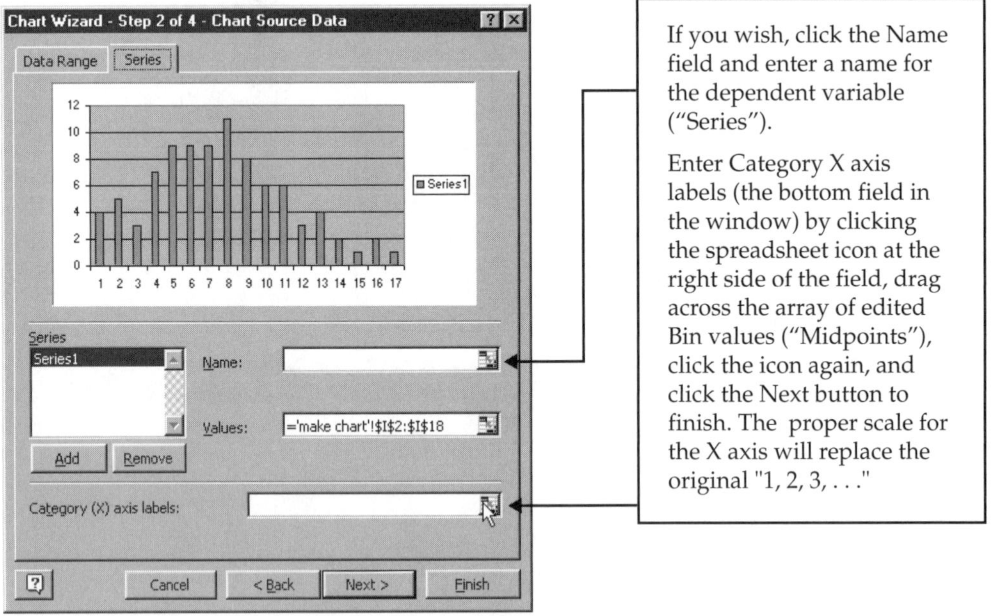
Chart Wizard - Step 2 of 4 - Chart Source Data
Data Range
Series
Series1
Series
Series1
Name:
Values:
='make chart'!$I$2:$I$18
Add
Remove
Category (X) axis labels:
Cancel
< Back
Next >
Finish

If you wish, click the Name field and enter a name for the dependent variable ("Series").

Enter Category X axis labels (the bottom field in the window) by clicking the spreadsheet icon at the right side of the field, drag across the array of edited Bin values ("Midpoints"), click the icon again, and click the Next button to finish. The proper scale for the X axis will replace the original "1, 2, 3, . . ."

Folder: 01 Descriptive Statistics
Workbook: Making Charts.xls
Worksheet: make chart

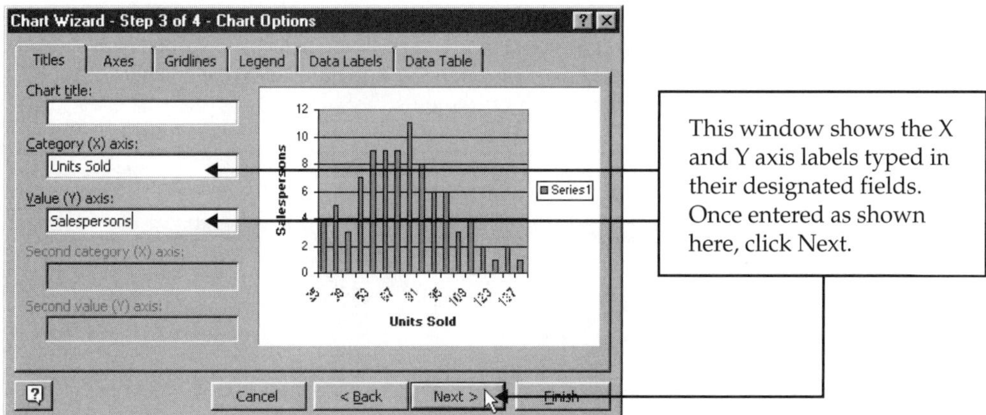
Chart Wizard - Step 3 of 4 - Chart Options
Titles
Axes
Gridlines
Legend
Data Labels
Data Table
Chart title:
Category (X) axis:
Units Sold
Value (Y) axis:
Salespersons
Second category (X) axis:
Second value (Y) axis:
Salespersons
Units Sold
Series1
Cancel
< Back
Next >
Finish
This window shows the X and Y axis labels typed in their designated fields. Once entered as shown here, click Next.

It is a matter of choice where you want the chart to appear – either on a new worksheet or on the resident "make chart" worksheet (select As object in). Editing seems to go more smoothly with the latter choice. You may always copy and paste the chart to its own worksheet later or just drag the chart to a blank area of the current worksheet. To print the chart, select it with a click inside its border (you will see the "handles" appear), and click File – Print.

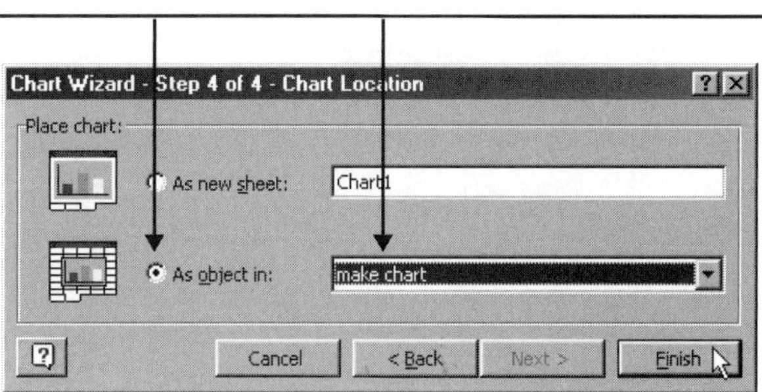
Chart Wizard - Step 4 of 4 - Chart Location
Place chart:
As new sheet:
Chart1
As object in:
make chart
Cancel
< Back
Next >
Finish

Folder: 01 Descriptive Statistics
Workbook: Making Charts.xls
Worksheet: make chart

This is what your Excel screen will look like if you select the As object in option to display your chart. The next step is to edit the crude chart to incorporate your appearance requirements.

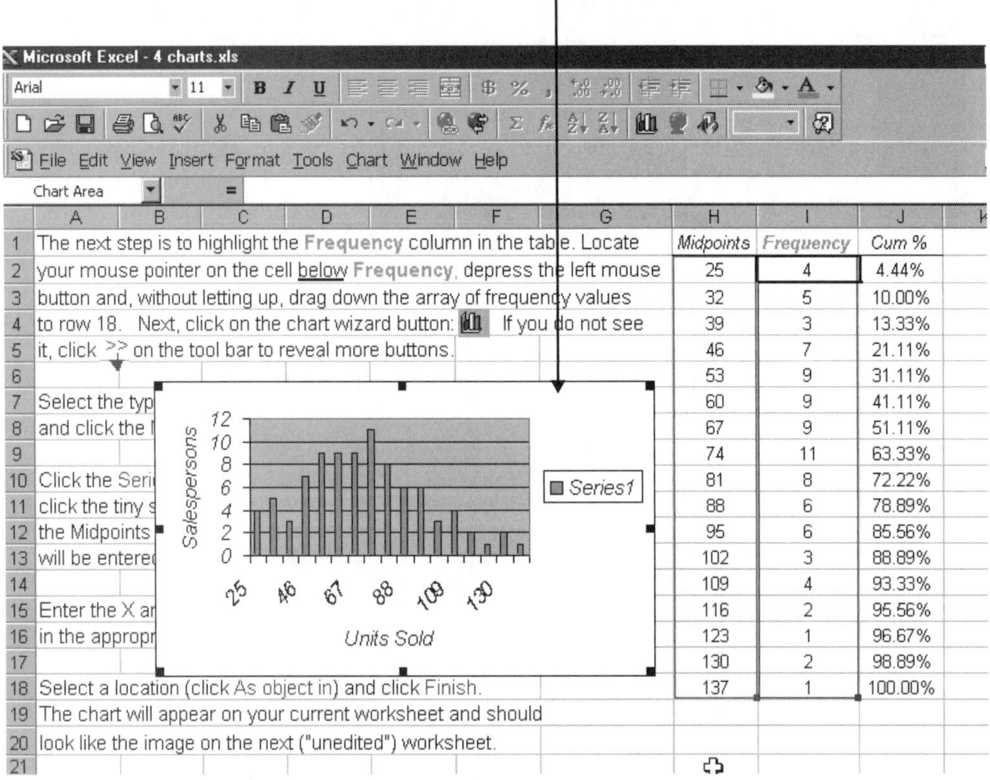
Microsoft Excel - 4 charts.xls
File Edit View Insert Format Tools Chart Window Help
Chart Area
The next step is to highlight the Frequency column in the table. Locate
your mouse pointer on the cell below Frequency, depress the left mouse
button and, without letting up, drag down the array of frequency values
to row 18. Next, click on the chart wizard button: If you do not see
it, click >> on the tool bar to reveal more buttons.
Select a location (click As object in) and click Finish.
The chart will appear on your current worksheet and should
look like the image on the next ("unedited") worksheet.
Salespersons
Units Sold
Series1
Midpoints
Frequency
Cum %
25 4 4.44%
32 5 10.00%
39 3 13.33%
46 7 21.11%
53 9 31.11%
60 9 41.11%
67 9 51.11%
74 11 63.33%
81 8 72.22%
88 6 78.89%
95 6 85.56%
102 3 88.89%
109 4 93.33%
116 2 95.56%
123 1 96.67%
130 2 98.89%
137 1 100.00%

Folder: 01 Descriptive Statistics
Workbook: Making Charts.xls
Worksheet: formatting

Right-click the legend box to access the shortcut menu that pertains to the legend. The appearance of "handles" around the box verify its selection.

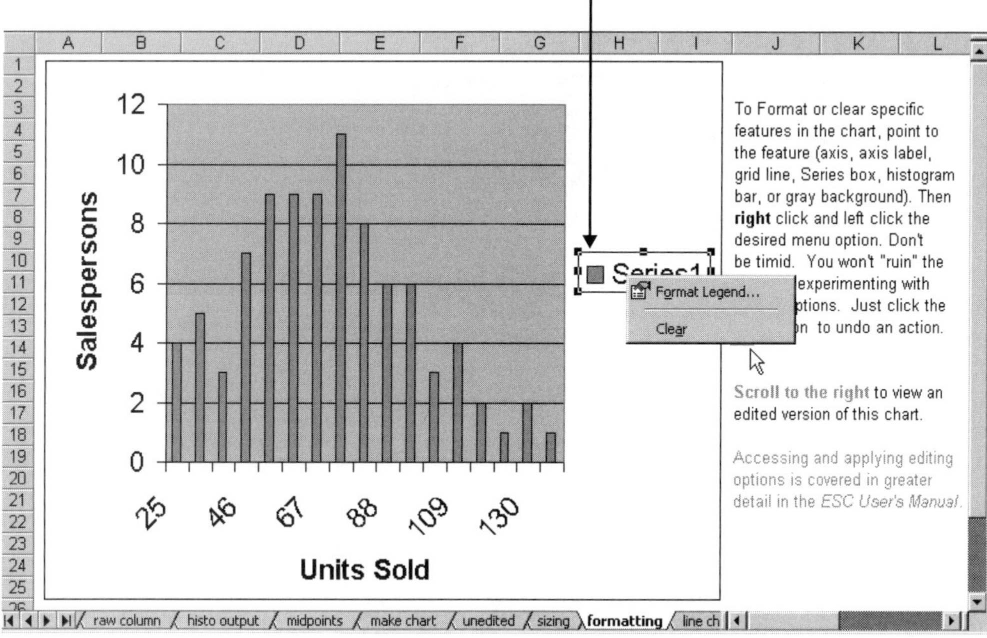
Salespersons
12
10
8
6
4
2
0
25
46
67
88
109
130
Units Sold
Format Legend...
Clear
To Format or clear specific features in the chart, point to the feature (axis, axis label, grid line, Series box, histogram bar, or gray background). Then **right** click and left click the desired menu option. Don't be timid. You won't "ruin" the
experimenting with
ptions. Just click the
n to undo an action.
Scroll to the right to view an edited version of this chart.
Accessing and applying editing options is covered in greater detail in the *ESC User's Manual*.
raw column
histo output
midpoints
make chart
unedited
sizing
formatting
line ch

Folder: 01 Descriptive Statistics
Workbook: Making Charts.xls
Worksheet: formatting

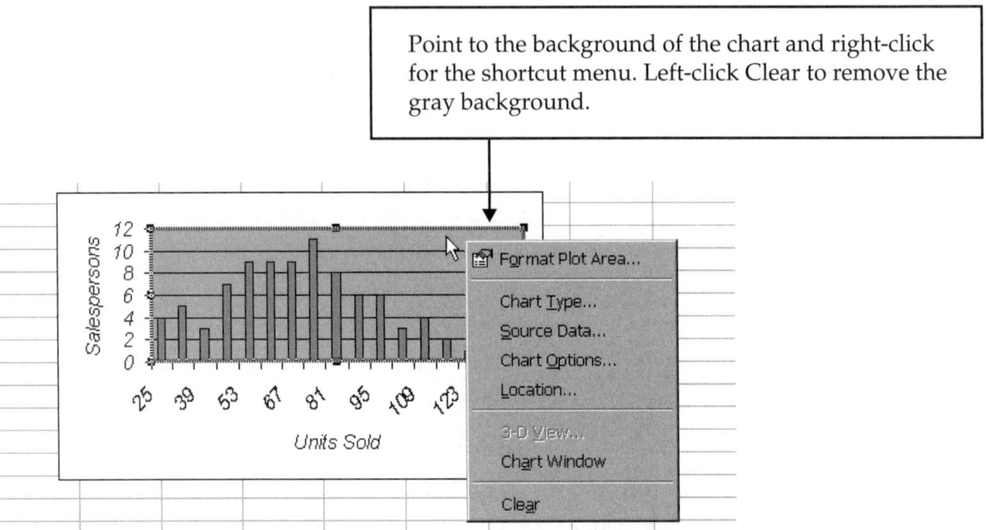
Point to the background of the chart and right-click for the shortcut menu. Left-click Clear to remove the gray background.
Salespersons
12
10
8
6
4
2
0
25
39
53
67
81
95
109
123
Units Sold
Format Plot Area...
Chart Type...
Source Data...
Chart Options...
Location...
3-D View...
Chart Window
Clear

Salespersons
12
10
8
6
4
2
0
25
39
53
67
81
95
109
123
137
Units Sold
Format Gridlines...
Clear
Use the same shortcut menu to clear the grid lines.

Folder: 01 Descriptive Statistics
Workbook: Making Charts.xls
Worksheet: sizing

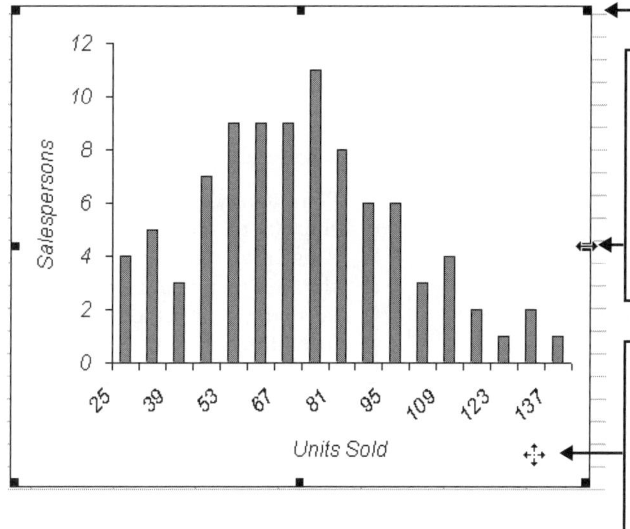
Salespersons
12
10
8
6
4
2
0
25
39
53
67
81
95
109
123
137
Units Sold

Click slightly within the chart border to expose the tiny square "handles." Then, position the mouse pointer on a handle until the pointer changes to a double-pointed arrow ⇹ and drag to resize.

Holding a left-click within the chart border changes the mouse pointer to an ornate plus sign (compass rose) and permits dragging the whole chart around the screen.

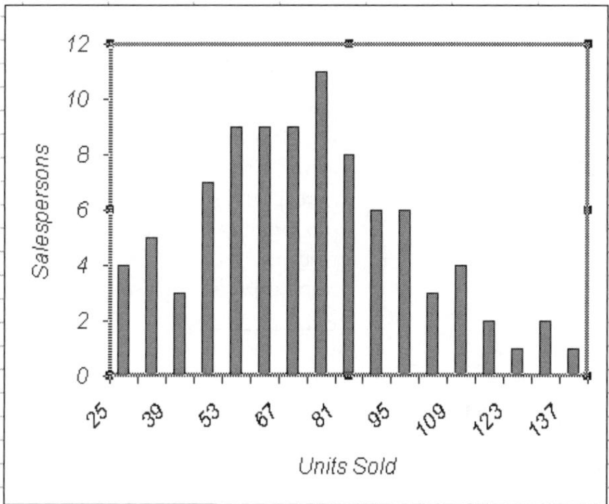
Salespersons
12
10
8
6
4
2
0
25
39
53
67
81
95
109
123
137
Units Sold

You may select the inner portion of the chart and apply the same drag operation, but resizing the inner portion is limited by the dimension of the outer portion.

Folder: 01 Descriptive Statistics
Workbook: Making Charts.xls
Worksheet: formatting

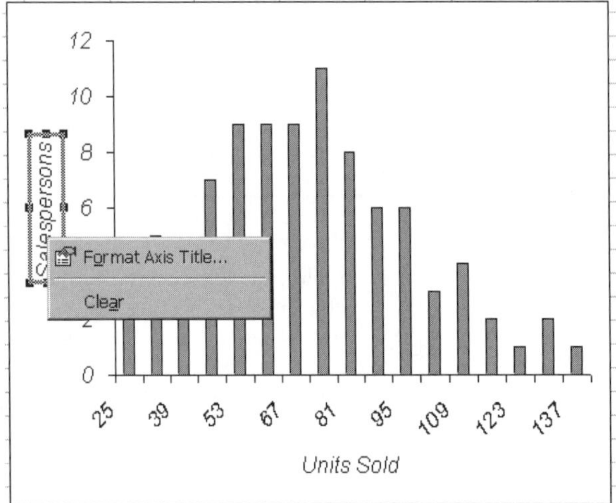
12
10
8
6
0
Salespersons
Format Axis Title...
Clear
25
39
53
67
81
95
109
123
137
Units Sold

Point to any element of the chart (here, illustrated with Axis Title), right-click for the shortcut menu, and left-click Format to access the relevant formatting option.

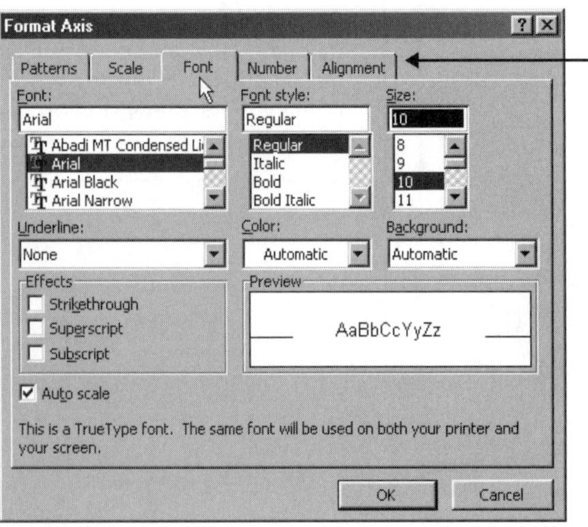
Format Axis
Patterns
Scale
Font
Number
Alignment
Font:
Arial
Abadi MT Condensed Li
Arial
Arial Black
Arial Narrow
Font style:
Regular
Regular
Italic
Bold
Bold Italic
Size:
10
8
9
10
11
Underline:
None
Color:
Automatic
Background:
Automatic
Effects
Strikethrough
Superscript
Subscript
Preview
AaBbCcYyZz
Auto scale
This is a TrueType font. The same font will be used on both your printer and your screen.
OK
Cancel

Each tab in the Format menu reveals a different formatting option. This image is the Font menu, which will enable you to control the size of the type used for the axis label selected in the above chart image.

Folder: 01 Descriptive Statistics
Workbook: Making Charts.xls
Worksheet: formatting

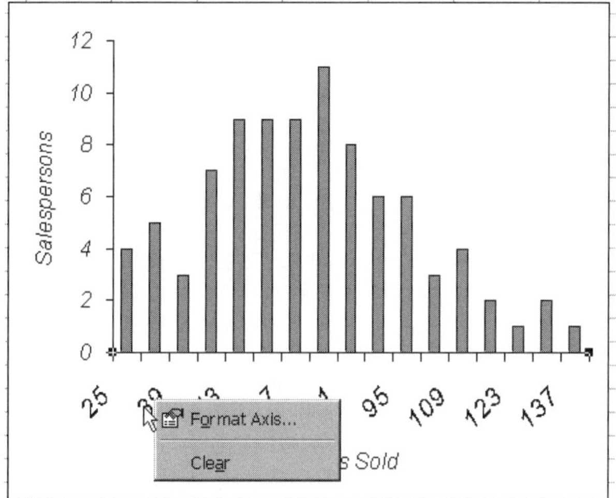
12
10
8
6
4
2
0
Salespersons
25
95
109
123
137
Format Axis...
Clear

If Excel displays your chart with print that is too large, just point to the axis value (as shown here), right-click, and left-click Format Axis. The Format menu will appear as above, and you may enter your change.

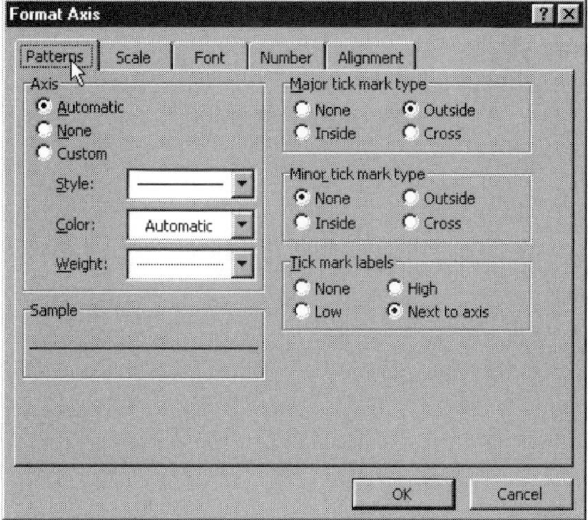
Format Axis
Patterns
Scale
Font
Number
Alignment
Axis
Automatic
None
Custom
Style:
Color:
Automatic
Weight:
Sample
Major tick mark type
None
Outside
Inside
Cross
Minor tick mark type
None
Outside
Inside
Cross
Tick mark labels
None
High
Low
Next to axis
OK
Cancel

Another editing option is to alter the appearance of the tick marks. Point to and right-click the chart's axis line, then left-click Format on the shortcut menu. Try different options and keep the one that meets your needs.

Folder: 01 Descriptive Statistics
Workbook: Making Charts.xls
Worksheet: formatting

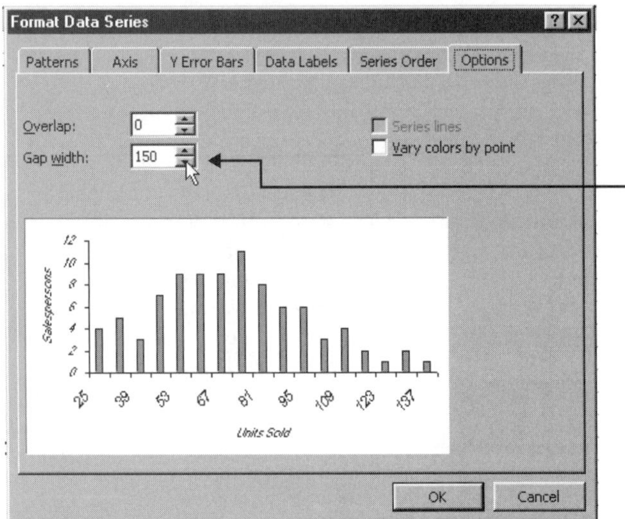
Format Data Series
Patterns
Axis
Y Error Bars
Data Labels
Series Order
Options
Overlap:
0
Gap width:
150
Series lines
Vary colors by point
Salespersons
Units Sold
OK
Cancel

It is usually desirable to widen the histogram bars. In fact, when the variable is continuous rather than categorical (as is the case with these sales data), the convention is to have the bars touch. Point to and right-click one of the bars on the chart. Left-click Format Data Series then the Options tab and this box will appear. A gap width of 3 should allow the bars to touch – just barely.

As you scroll this number to a lower value, the bars will widen.

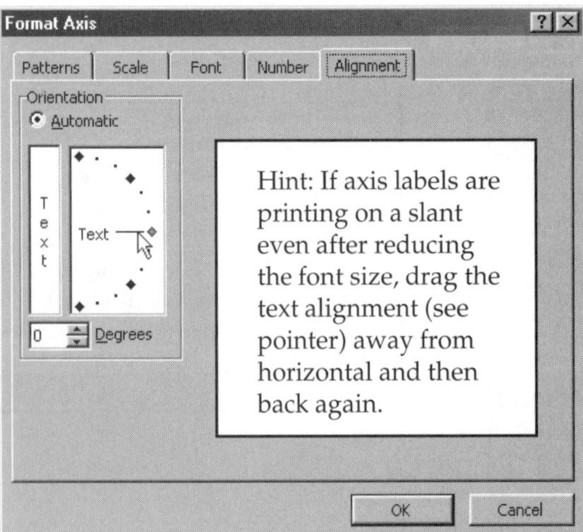
Format Axis
Patterns
Scale
Font
Number
Alignment
Orientation
Automatic
Text
Text
0
Degrees
Hint: If axis labels are printing on a slant even after reducing the font size, drag the text alignment (see pointer) away from horizontal and then back again.
OK
Cancel

Folder: 01 Descriptive Statistics
Workbook: Making Charts.xls
Worksheet: formatting

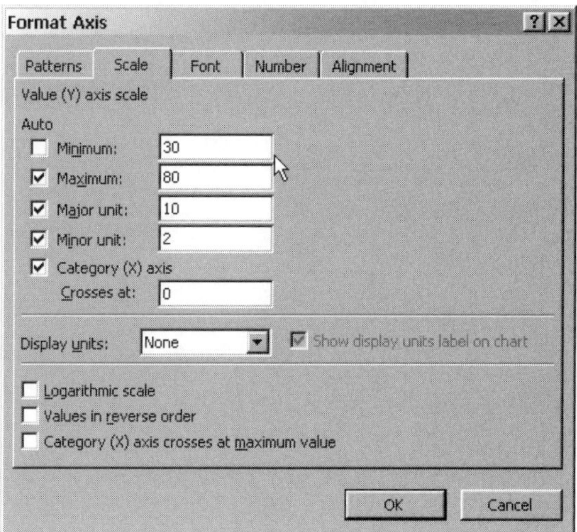
Format Axis
Patterns
Scale
Font
Number
Alignment
Value (Y) axis scale
Auto
Minimum: 30
Maximum: 80
Major unit: 10
Minor unit: 2
Category (X) axis
Crosses at: 0
Display units: None
Show display units label on chart
Logarithmic scale
Values in reverse order
Category (X) axis crosses at maximum value
OK
Cancel

Another useful option on the Format Axis dialog box is for resetting the minimum and maximum of an axis scale. Consider the two line charts below. The one on the left has a good deal of empty space below the data points. By raising the minimum of the axis scale from zero to 30, the whole chart area is used for the display.

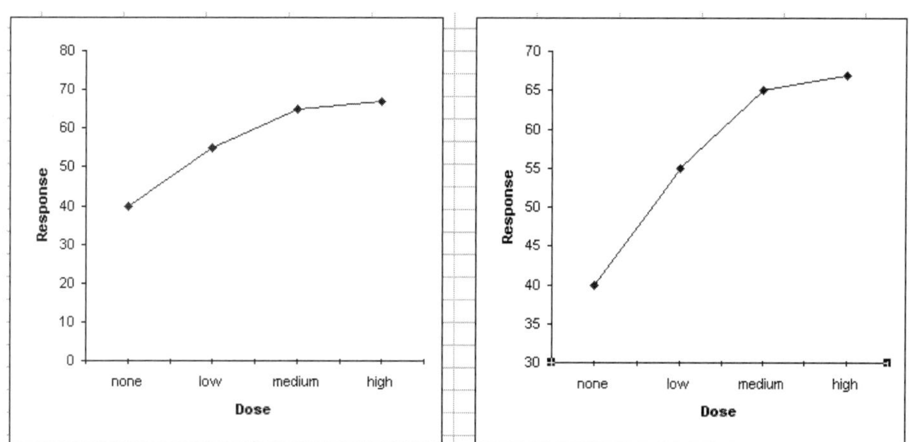
Response
0
10
20
30
40
50
60
70
80
none
low
medium
high
Dose
Response
30
35
40
45
50
55
60
65
70
none
low
medium
high
Dose

Changing the minimum to 30 shortens the Y-axis scale, as seen on the right-hand chart above. You will notice that the response now appears to react more sharply to the dose. It is not proper practice to manipulate the scale of a variable simply to create the appearance of an experimental effect. So, use this editing capability with restraint.

CHAPTER 2

The *z* Statistic

Folder: 02 The z Statistic
Workbook: Comparing Distributions.xls
Worksheet: experiment 1

On this worksheet, as well as in many of the worksheets to come, you are asked to select a cell (here, **D5**) and type the **<delete>** key to generate new data. There is really nothing special about cell D5 – it is just an empty cell. Why not use any empty cell? The instructions specify cell D5 rather than take a chance that the user will select an empty cell too far off to the right or too low, which can sometimes cause the screen to scroll abruptly right/left or up/down.

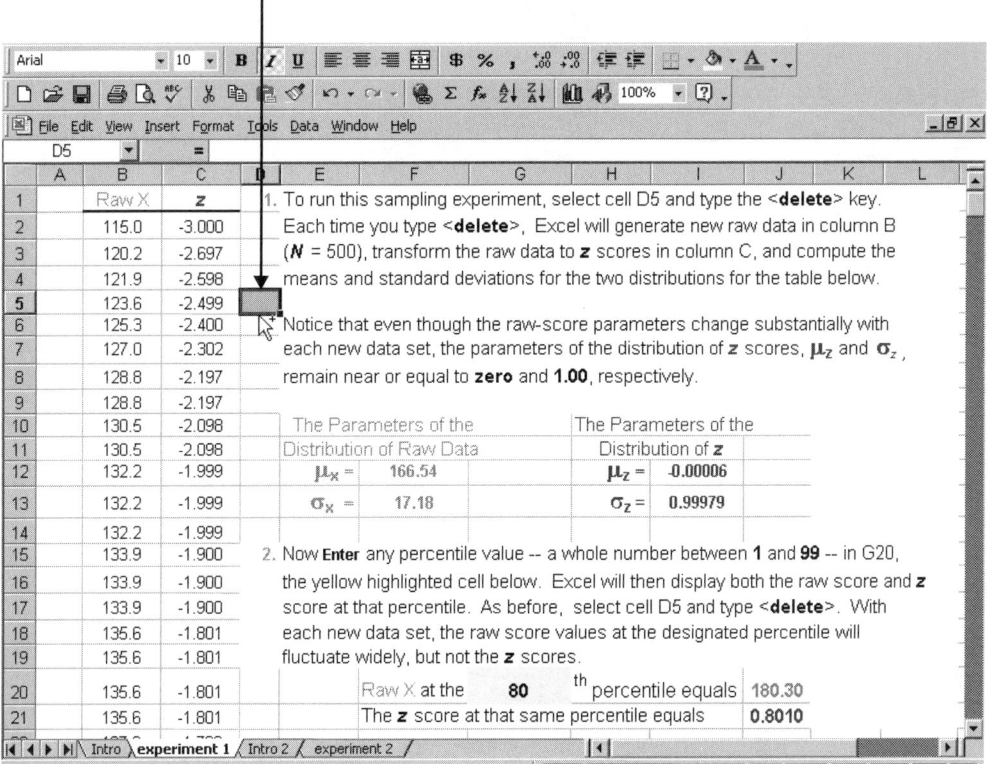
File Edit View Insert Format Tools Data Window Help
D5
Raw X
z
1. To run this sampling experiment, select cell D5 and type the <delete> key. Each time you type <delete>, Excel will generate new raw data in column B (N = 500), transform the raw data to z scores in column C, and compute the means and standard deviations for the two distributions for the table below.
Notice that even though the raw-score parameters change substantially with each new data set, the parameters of the distribution of z scores, μz and σz, remain near or equal to zero and 1.00, respectively.
The Parameters of the Distribution of Raw Data
μX = 166.54
σX = 17.18
The Parameters of the Distribution of z
μz = -0.00006
σz = 0.99979
2. Now Enter any percentile value -- a whole number between 1 and 99 -- in G20, the yellow highlighted cell below. Excel will then display both the raw score and z score at that percentile. As before, select cell D5 and type <delete>. With each new data set, the raw score values at the designated percentile will fluctuate widely, but not the z scores.
Raw X at the 80 th percentile equals 180.30
The z score at that same percentile equals 0.8010
115.0 -3.000
120.2 -2.697
121.9 -2.598
123.6 -2.499
125.3 -2.400
127.0 -2.302
128.8 -2.197
128.8 -2.197
130.5 -2.098
130.5 -2.098
132.2 -1.999
132.2 -1.999
132.2 -1.999
133.9 -1.900
133.9 -1.900
133.9 -1.900
135.6 -1.801
135.6 -1.801
135.6 -1.801
135.6 -1.801
Intro
experiment 1
Intro 2
experiment 2

Folder: 02 The z statistic
Workbook: Comparing Distributions.xls
Worksheet: final grades

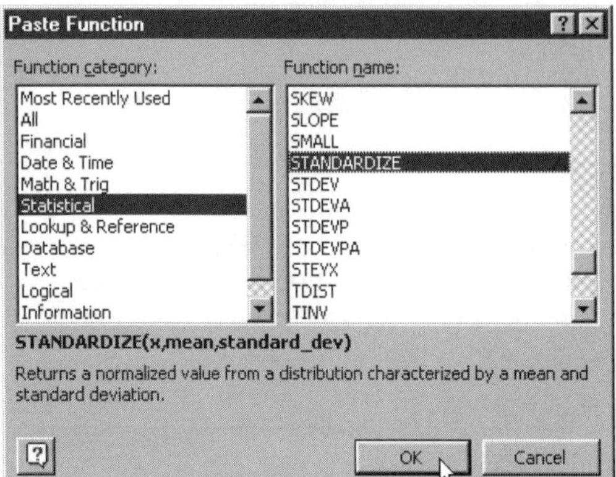
Paste Function
Function category:
Most Recently Used
All
Financial
Date & Time
Math & Trig
Statistical
Lookup & Reference
Database
Text
Logical
Information
Function name:
SKEW
SLOPE
SMALL
STANDARDIZE
STDEV
STDEVA
STDEVP
STDEVPA
STEYX
TDIST
TINV
STANDARDIZE(x,mean,standard_dev)
Returns a normalized value from a distribution characterized by a mean and standard deviation.
OK
Cancel

Click the f_x button to bring up this box. Then select Statistical from the list on the left (Function category) and STANDARDIZE from the list on the right (Function name) and click **OK**.

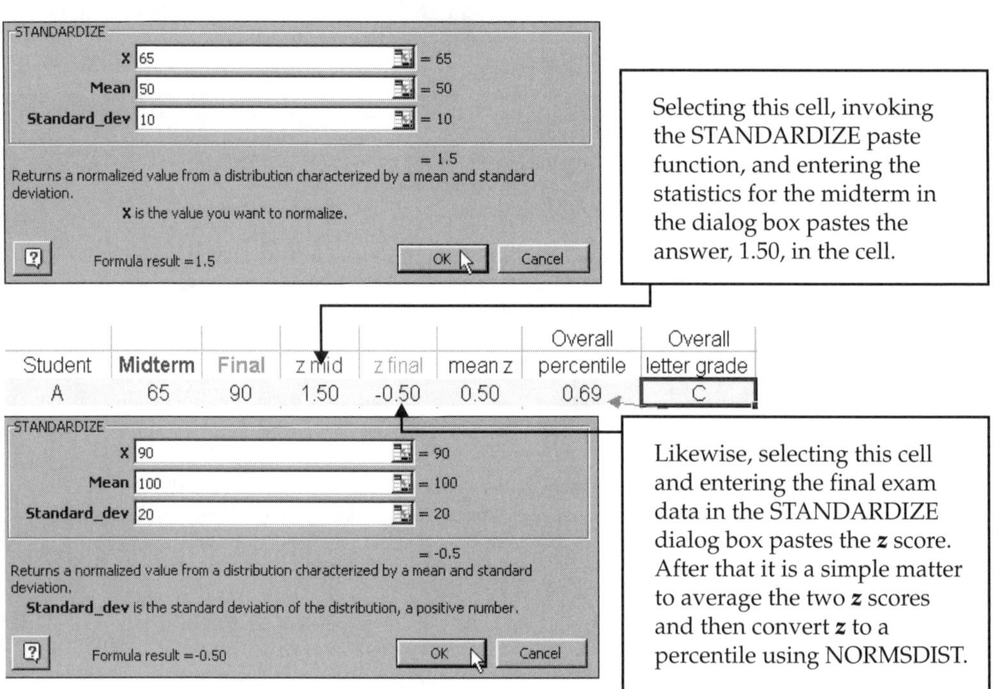
STANDARDIZE
X 65 = 65
Mean 50 = 50
Standard_dev 10 = 10
= 1.5
Returns a normalized value from a distribution characterized by a mean and standard deviation.
X is the value you want to normalize.
Formula result =1.5
OK
Cancel
Selecting this cell, invoking the STANDARDIZE paste function, and entering the statistics for the midterm in the dialog box pastes the answer, 1.50, in the cell.
Student
Midterm
Final
z mid
z final
mean z
Overall percentile
Overall letter grade
A
65
90
1.50
-0.50
0.50
0.69
C
STANDARDIZE
X 90 = 90
Mean 100 = 100
Standard_dev 20 = 20
= -0.5
Returns a normalized value from a distribution characterized by a mean and standard deviation.
Standard_dev is the standard deviation of the distribution, a positive number.
Formula result =-0.50
OK
Cancel
Likewise, selecting this cell and entering the final exam data in the STANDARDIZE dialog box pastes the z score. After that it is a simple matter to average the two z scores and then convert z to a percentile using NORMSDIST.

Folder: 02 The z statistic
Workbook: Comparing Distributions.xls
Worksheet: final grades

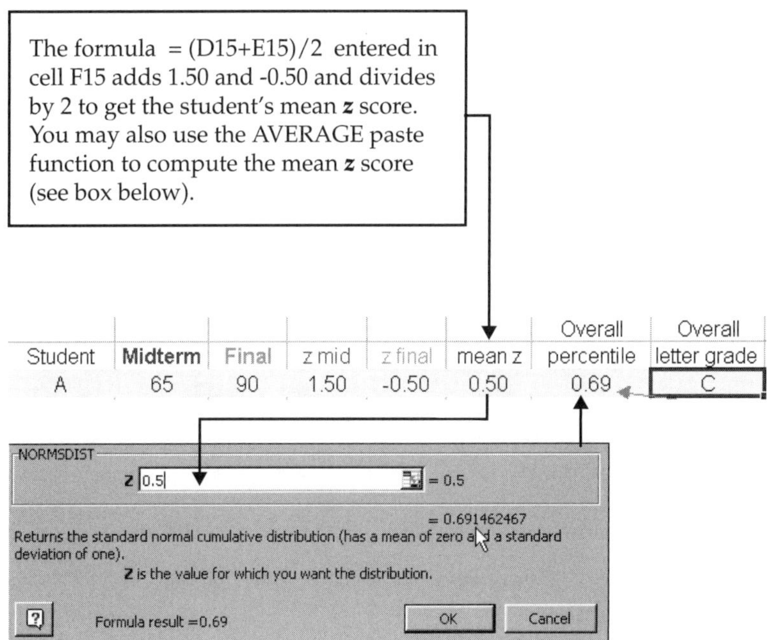
The formula = (D15+E15)/2 entered in cell F15 adds 1.50 and -0.50 and divides by 2 to get the student's mean ***z*** score. You may also use the AVERAGE paste function to compute the mean ***z*** score (see box below).
Student | Midterm | Final | z mid | z final | mean z | Overall percentile | Overall letter grade
A | 65 | 90 | 1.50 | -0.50 | 0.50 | 0.69 | C
NORMSDIST
Z 0.5 = 0.5
= 0.691462467
Returns the standard normal cumulative distribution (has a mean of zero and a standard deviation of one).
Z is the value for which you want the distribution.
Formula result =0.69
OK
Cancel

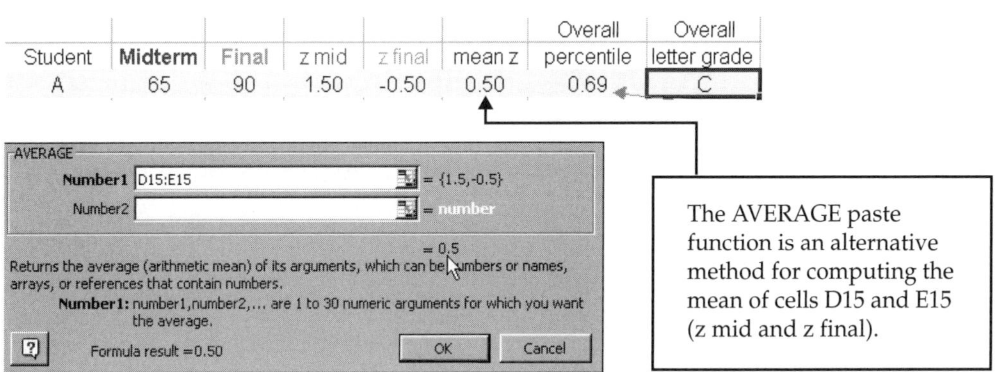
Student | Midterm | Final | z mid | z final | mean z | Overall percentile | Overall letter grade
A | 65 | 90 | 1.50 | -0.50 | 0.50 | 0.69 | C
AVERAGE
Number1 D15:E15 = {1.5,-0.5}
Number2 = number
= 0.5
Returns the average (arithmetic mean) of its arguments, which can be numbers or names, arrays, or references that contain numbers.
Number1: number1,number2,... are 1 to 30 numeric arguments for which you want the average.
Formula result =0.50
OK
Cancel
The AVERAGE paste function is an alternative method for computing the mean of cells D15 and E15 (z mid and z final).

Folder: 02 The z statistic
Workbook: Comparing Distributions.xls
Worksheet: practice

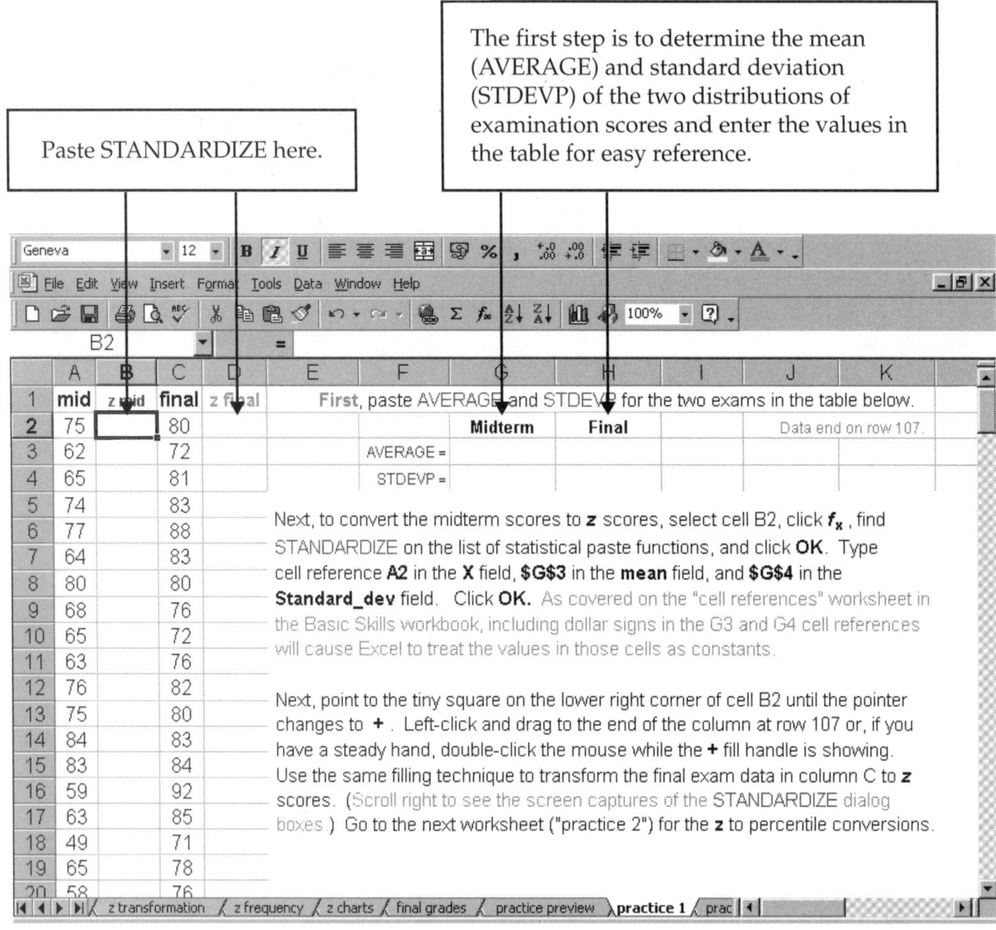

The first step is to determine the mean (AVERAGE) and standard deviation (STDEVP) of the two distributions of examination scores and enter the values in the table for easy reference.
Paste STANDARDIZE here.
mid
z mid
final
z final
First, paste AVERAGE and STDEVP for the two exams in the table below.
Midterm
Final
Data end on row 107.
AVERAGE =
STDEVP =
Next, to convert the midterm scores to z scores, select cell B2, click fx, find STANDARDIZE on the list of statistical paste functions, and click OK. Type cell reference A2 in the X field, $G$3 in the mean field, and $G$4 in the Standard_dev field. Click OK. As covered on the "cell references" worksheet in the Basic Skills workbook, including dollar signs in the G3 and G4 cell references will cause Excel to treat the values in those cells as constants.
Next, point to the tiny square on the lower right corner of cell B2 until the pointer changes to +. Left-click and drag to the end of the column at row 107 or, if you have a steady hand, double-click the mouse while the + fill handle is showing. Use the same filling technique to transform the final exam data in column C to z scores. (Scroll right to see the screen captures of the STANDARDIZE dialog boxes.) Go to the next worksheet ("practice 2") for the z to percentile conversions.
z transformation
z frequency
z charts
final grades
practice preview
practice 1

Folder: 02 The z statistic
Workbook: Comparing Distributions.xls
Worksheet: practice 1

Your practice 1 worksheet should look like this once you are finished converting all the scores to ***z*** scores.

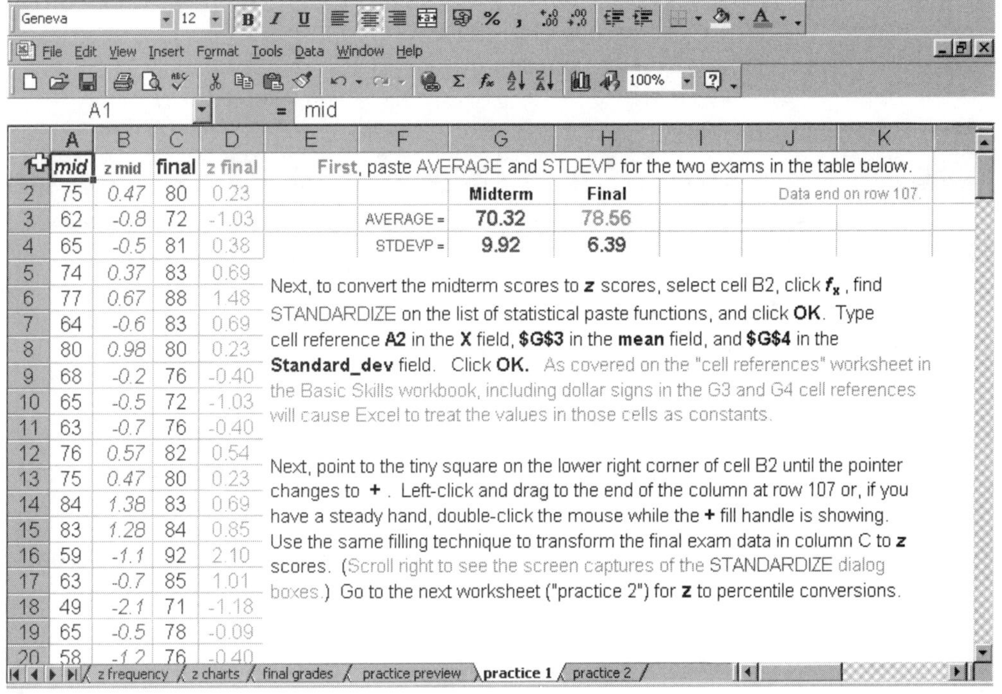

Geneva
12
File Edit View Insert Format Tools Data Window Help
100%
A1
= mid
First, paste AVERAGE and STDEVP for the two exams in the table below.
Midterm
Final
Data end on row 107.
AVERAGE = 70.32 78.56
STDEVP = 9.92 6.39
Next, to convert the midterm scores to z scores, select cell B2, click fx , find STANDARDIZE on the list of statistical paste functions, and click OK. Type cell reference A2 in the X field, $G$3 in the mean field, and $G$4 in the Standard_dev field. Click OK. As covered on the "cell references" worksheet in the Basic Skills workbook, including dollar signs in the G3 and G4 cell references will cause Excel to treat the values in those cells as constants.
Next, point to the tiny square on the lower right corner of cell B2 until the pointer changes to + . Left-click and drag to the end of the column at row 107 or, if you have a steady hand, double-click the mouse while the + fill handle is showing. Use the same filling technique to transform the final exam data in column C to z scores. (Scroll right to see the screen captures of the STANDARDIZE dialog boxes.) Go to the next worksheet ("practice 2") for z to percentile conversions.
z frequency
z charts
final grades
practice preview
practice 1
practice 2

	mid	z mid	final	z final
2	75	0.47	80	0.23
3	62	-0.8	72	-1.03
4	65	-0.5	81	0.38
5	74	0.37	83	0.69
6	77	0.67	88	1.48
7	64	-0.6	83	0.69
8	80	0.98	80	0.23
9	68	-0.2	76	-0.40
10	65	-0.5	72	-1.03
11	63	-0.7	76	-0.40
12	76	0.57	82	0.54
13	75	0.47	80	0.23
14	84	1.38	83	0.69
15	83	1.28	84	0.85
16	59	-1.1	92	2.10
17	63	-0.7	85	1.01
18	49	-2.1	71	-1.18
19	65	-0.5	78	-0.09
20	58	-1.2	76	-0.40

Folder: 02 The z statistic
Workbook: Comparing Distributions.xls
Worksheet: practice

This worksheet is one of many in *ESC* that allow the user to input information and then practice solving problems that rely on that information. The solutions appear off to the right – in an area of the spreadsheet that is out of the initial viewing area – and are dynamically linked to the requested user inputs. For such a worksheet to function as intended, it is important not to disturb the contents of any cells outside of those that require user input. This screen capture points out one of these "out-of-bounds" cells.

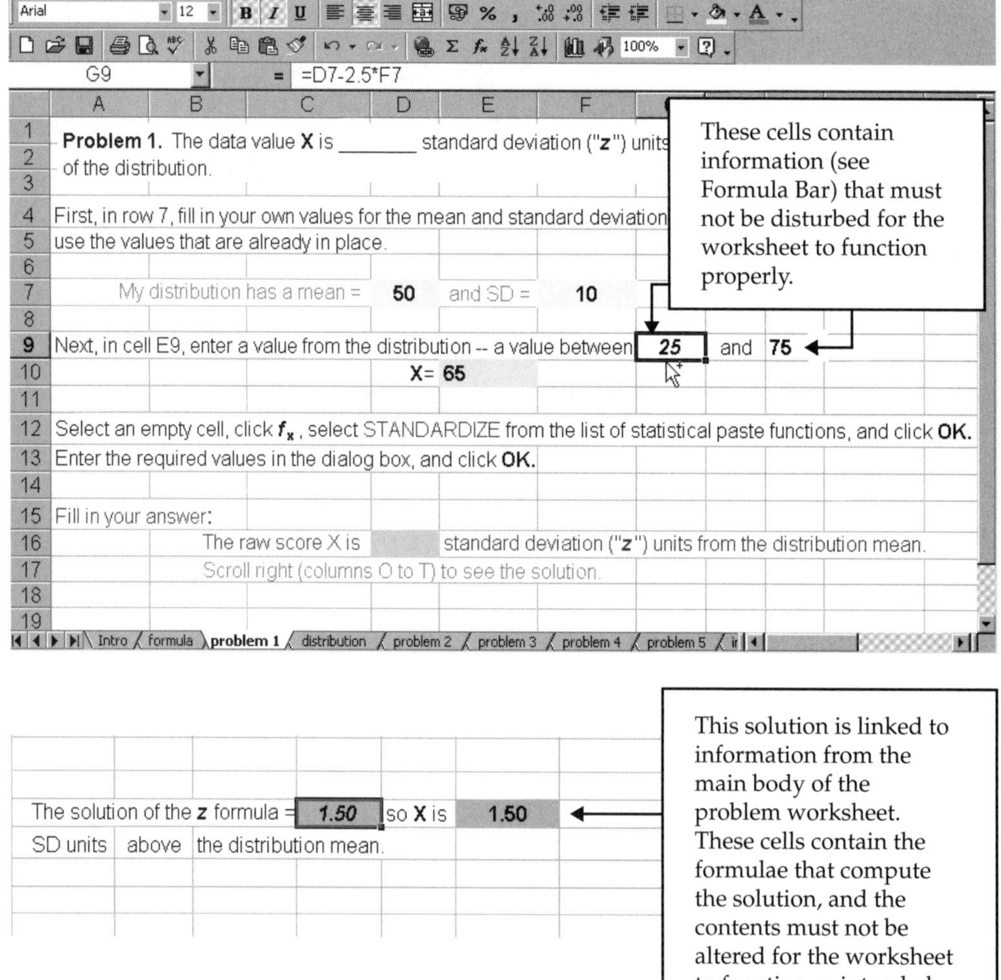
G9
=D7-2.5*F7
Problem 1. The data value X is _______ standard deviation ("z") units
of the distribution.
First, in row 7, fill in your own values for the mean and standard deviation
use the values that are already in place.
My distribution has a mean = 50 and SD = 10
Next, in cell E9, enter a value from the distribution -- a value between 25 and 75
X= 65
Select an empty cell, click fx, select STANDARDIZE from the list of statistical paste functions, and click OK.
Enter the required values in the dialog box, and click OK.
Fill in your answer:
The raw score X is standard deviation ("z") units from the distribution mean.
Scroll right (columns O to T) to see the solution.
Intro formula problem 1 distribution problem 2 problem 3 problem 4 problem 5
These cells contain information (see Formula Bar) that must not be disturbed for the worksheet to function properly.
The solution of the z formula = 1.50 so X is 1.50
SD units above the distribution mean.
This solution is linked to information from the main body of the problem worksheet. These cells contain the formulae that compute the solution, and the contents must not be altered for the worksheet to function as intended.

CHAPTER 3

Correlation and Regression

Folder: 03 Correlation and Regression
Workbook: Type 1 Error.xls
Worksheet: exercise

Highlight a random data matrix with a left-click and drag operation. Then, with the mouse pointer over the matrix, right-click Copy. Finally, Paste Special (with Values selected) over the existing matrix in the "my saved data' worksheet. Be careful to select only the data – no column labels.

sample 1	sample 2	sample 3	sample 4	sample 5	sample 6	sample 7	sample 8	sample 9
14	11	10	4	53	45	72	89	99
71	40	65	2	98	20	24	94	60
11	67	4	95	34	36	15	20	48
58	45	12	19	80	68	34	44	45
86	99	85	39	53	3	92	28	77
91	79	16	14	68	69	74	7	41
74	31	79	21	69	43	67	11	45
64	45	78	16	42	10	55	70	25
77	60	41	86	24	29	66	44	3
89	50	5	74	49	16	66	19	57
77	54	49	66	76	38	69	75	40
77	20	54	56	64	9	55	71	40
41	21	91	96	94	19	19	17	28
26	17	13	31	68	3	77	36	80
57	39	92	41	17	32	33	52	28
16	5	43	23	92	11	34	23	96
13	38	96	95	50	10	90	85	21
16	96	59	79	32	30	28	90	70
46	69	23	22	9	55	43	76	16
59	58	16	9	17	32	1	68	2
28	96	79	41	38	56	95	32	24

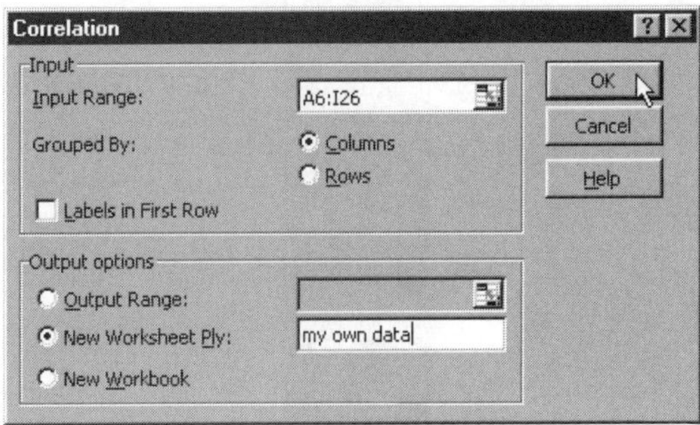
Correlation
Input
Input Range:
A6:I26
Grouped By:
Columns
Rows
Labels in First Row
OK
Cancel
Help
Output options
Output Range:
New Worksheet Ply:
my own data
New Workbook

Your Correlation tool dialog box should look like this. The Input Range is from cell A6 to cell I26. Once you click **OK** the new matrix will appear on a new "my own data" worksheet.

Folder: 03 Correlation and Regression
Workbook: Pearson r.xls
Worksheet: Definitional 2

For purposes of this demonstration, formulae are already written to cells D2, E2, and F2. For example, the formula in D2 computes the square of the deviation between X_1 and the mean of all the X values.

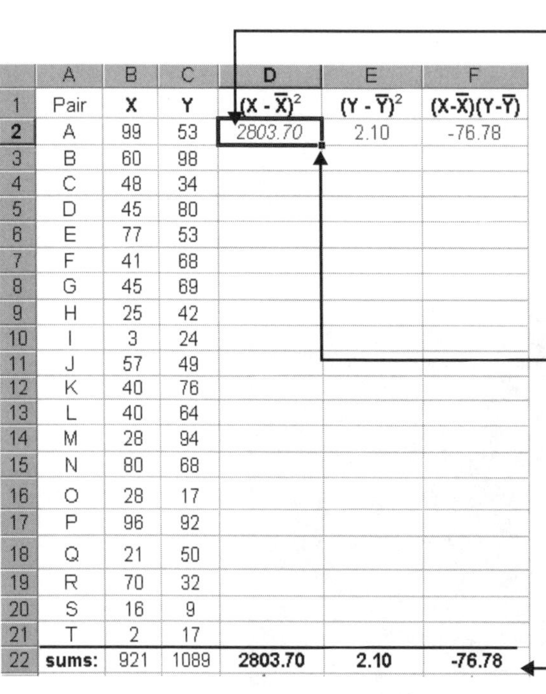

	A	B	C	D	E	F
1	Pair	X	Y	$(X - \bar{X})^2$	$(Y - \bar{Y})^2$	$(X-\bar{X})(Y-\bar{Y})$
2	A	99	53	2803.70	2.10	-76.78
3	B	60	98			
4	C	48	34			
5	D	45	80			
6	E	77	53			
7	F	41	68			
8	G	45	69			
9	H	25	42			
10	I	3	24			
11	J	57	49			
12	K	40	76			
13	L	40	64			
14	M	28	94			
15	N	80	68			
16	O	28	17			
17	P	96	92			
18	Q	21	50			
19	R	70	32			
20	S	16	9			
21	T	2	17			
22	**sums:**	921	1089	**2803.70**	**2.10**	**-76.78**

The pointer will change to a plus sign (or a square on a Macintosh) when positioned over the tiny box in the lower right corner of the cell. Once the plus sign appears, hold down the left mouse button and drag down the column to the last X-Y pair as shown below.

Ignore these sums until after you complete the drag-to-fill procedure.

	A	B	C	D	E	F
1	Pair	X	Y	$(X - \bar{X})^2$	$(Y - \bar{Y})^2$	$(X-\bar{X})(Y-\bar{Y})$
2	A	99	53	2803.70	2.10	-76.78
3	B	60	98	194.60		
4	C	48	34	3.80		
5	D	45	80	1.10		
6	E	77	53	957.90		
7	F	41	68	25.50		
8	G	45	69	1.10		
9	H	25	42	443.10		
10	I	3	24	1853.30		
11	J	57	49	119.90		
12	K	40	76	36.60		
13	L	40	64	36.60		
14	M	28	94	325.80		
15	N	80	68	1152.60		
16	O	28	17	325.80		
17	P	96	92	2495.00		
18	Q	21	50	627.50		
19	R	70	32	573.60		

After the column D drag-to-fill operation your screen will look like this. The SUM of the column entries appears on line 22. (Be careful not to include line 22 in your fill operation. Stop where the data stops – on line 21.) Now carry out drag-to-fill operations on columns E and F and the solutions for the formula entries swill appear in the highlighted cells on the lower right portion of the screen.

Folder: 03 Correlation and Regression
Workbook: Spearman rho.xls
Worksheet: easy rank 1

This is how your computer screen should look after following the directions on the "easy rank 1" worksheet. Completion of this worksheet employs a number of Excel skills: accessing a paste function, entering a formula into a field in the paste function dialog box, the use of $$ to control the values in a fill operation, the fill operation itself, and running a descending sort. If your screen looks like the one below, pat yourself on the back!

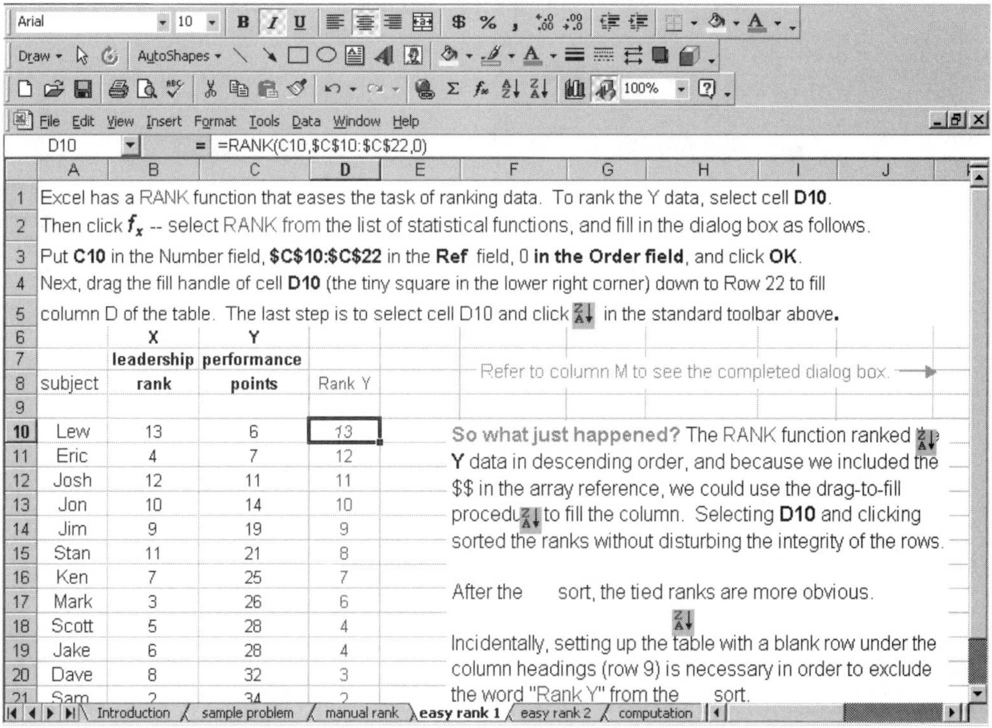
D10 = =RANK(C10,$C$10:$C$22,0)
Excel has a RANK function that eases the task of ranking data. To rank the Y data, select cell D10.
Then click fx -- select RANK from the list of statistical functions, and fill in the dialog box as follows.
Put C10 in the Number field, $C$10:$C$22 in the Ref field, 0 in the Order field, and click OK.
Next, drag the fill handle of cell D10 (the tiny square in the lower right corner) down to Row 22 to fill
column D of the table. The last step is to select cell D10 and click in the standard toolbar above.
Refer to column M to see the completed dialog box.
So what just happened? The RANK function ranked the Y data in descending order, and because we included the $$ in the array reference, we could use the drag-to-fill procedure to fill the column. Selecting D10 and clicking sorted the ranks without disturbing the integrity of the rows.
After the sort, the tied ranks are more obvious.
Incidentally, setting up the table with a blank row under the column headings (row 9) is necessary in order to exclude the word "Rank Y" from the sort.
Introduction
sample problem
manual rank
easy rank 1
easy rank 2
computation

subject	X leadership rank	Y performance points	Rank Y
Lew	13	6	13
Eric	4	7	12
Josh	12	11	11
Jon	10	14	10
Jim	9	19	9
Stan	11	21	8
Ken	7	25	7
Mark	3	26	6
Scott	5	28	4
Jake	6	28	4
Dave	8	32	3
Sam	2	34	2

Folder: 03 Correlation and Regression
Workbook: Linear Regression.xls
Worksheet: computation

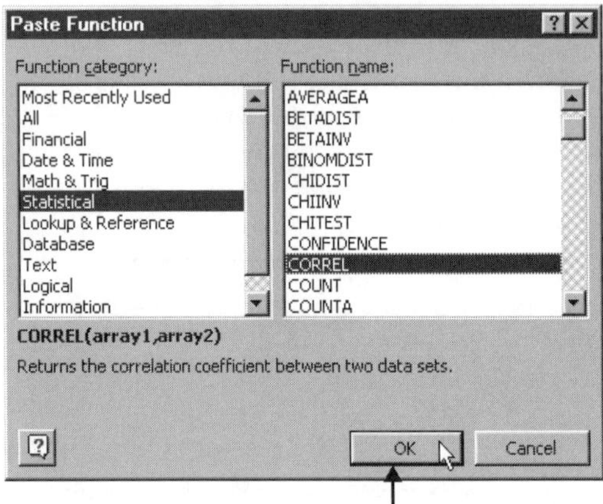
Paste Function
Function category:
Most Recently Used
All
Financial
Date & Time
Math & Trig
Statistical
Lookup & Reference
Database
Text
Logical
Information
Function name:
AVERAGEA
BETADIST
BETAINV
BINOMDIST
CHIDIST
CHIINV
CHITEST
CONFIDENCE
CORREL
COUNT
COUNTA
CORREL(array1,array2)
Returns the correlation coefficient between two data sets.
OK
Cancel

Your paste function dialog box should look like this (Function category = Statistical and Function name = CORREL) when running the CORREL paste function.

After clicking **OK**, the box below will pop up. Position the mouse pointer over the spreadsheet icon for Array 1 and left-click. The dialog box will "roll up" and wait for you to drag the dotted marquee around the data of Array 1 (say, the **X** values). Click the Array 2 field and drag the marquee around Array 2 (**Y**). When using CORREL it does not matter how you label the arrays. X can be Array 1 and Y Array 2, or the reverse.

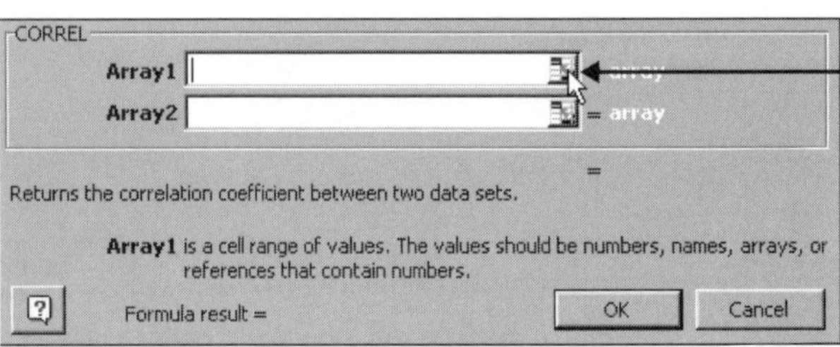
CORREL
Array1
Array2
= array
Returns the correlation coefficient between two data sets.
Array1 is a cell range of values. The values should be numbers, names, arrays, or references that contain numbers.
Formula result =
OK
Cancel

Folder: 03 Correlation and Regression
Workbook: Linear Regression.xls
Worksheet: paste functions

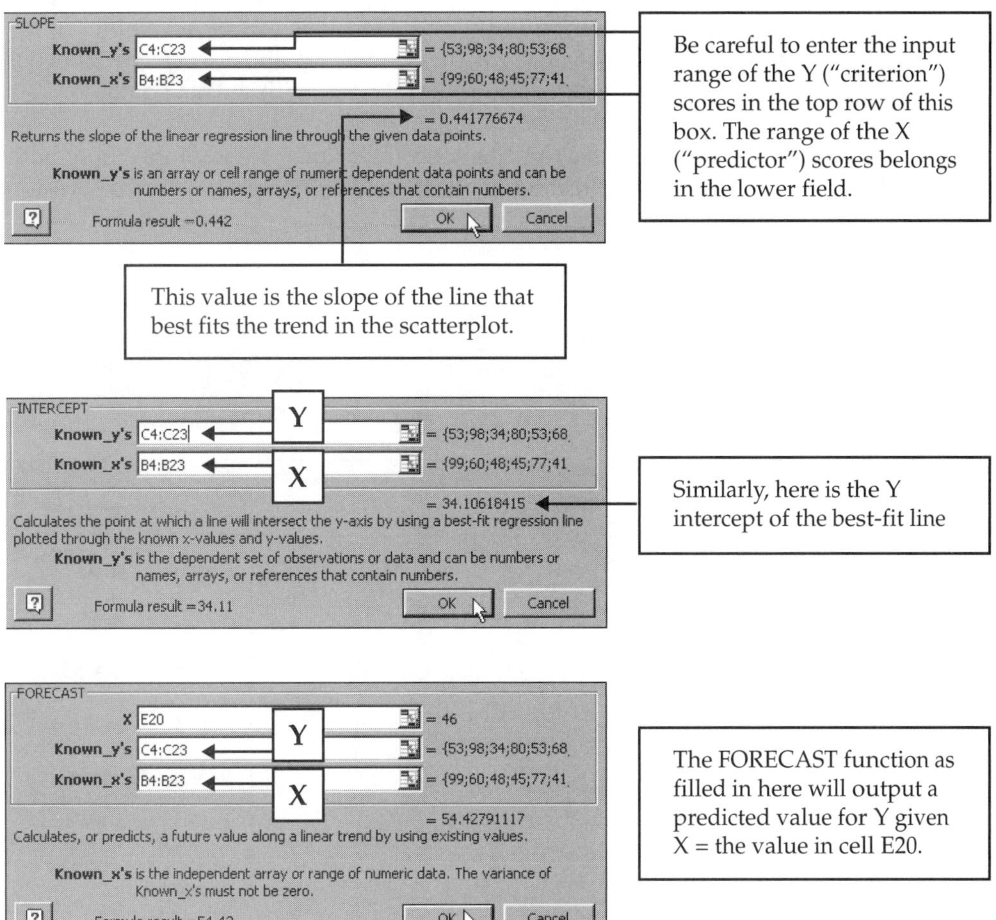
SLOPE
Known_y's C4:C23 = {53;98;34;80;53;68
Known_x's B4:B23 = {99;60;48;45;77;41
= 0.441776674
Returns the slope of the linear regression line through the given data points.
Known_y's is an array or cell range of numeric dependent data points and can be numbers or names, arrays, or references that contain numbers.
Formula result =0.442
OK
Cancel
Be careful to enter the input range of the Y ("criterion") scores in the top row of this box. The range of the X ("predictor") scores belongs in the lower field.
This value is the slope of the line that best fits the trend in the scatterplot.
INTERCEPT
Y
X
Known_y's C4:C23 = {53;98;34;80;53;68
Known_x's B4:B23 = {99;60;48;45;77;41
= 34.10618415
Calculates the point at which a line will intersect the y-axis by using a best-fit regression line plotted through the known x-values and y-values.
Known_y's is the dependent set of observations or data and can be numbers or names, arrays, or references that contain numbers.
Formula result =34.11
OK
Cancel
Similarly, here is the Y intercept of the best-fit line
FORECAST
X E20 = 46
Y
X
Known_y's C4:C23 = {53;98;34;80;53;68
Known_x's B4:B23 = {99;60;48;45;77;41
= 54.42791117
Calculates, or predicts, a future value along a linear trend by using existing values.
Known_x's is the independent array or range of numeric data. The variance of Known_x's must not be zero.
Formula result =54.43
OK
Cancel
The FORECAST function as filled in here will output a predicted value for Y given X = the value in cell E20.

Folder: 03 Correlation and Regression
Workbook: Linear Regression.xls
Worksheet: analysis

Put your mouse pointer on one of the scatterplot dots and a box will appear [not shown] revealing its X-Y coordinates. Find that pair of X-Y values in the table on the left, change them, and the scatterplot and associated statistics (columns K and L) will update instantly in concert with the new data.

As you alter the coordinates to form a stronger linear trend, notice how both the image of the scatterplot and the statistics of correlation and regression reflect the stronger trend.

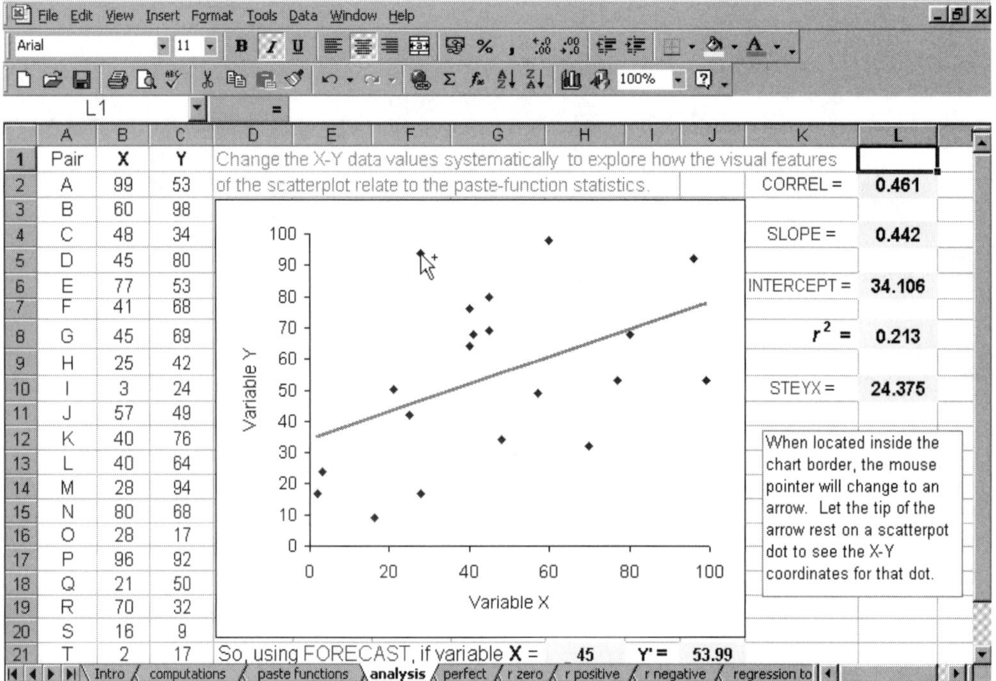
File Edit View Insert Format Tools Data Window Help
Arial 11
100%
L1
Pair X Y
A 99 53
B 60 98
C 48 34
D 45 80
E 77 53
F 41 68
G 45 69
H 25 42
I 3 24
J 57 49
K 40 76
L 40 64
M 28 94
N 80 68
O 28 17
P 96 92
Q 21 50
R 70 32
S 16 9
T 2 17
Change the X-Y data values systematically to explore how the visual features
of the scatterplot relate to the paste-function statistics.
CORREL = 0.461
SLOPE = 0.442
INTERCEPT = 34.106
r^2 = 0.213
STEYX = 24.375
Variable Y
Variable X
When located inside the chart border, the mouse pointer will change to an arrow. Let the tip of the arrow rest on a scatterpot dot to see the X-Y coordinates for that dot.
So, using FORECAST, if variable X = 45 Y' = 53.99
Intro computations paste functions analysis perfect r zero r positive r negative regression to

CHAPTER 4

Sampling Distributions

Folder: 04 Sampling Distributions
Workbook: The Binomial.xls
Worksheet: Bernoulli

The Random Number Generation dialog box will appear once you click the Tools menu, select Random Number Generation, and click **OK**. When you get to the Distribution entry, click the scroll arrow for the Distribution field, then find and click Bernoulli on the list that appears.

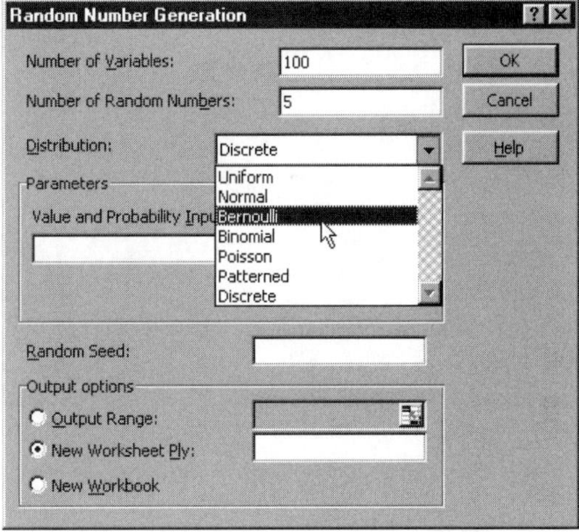
Random Number Generation
Number of Variables:
100
Number of Random Numbers:
5
Distribution:
Discrete
Parameters
Value and Probability Input
Uniform
Normal
Bernoulli
Binomial
Poisson
Patterned
Discrete
OK
Cancel
Help
Random Seed:
Output options
Output Range:
New Worksheet Ply:
New Workbook

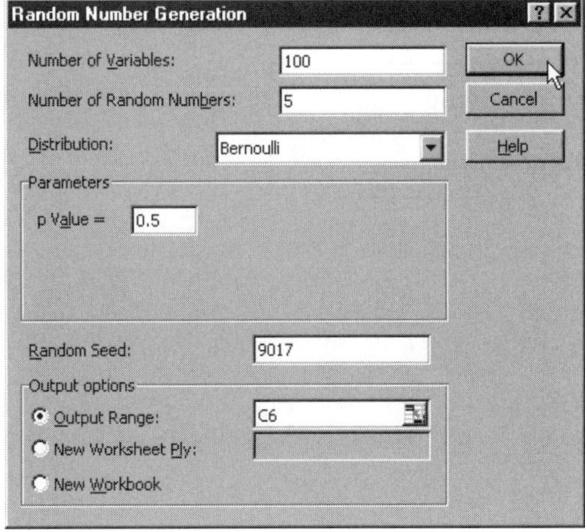
Random Number Generation
Number of Variables:
100
Number of Random Numbers:
5
Distribution:
Bernoulli
Parameters
p Value =
0.5
OK
Cancel
Help
Random Seed:
9017
Output options
Output Range:
C6
New Worksheet Ply:
New Workbook

Here is the Random Number Generation dialog box filled in with the appropriate entries. Clicking **OK** will rerun the Bernoulli experiment for the specific random number entered. Be sure to use a different Random Seed in subsequent reruns. Click **OK** to the warning about overwriting existing data.

Folder: 04 Sampling Distributions
Workbook: The Binomial.xls
Worksheet: Binomial exp

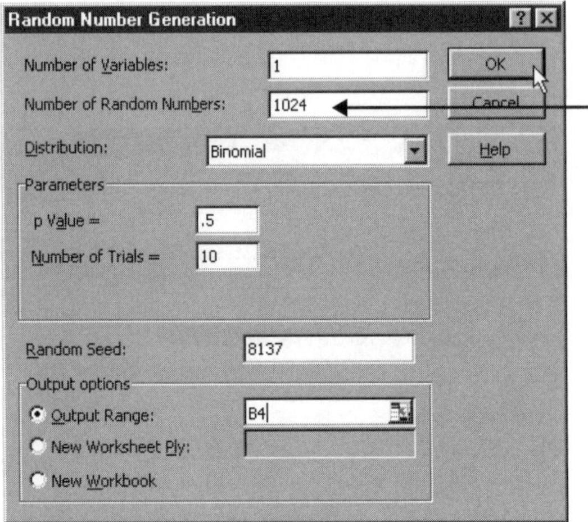
Random Number Generation
Number of Variables:
1
Number of Random Numbers:
1024
OK
Cancel
Help
Distribution:
Binomial
Parameters
p Value =
.5
Number of Trials =
10
Random Seed:
8137
Output options
Output Range:
B4
New Worksheet Ply:
New Workbook

When filled in as shown on the left, the Random Number Generation tool selects 1024 new samples for the binomial sampling experiment in which ***n***=10 and *p*=.50. By entering 1024 in the Number of Random Numbers field of the ten-flip experiment, every one of the 210 = 1024 possible patterns of heads and tails has some chance of occurring.

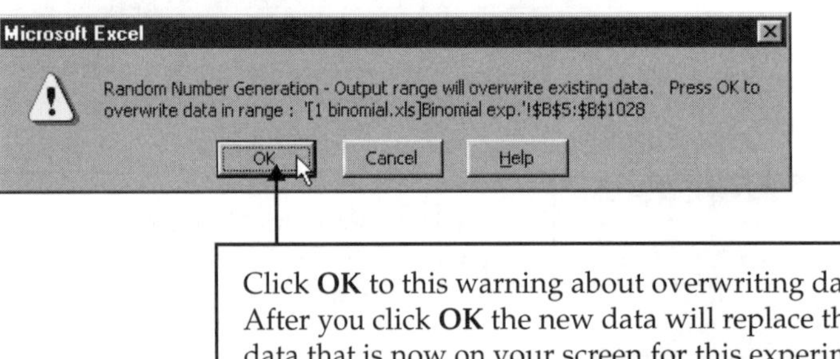
Microsoft Excel
Random Number Generation - Output range will overwrite existing data. Press OK to overwrite data in range : '[1 binomial.xls]Binomial exp.'!$B$5:$B$1028
OK
Cancel
Help

Click **OK** to this warning about overwriting data. After you click **OK** the new data will replace the the data that is now on your screen for this experiment.

Folder: 04 Sampling Distributions
Workbook: Central Limit Theorem.xls
Worksheet: your data (n=9)

The "your data" sequence of worksheets permit an empirical test of the central limit theorem with a variety of sample sizes (9, 16, 25, and 100). The sheet show here uses the sample size ***n*=9.** Scroll to the right of the Excel worksheet to see the actual sample values.

Be sure to use a different random seed for each repetition of the experiment, and just click **OK** if a warning pops up about overwriting existing data.

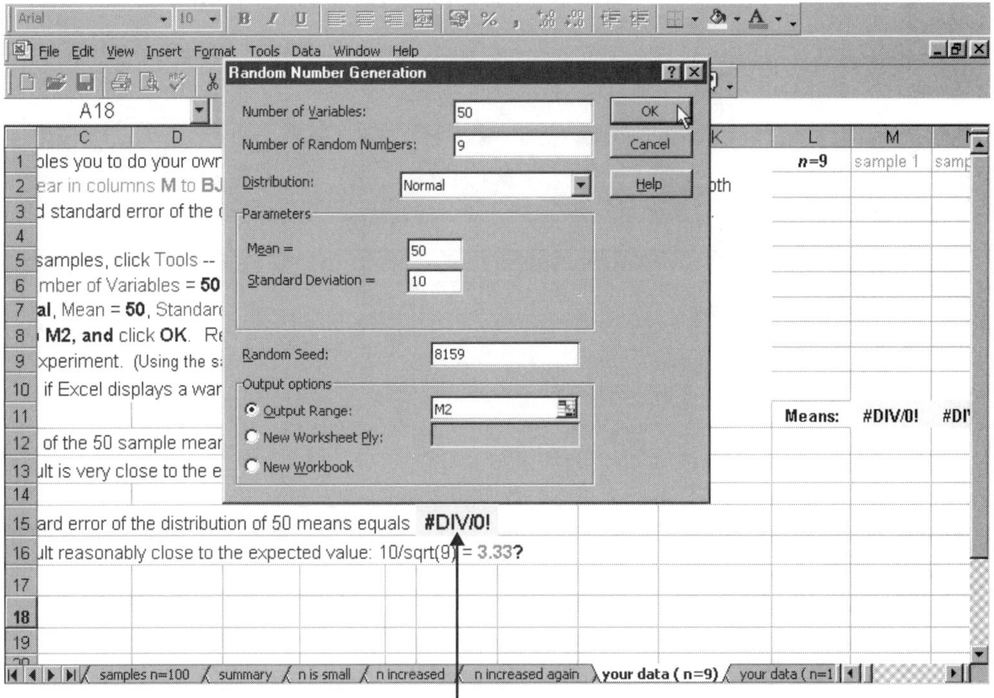
File Edit View Insert Format Tools Data Window Help
A18
Random Number Generation
Number of Variables: 50
Number of Random Numbers: 9
Distribution: Normal
Parameters
Mean = 50
Standard Deviation = 10
Random Seed: 8159
Output options
Output Range: M2
New Worksheet Ply:
New Workbook
OK
Cancel
Help
n=9
sample 1
Means: #DIV/0!
ard error of the distribution of 50 means equals #DIV/0!
ult reasonably close to the expected value: 10/sqrt(9) = 3.33?
samples n=100
summary
n is small
n increased
n increased again
your data (n=9)

Once you click **OK** in the above Random Number Generation dialog box, the #DIV/0! error messages will be replaced by the output of the experiment.

Folder: 04 Sampling Distributions
Workbook: Central Limit Theorem.xls
Worksheet: your parameters (n=9)

On the "your parameter" series of worksheets you may repeat the sampling experiments using your own values for the mean and standard deviation. As before, the sample sizes are held at 9, 16, 25, and 100.

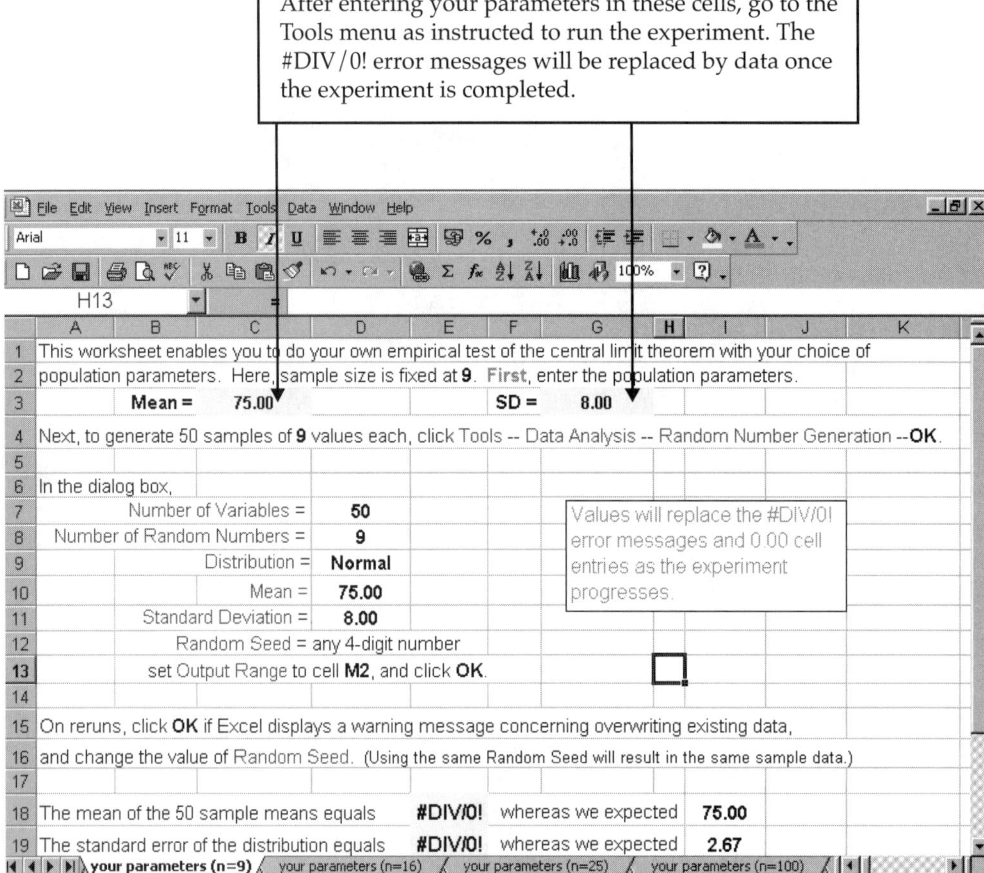
After entering your parameters in these cells, go to the Tools menu as instructed to run the experiment. The #DIV/0! error messages will be replaced by data once the experiment is completed.
File Edit View Insert Format Tools Data Window Help
Arial
11
100%
H13
This worksheet enables you to do your own empirical test of the central limit theorem with your choice of
population parameters. Here, sample size is fixed at 9. First, enter the population parameters.
Mean = 75.00
SD = 8.00
Next, to generate 50 samples of 9 values each, click Tools -- Data Analysis -- Random Number Generation --OK.
In the dialog box,
Number of Variables = 50
Number of Random Numbers = 9
Distribution = Normal
Mean = 75.00
Standard Deviation = 8.00
Random Seed = any 4-digit number
set Output Range to cell M2, and click OK.
Values will replace the #DIV/0! error messages and 0.00 cell entries as the experiment progresses.
On reruns, click OK if Excel displays a warning message concerning overwriting existing data,
and change the value of Random Seed. (Using the same Random Seed will result in the same sample data.)
The mean of the 50 sample means equals #DIV/0! whereas we expected 75.00
The standard error of the distribution equals #DIV/0! whereas we expected 2.67
your parameters (n=9)
your parameters (n=16)
your parameters (n=25)
your parameters (n=100)

CHAPTER 5

Probability

Folder: 05 Probability
Workbook: Computing Probability.xls
Worksheets: exact / X or fewer / X or more

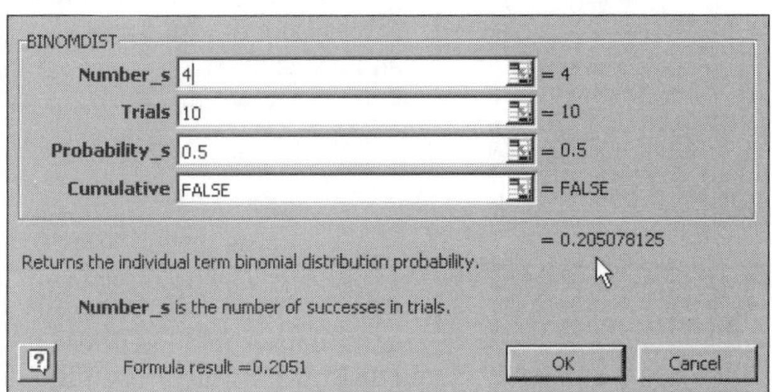
BINOMDIST
Number_s 4 = 4
Trials 10 = 10
Probability_s 0.5 = 0.5
Cumulative FALSE = FALSE
= 0.205078125
Returns the individual term binomial distribution probability.
Number_s is the number of successes in trials.
Formula result =0.2051
OK
Cancel

With these values entered into the four fields, the BINOMDIST paste function outputs the probability of **exactly** 4 successes in 10 trials when p(success) = .50.

BINOMDIST
Number_s 4 = 4
Trials 10 = 10
Probability_s 0.5 = 0.5
Cumulative TRUE = TRUE
= 0.376953125
Returns the individual term binomial distribution probability.
Number_s is the number of successes in trials.
Formula result =0.3770
OK
Cancel

By changing the FALSE entry to TRUE, the BINOMDIST paste function outputs the probability of **4 or fewer** successes in 10 trials when p(success) = .50.

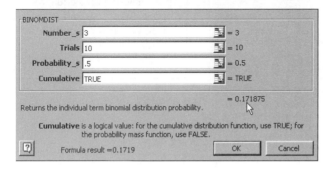

BINOMDIST
Number_s 3 = 3
Trials 10 = 10
Probability_s .5 = 0.5
Cumulative TRUE = TRUE
= 0.171875
Returns the individual term binomial distribution probability.
Cumulative is a logical value: for the cumulative distribution function, use TRUE; for the probability mass function, use FALSE.
Formula result =0.1719
OK
Cancel

The probability of 4 or more successes is the same as 1 minus the probability of 3 or fewer successes. Here, the result (.172) is for 3 or fewer successes. So, the probability of 4 or more successes equals 1 – .172 = **.828.**

Folder: 05 Probability
Workbook: Computing Probability.xls
Worksheet: =, < or =

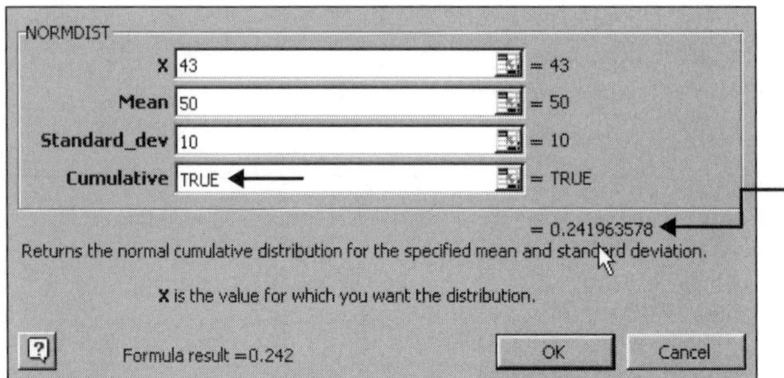
NORMDIST
X 43 = 43
Mean 50 = 50
Standard_dev 10 = 10
Cumulative TRUE = TRUE
= 0.241963578
Returns the normal cumulative distribution for the specified mean and standard deviation.
X is the value for which you want the distribution.
Formula result =0.242
OK
Cancel

NORMDIST tells us that the probability of selecting a random value from the population (μ=50, σ=10) that is **less than or equal to** 43 equals .242.

NORMDIST
X 43 = 43
Mean 50 = 50
Standard_dev 10 = 10
Cumulative FALSE = FALSE
= 0.031225393
Returns the normal cumulative distribution for the specified mean and standard deviation.
X is the value for which you want the distribution.
Formula result =0.031
OK Cancel

By entering FALSE in the Cumulative field, NORMDIST outputs the probability (.03) of a sample that equals **exactly** 43. But bear in mind that because the true limits of the number 43 are **42.5** and **43.5**, computing exactly 43 is really the same as computing between 42.5 and 43.5.

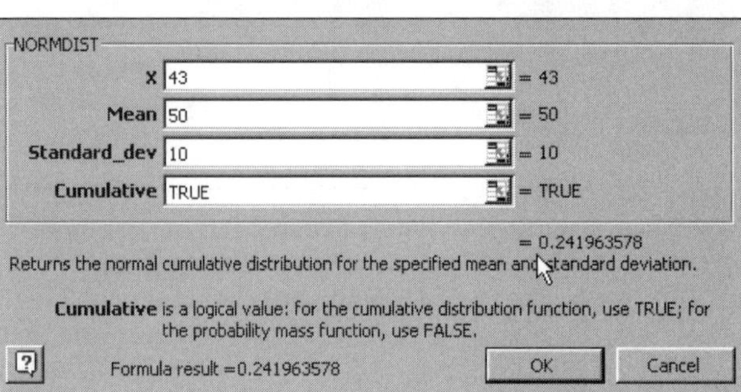
NORMDIST
X 43 = 43
Mean 50 = 50
Standard_dev 10 = 10
Cumulative TRUE = TRUE
= 0.241963578
Returns the normal cumulative distribution for the specified mean and standard deviation.
Cumulative is a logical value: for the cumulative distribution function, use TRUE; for the probability mass function, use FALSE.
Formula result =0.241963578
OK
Cancel

Because the Cumulative = TRUE specification causes NORMDIST to output a proportion of area equal to or less than X, to find 43 **or more** we must compute 1 minus ***p***(X or less). Here, the answer is **1 – .24 = .76**

Folder: 05 Probability
Workbook: Solving Problems.xls
Worksheet: problem set 1

This screen shows the first of two problem sets in this workbook. The solutions (on the next "answers" worksheet) are linked to the values listed for the basket (highlighted yellow in column H), so they will automatically update following any changes to the original basket of red, white, and blue balls.

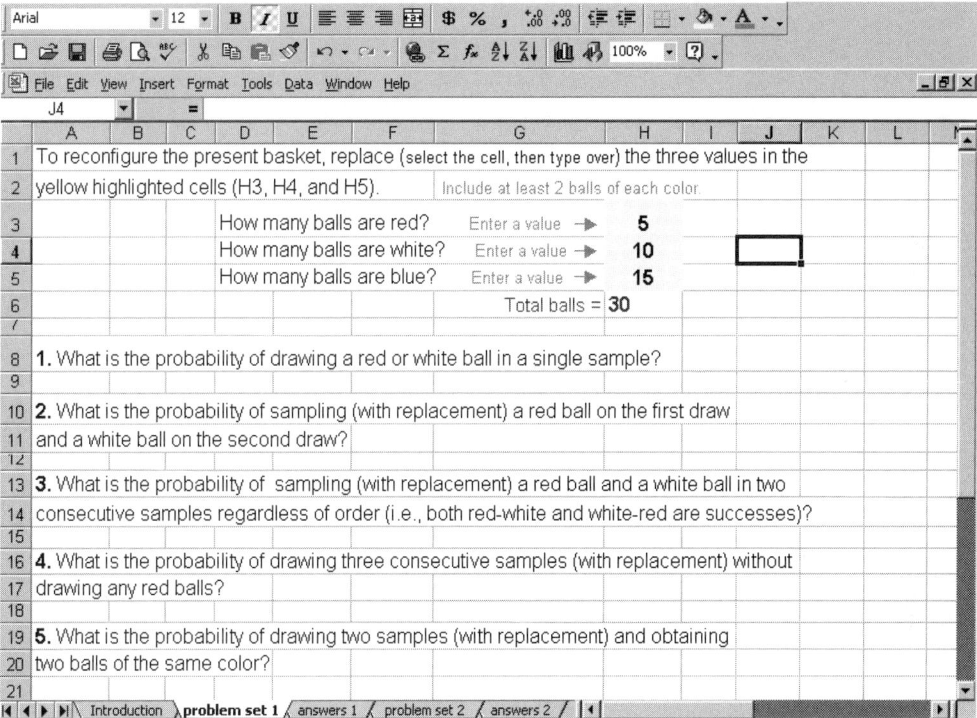
To reconfigure the present basket, replace (select the cell, then type over) the three values in the
yellow highlighted cells (H3, H4, and H5).
Include at least 2 balls of each color.
How many balls are red? Enter a value 5
How many balls are white? Enter a value 10
How many balls are blue? Enter a value 15
Total balls = 30
1. What is the probability of drawing a red or white ball in a single sample?
2. What is the probability of sampling (with replacement) a red ball on the first draw
and a white ball on the second draw?
3. What is the probability of sampling (with replacement) a red ball and a white ball in two
consecutive samples regardless of order (i.e., both red-white and white-red are successes)?
4. What is the probability of drawing three consecutive samples (with replacement) without
drawing any red balls?
5. What is the probability of drawing two samples (with replacement) and obtaining
two balls of the same color?
Introduction
problem set 1
answers 1
problem set 2
answers 2

CHAPTER 6

The *t* Statistic – One Sample

Folder: 06 The t Statistic - 1 Sample
Workbook: Estimating Error.xls
Worksheet: experiment

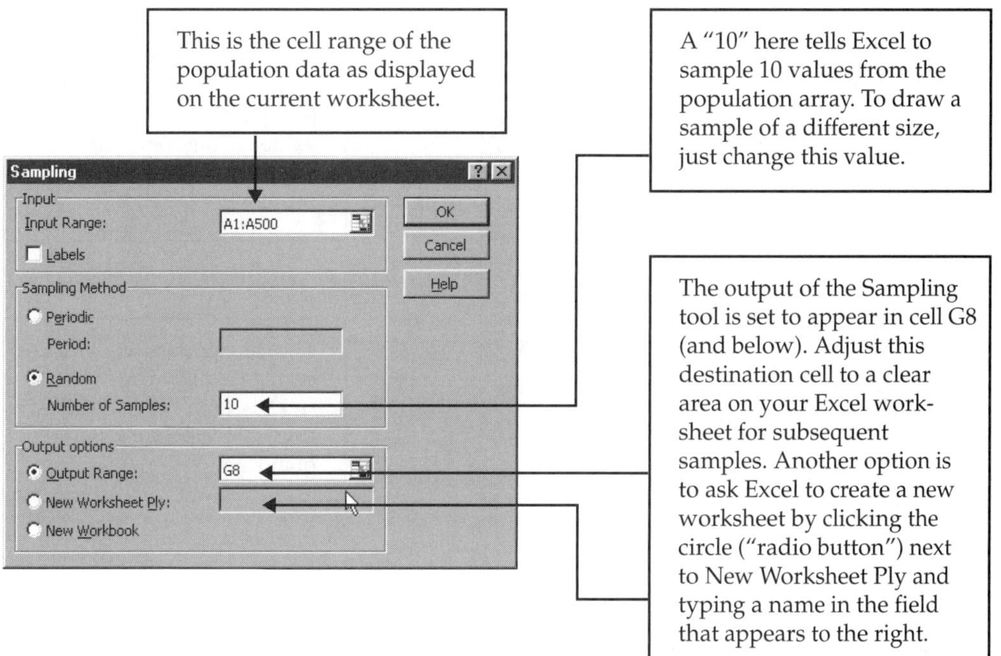
This is the cell range of the population data as displayed on the current worksheet.
A "10" here tells Excel to sample 10 values from the population array. To draw a sample of a different size, just change this value.
Sampling
Input
Input Range:
A1:A500
Labels
OK
Cancel
Help
Sampling Method
Periodic
Period:
Random
Number of Samples:
10
Output options
Output Range:
G8
New Worksheet Ply:
New Workbook
The output of the Sampling tool is set to appear in cell G8 (and below). Adjust this destination cell to a clear area on your Excel worksheet for subsequent samples. Another option is to ask Excel to create a new worksheet by clicking the circle ("radio button") next to New Worksheet Ply and typing a name in the field that appears to the right.

The AVERAGE, STDEV, and STDEVP dialog boxes are virtually the same. The only field to fill in (Number 1) is the range of cells that hold the data on which you wish the function to operate.

AVERAGE
Number1 C8:C17 = {53;46;50;58;39;36
Number2 = number
= 49.9
Returns the average (arithmetic mean) of its arguments, which can be numbers or names, arrays, or references that contain numbers.
Number1: number1,number2,... are 1 to 30 numeric arguments for which you want the average.
Formula result =49.90
OK Cancel

Folder: 06 The t Statistic - 1 Sample
Workbook: Rationale of the t Test.xls
Worksheet: experiment / t formula

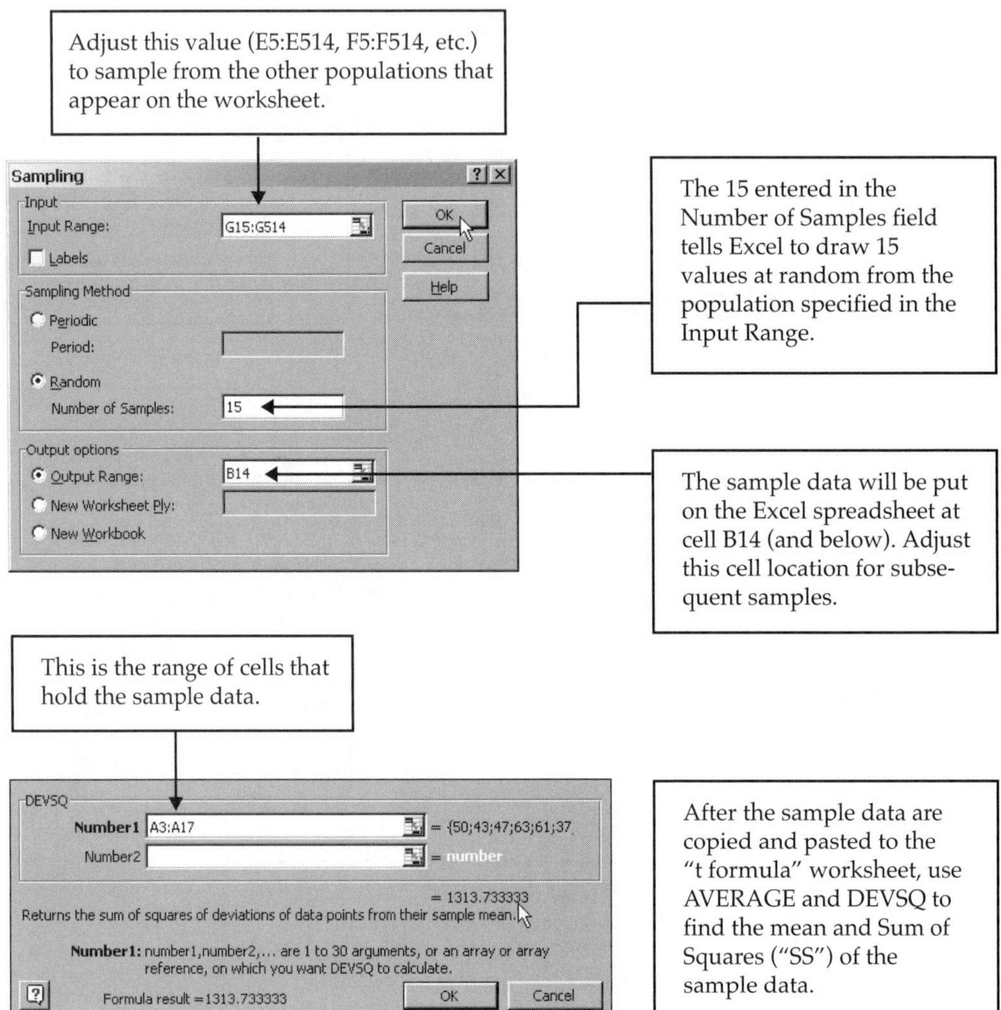
Adjust this value (E5:E514, F5:F514, etc.) to sample from the other populations that appear on the worksheet.
Sampling
Input
Input Range:
G15:G514
Labels
OK
Cancel
Help
Sampling Method
Periodic
Period:
Random
Number of Samples:
15
Output options
Output Range:
B14
New Worksheet Ply:
New Workbook
The 15 entered in the Number of Samples field tells Excel to draw 15 values at random from the population specified in the Input Range.
The sample data will be put on the Excel spreadsheet at cell B14 (and below). Adjust this cell location for subsequent samples.

This is the range of cells that hold the sample data.
DEVSQ
Number1
A3:A17
= {50;43;47;63;61;37
Number2
= number
= 1313.733333
Returns the sum of squares of deviations of data points from their sample mean.
Number1: number1,number2,... are 1 to 30 arguments, or an array or array reference, on which you want DEVSQ to calculate.
Formula result =1313.733333
OK
Cancel
After the sample data are copied and pasted to the "t formula" worksheet, use AVERAGE and DEVSQ to find the mean and Sum of Squares ("SS") of the sample data.

Folder: 06 The t Statistic - 1 Sample
Workbook: Confidence Intervals.xls
Worksheet: demo2

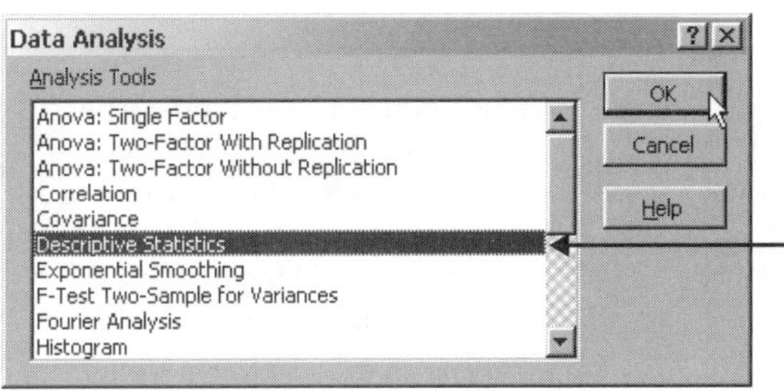
Data Analysis
Analysis Tools
Anova: Single Factor
Anova: Two-Factor With Replication
Anova: Two-Factor Without Replication
Correlation
Covariance
Descriptive Statistics
Exponential Smoothing
F-Test Two-Sample for Variances
Fourier Analysis
Histogram
OK
Cancel
Help

As usual, the first step in running a data analysis tool is to access the Data Analysis menu from the Tools drop-down menu. Find Descriptive Statistics on the list of Analysis Tools and click **OK**.

This is the input range of the sample data.

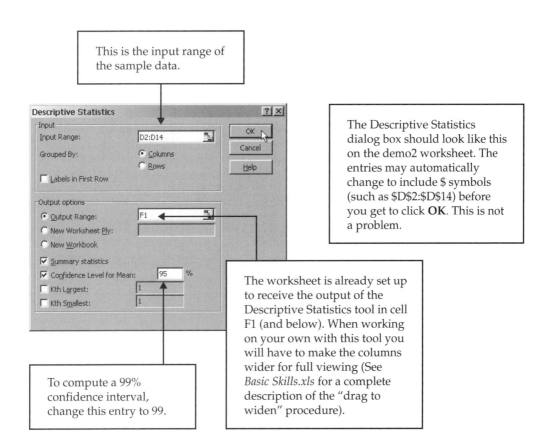

The Descriptive Statistics dialog box should look like this on the demo2 worksheet. The entries may automatically change to include $ symbols (such as $D$2:$D$14) before you get to click **OK**. This is not a problem.

The worksheet is already set up to receive the output of the Descriptive Statistics tool in cell F1 (and below). When working on your own with this tool you will have to make the columns wider for full viewing (See *Basic Skills.xls* for a complete description of the "drag to widen" procedure).

To compute a 99% confidence interval, change this entry to 99.

Folder: 06 The t Statistic - 1 Sample
Workbook: Confidence Intervals.xls
Worksheet: your data (1)

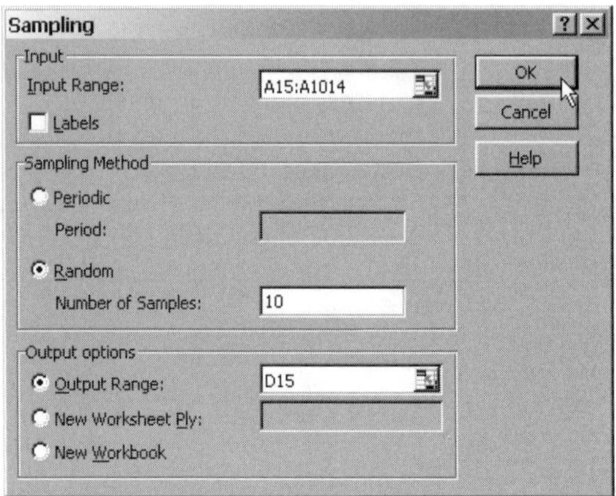
Sampling
Input
Input Range:
A15:A1014
Labels
OK
Cancel
Help
Sampling Method
Periodic
Period:
Random
Number of Samples:
10
Output options
Output Range:
D15
New Worksheet Ply:
New Workbook

Once you click **OK**, the entries in this Sampling tool dialog box direct Excel to take a sample of 10 values from the 1000-score population and locate the sample data in cell D15 (and below).

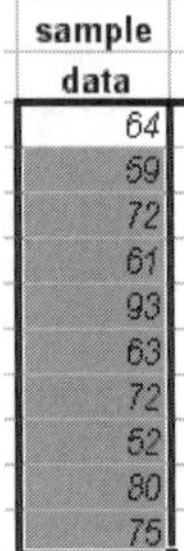
sample data
64
59
72
61
93
63
72
52
80
75

Holding a left-click while dragging down the sample array will highlight the data. With your mouse pointer within the highlighted area, right-click and select Copy from the shortcut menu (in preparation for pasting on the next worksheet). An alternative is to click Edit on the toolbar at the top of your computer screen. The copy and paste options appear here as well.

Some users prefer to complete copy and pasting with key strokes. As you will see in the Edit menu, typing Ctrl and the C key at the same time (written in the menu as "Ctrl+C") completes a copy and Ctrl+V completes a paste.

Folder: 06 The t Statistic - 1 Sample
Workbook: Confidence Intervals
Worksheet: your data (2)

This screen capture shows what the yo ur data (2)" worksheet should look like after pasting the sample data gathered in "your data (1)" to cell A15. Your actual data will, of course, be different from the values shown here.

8			
9	You should repeat this exercise several times with different size samples then evaluate:		
10	**1.** Did your confidence intervals always include **μ**, the mean of the population from which the sample		
11	was drawn? (For your reference, μ=70.14 for the original data set.)		
12	**2.** What was the effect of sample size on the width ("precision") of the intervals?		
13	sample		
14	data		**lower limit =**
15	64		
16	59		**upper limit =**
17	72		
18	61		
19	93		
20	63		
21	72		
22	52		
23	80		
24	75		

You may locate the necessary computations in a vacant area of this same worksheet or, if you wish, ask Excel to locate your output on a new worksheet. The easier of the two methods for determining the confidence interval uses Excel's Descriptive Statistics tool – with Summary Statistics and Confidence Level selected. With your output in hand, determine the upper limit by adding the confidence level value to the sample mean and, to determine the lower limit of the interval, subtract the confidence level value from the sample mean.

Folder: 06 The t Statistic - 1 Sample
Workbook: Confidence Intervals.xls
Worksheet: your data (1)

These instructions for generating new population data also appear in column N (scroll to the right of the main display) of the your data (1) worksheet.

To generate new population data using the Random Number Generation tool: Click Tools – Data Analysis – Random Number Generation – **OK**. In the Random Number Generation dialog box, set Number of Variables = 1, Number of Random Numbers = the number of values you wish to be in your population. Set Distribution to Normal, Mean = your chosen value for μ, Standard Deviation = your chosen SD value, and Random Seed = any 4-digit number. Set Output Range to A15, the location of the first cell of population data.

Click **OK** and leave the data highlighted. Then click Format – Cells – Number tab – Custom. Click "0" on the list, then **OK**. The population data will now show as integers.

Be advised that using the same Random Seed will result in the same data.

Once you have the population in place, click Tools – Sampling – **OK** to collect sample data. The Input Range spans the population data array you generated in column A. For example, if you elected to have 100 values in the population, you would enter A15:A114 . After selecting Random, let Number of Random Numbers equal your chosen sample size. The Output Range = the cell under the sample column heading (D15). If you wish the data to display as integers use the same procedure described above (leave the data highlighted, etc.).

Folder: 06 The t Statistic - 1 Sample
Workbook: Confidence Intervals.xls
Worksheet: sampling experiment

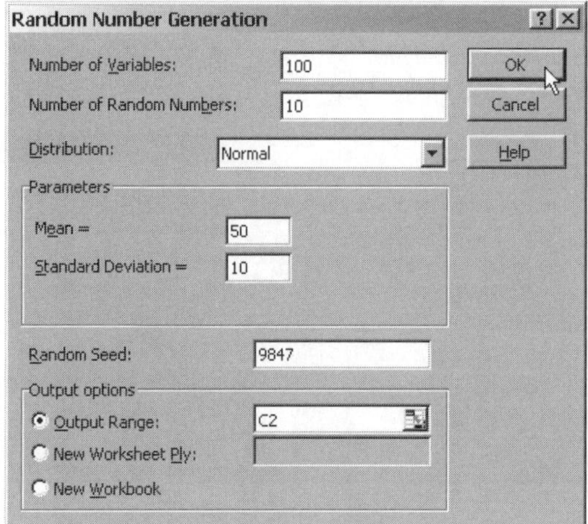
Random Number Generation
Number of Variables:
100
Number of Random Numbers:
10
Distribution:
Normal
Parameters
Mean =
50
Standard Deviation =
10
Random Seed:
9847
Output options
Output Range:
C2
New Worksheet Ply:
New Workbook
OK
Cancel
Help

This image shows the dialog box entries you need for repeating the experiment on the "sampling experiment" worksheet. Be sure to use a new random seed for each subsequent repetition. The other entries need not be changed when repeating the experiment.

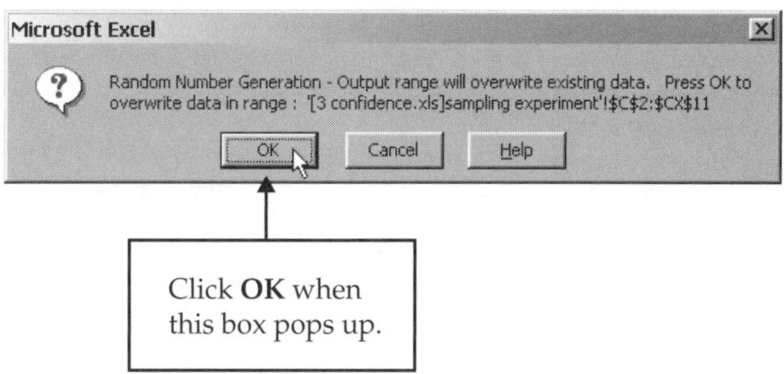
Microsoft Excel
Random Number Generation - Output range will overwrite existing data. Press OK to overwrite data in range : '[3 confidence.xls]sampling experiment'!$C$2:$CX$11
OK
Cancel
Help

Click **OK** when this box pops up.

Folder: 06 The t Statistic - 1 Sample
Workbook: Confidence Intervals.xls
Worksheet: sampling experiment

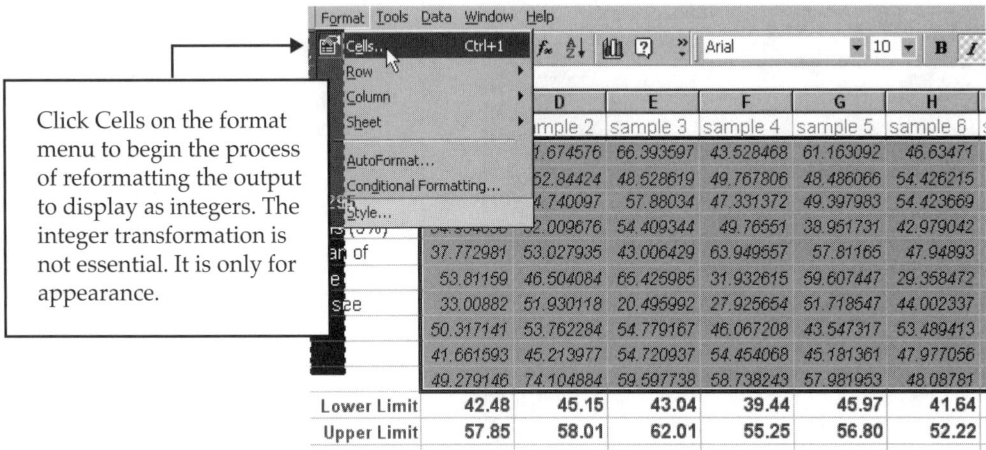
Click Cells on the format menu to begin the process of reformatting the output to display as integers. The integer transformation is not essential. It is only for appearance.
Format Tools Data Window Help
Cells... Ctrl+1
Row
Column
Sheet
AutoFormat...
Conditional Formatting...
Style...
Arial
10
D E F G H
sample 3 sample 4 sample 5 sample 6
Lower Limit 42.48 45.15 43.04 39.44 45.97 41.64
Upper Limit 57.85 58.01 62.01 55.25 56.80 52.22

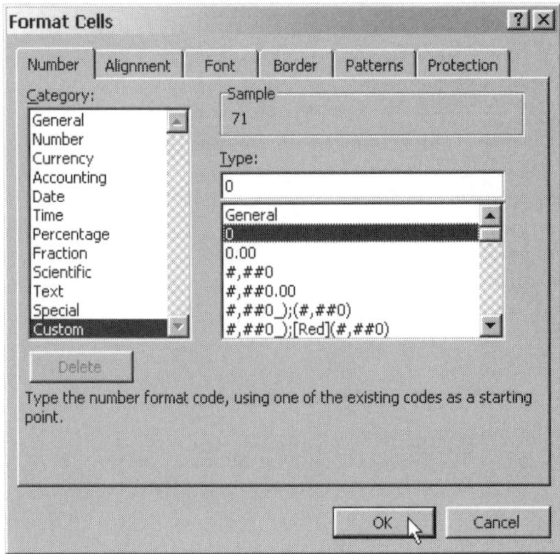
Format Cells
Number Alignment Font Border Patterns Protection
Category:
General
Number
Currency
Accounting
Date
Time
Percentage
Fraction
Scientific
Text
Special
Custom
Sample
71
Type:
0
General
0
0.00
#,##0
#,##0.00
#,##0_);(#,##0)
#,##0_);[Red](#,##0)
Delete
Type the number format code, using one of the existing codes as a starting point.
OK
Cancel

Once you click Cell on the Format drop-down menu, this menu appears. Click the Number tab at the top, select Custom from the list on the left and 0 from the list on the right, then **OK**. The new sample data will then display as integers.

CHAPTER 7

The *t* Statistic – Two Samples

Folder: 06 The t Statistic - 2 Samples
Workbook: Inside the t Test.xls
Worksheet: variability

This worksheet provides extensive opportunity to explore the features of data that affect the determination of significance and statistical power. Prove to yourself that a small difference between means can be significant if the within-sample variability is small enough, and that a relatively large difference between means may not be significant if the within-sample variability is high. Each change you make to either of the two data sets will be instantly reflected in the statistical output in rows 16 to 21.

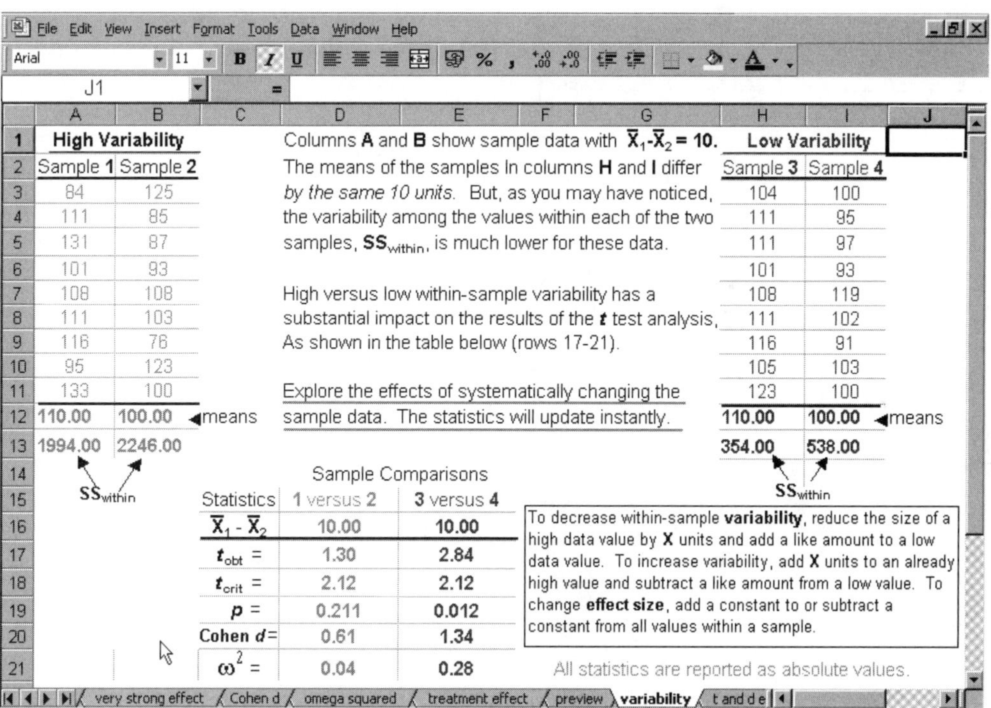

High Variability
Sample 1 Sample 2
84 125
111 85
131 87
101 93
108 108
111 103
116 76
95 123
133 100
110.00 100.00 means
1994.00 2246.00
SSwithin
Columns A and B show sample data with X1-X2 = 10.
The means of the samples In columns H and I differ by the same 10 units. But, as you may have noticed, the variability among the values within each of the two samples, SSwithin, is much lower for these data.
High versus low within-sample variability has a substantial impact on the results of the t test analysis, As shown in the table below (rows 17-21).
Explore the effects of systematically changing the sample data. The statistics will update instantly.
Low Variability
Sample 3 Sample 4
104 100
111 95
111 97
101 93
108 119
111 102
116 91
105 103
123 100
110.00 100.00 means
354.00 538.00
SSwithin
Sample Comparisons
Statistics 1 versus 2 3 versus 4
X1 - X2 10.00 10.00
tobt = 1.30 2.84
tcrit = 2.12 2.12
p = 0.211 0.012
Cohen d= 0.61 1.34
ω2 = 0.04 0.28
To decrease within-sample variability, reduce the size of a high data value by X units and add a like amount to a low data value. To increase variability, add X units to an already high value and subtract a like amount from a low value. To change effect size, add a constant to or subtract a constant from all values within a sample.
All statistics are reported as absolute values.
very strong effect Cohen d omega squared treatment effect preview variability t and d e

Folder: 06 The t Statistic - 2 Samples
Workbook: Estimating Errors.xls
Worksheet: experiment

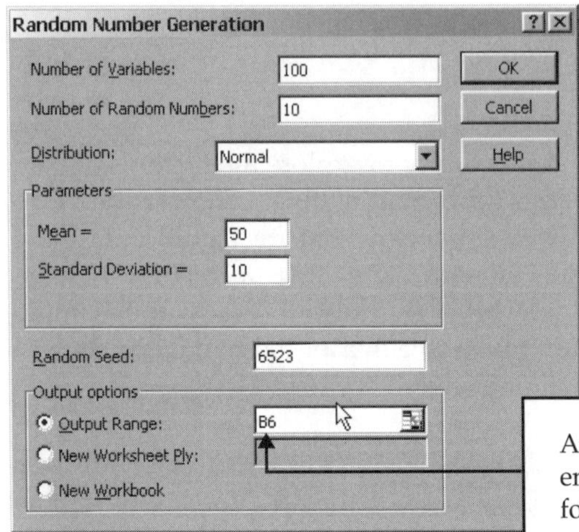
Random Number Generation
Number of Variables: 100
Number of Random Numbers: 10
Distribution: Normal
OK
Cancel
Help
Parameters
Mean = 50
Standard Deviation = 10
Random Seed: 6523
Output options
Output Range: B6
New Worksheet Ply:
New Workbook

This box shows the entries in the Random Number Generation dialog box for generating the first set of sample data. In subsequent reruns you need only change the Random Seed. The other entries remain the same.

As pointed out in the instructions, enter **B6** for the **first** run and B19 for the second run.

After clicking **OK** you will see a warning about overwriting data. Click **OK** to continue.

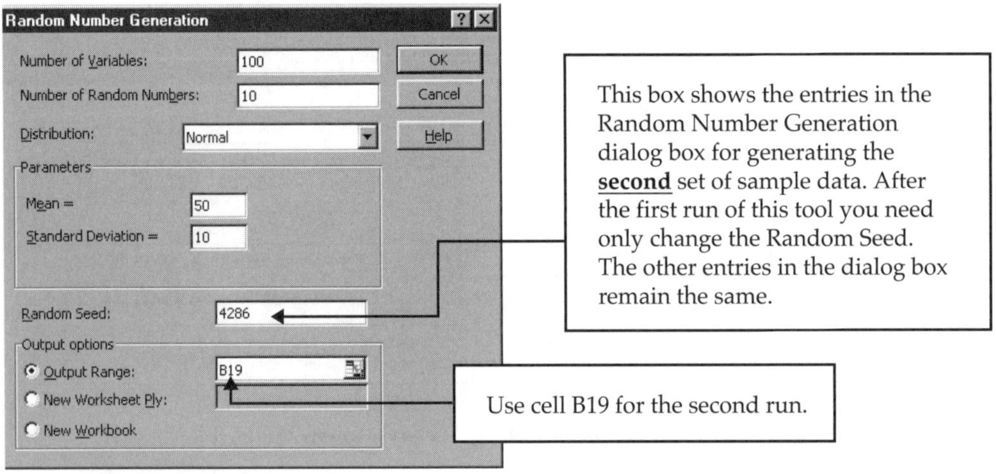
Random Number Generation
Number of Variables: 100
Number of Random Numbers: 10
Distribution: Normal
OK
Cancel
Help
Parameters
Mean = 50
Standard Deviation = 10
Random Seed: 4286
Output options
Output Range: B19
New Worksheet Ply:
New Workbook
This box shows the entries in the Random Number Generation dialog box for generating the second set of sample data. After the first run of this tool you need only change the Random Seed. The other entries in the dialog box remain the same.
Use cell B19 for the second run.

Folder: 06 The t Statistic - 2 Samples
Workbook: Independent vs Related.xls
Worksheet: DEVSQ

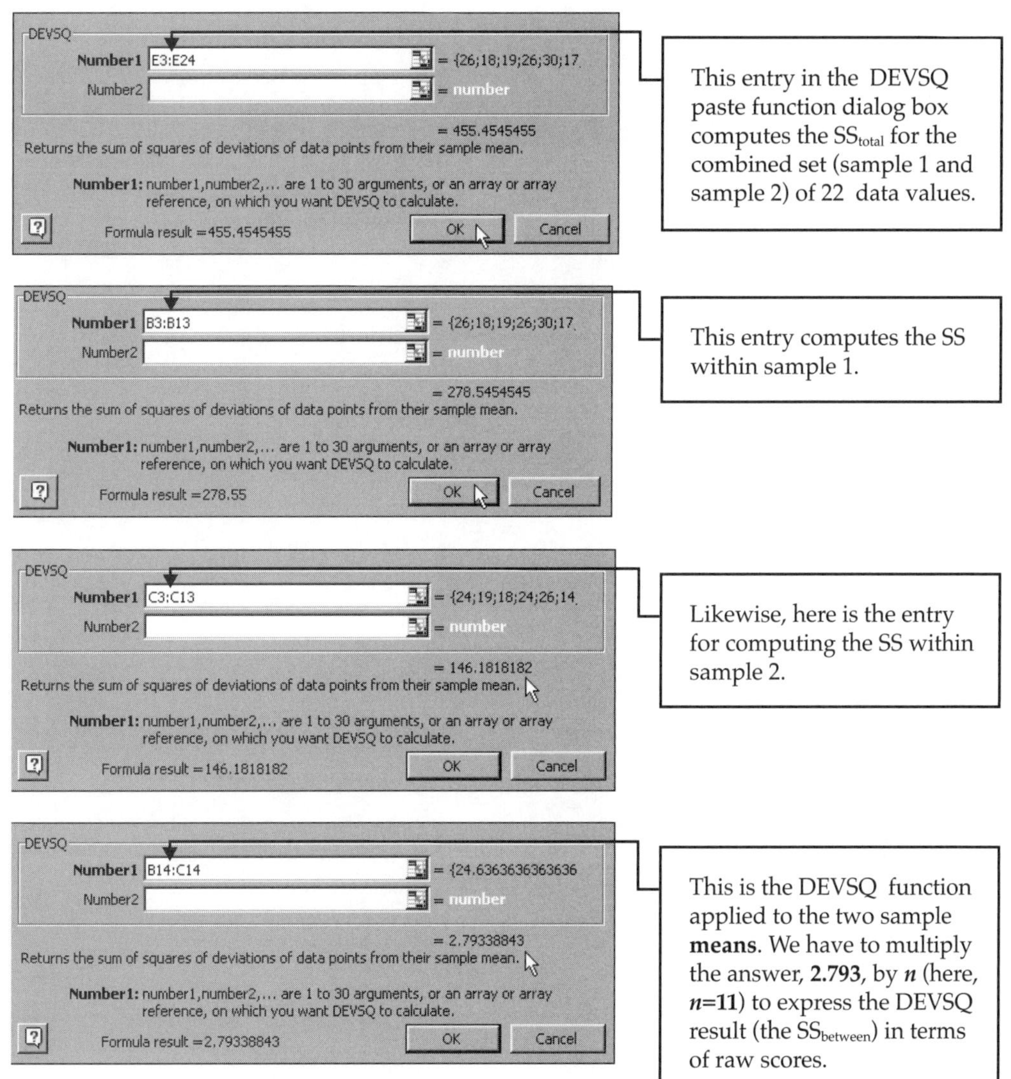
DEVSQ
Number1 E3:E24
= {26;18;19;26;30;17
Number2
= number
= 455.4545455
Returns the sum of squares of deviations of data points from their sample mean.
Number1: number1,number2,... are 1 to 30 arguments, or an array or array reference, on which you want DEVSQ to calculate.
Formula result =455.4545455
OK
Cancel
This entry in the DEVSQ paste function dialog box computes the SS_{total} for the combined set (sample 1 and sample 2) of 22 data values.
DEVSQ
Number1 B3:B13
= {26;18;19;26;30;17
Number2
= number
= 278.5454545
Returns the sum of squares of deviations of data points from their sample mean.
Number1: number1,number2,... are 1 to 30 arguments, or an array or array reference, on which you want DEVSQ to calculate.
Formula result =278.55
OK
Cancel
This entry computes the SS within sample 1.
DEVSQ
Number1 C3:C13
= {24;19;18;24;26;14
Number2
= number
= 146.1818182
Returns the sum of squares of deviations of data points from their sample mean.
Number1: number1,number2,... are 1 to 30 arguments, or an array or array reference, on which you want DEVSQ to calculate.
Formula result =146.1818182
OK
Cancel
Likewise, here is the entry for computing the SS within sample 2.
DEVSQ
Number1 B14:C14
= {24.6363636363636
Number2
= number
= 2.79338843
Returns the sum of squares of deviations of data points from their sample mean.
Number1: number1,number2,... are 1 to 30 arguments, or an array or array reference, on which you want DEVSQ to calculate.
Formula result =2.79338843
OK
Cancel
This is the DEVSQ function applied to the two sample **means**. We have to multiply the answer, **2.793**, by ***n*** (here, ***n*=11**) to express the DEVSQ result (the $SS_{between}$) in terms of raw scores.

CHAPTER 8

Single-Factor ANOVA

Folder: 08 Single-Factor ANOVA
Workbook: The ANOVA Model.xls
Worksheet: interactive demo 1

In this interactive demonstration you may change the sample data by selecting cell D5 and typing the <**delete**> key. Do not change the sample data themselves (rows 5 to 19). If you do you will disrupt the functions that reside in those cells. You may, however, change the model assumptions in the yellow-highlighted cells at the top of the worksheet in columns B, D, and G.

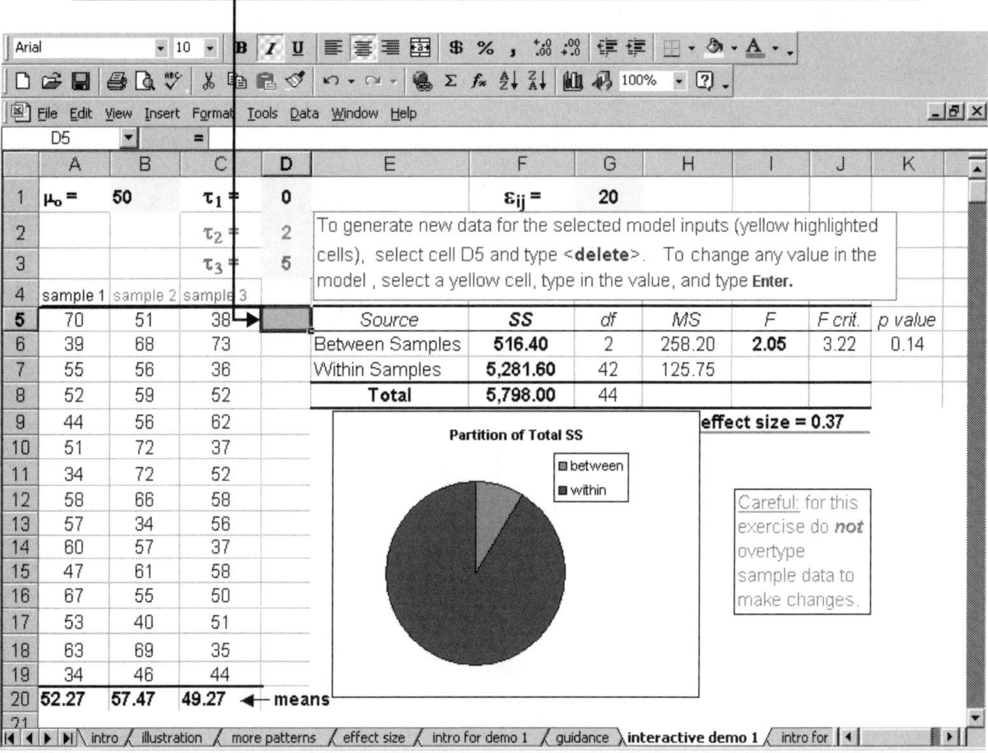

	A	B	C	D
1	μ_o =	50	τ_1 =	0
2			τ_2 =	2
3			τ_3 =	5
4	sample 1	sample 2	sample 3	
5	70	51	38	
6	39	68	73	
7	55	56	36	
8	52	59	52	
9	44	56	62	
10	51	72	37	
11	34	72	52	
12	58	66	58	
13	57	34	56	
14	60	57	37	
15	47	61	58	
16	67	55	50	
17	53	40	51	
18	63	69	35	
19	34	46	44	
20	52.27	57.47	49.27	← means

ε_{ij} = 20

To generate new data for the selected model inputs (yellow highlighted cells), select cell D5 and type <**delete**>. To change any value in the model , select a yellow cell, type in the value, and type **Enter.**

Source	***SS***	*df*	*MS*	*F*	*F crit.*	*p value*
Between Samples	**516.40**	2	258.20	**2.05**	3.22	0.14
Within Samples	**5,281.60**	42	125.75			
Total	**5,798.00**	44				

effect size = 0.37

Partition of Total SS
between
within
Careful: for this exercise do ***not*** overtype sample data to make changes.
intro
illustration
more patterns
effect size
intro for demo 1
guidance
interactive demo 1
intro for

Folder: 08 Single-Factor ANOVA
Workbook: The ANOVA Model
Worksheet: interactive demo 1

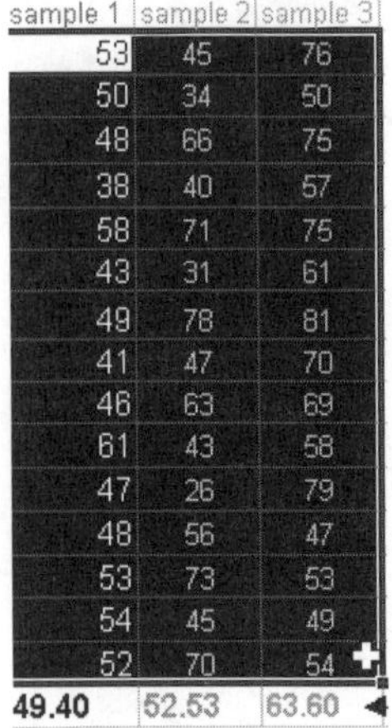

sample 1	sample 2	sample 3
53	45	76
50	34	50
48	66	75
38	40	57
58	71	75
43	31	61
49	78	81
41	47	70
46	63	69
61	43	58
47	26	79
48	56	47
53	73	53
54	45	49
52	70	54
49.40	52.53	63.60

The first step in sampling new data is to highlight the existing data matrix. Position the mouse pointer over the cell in the top left corner. Then, while holding a left-click on your mouse, drag the mouse pointer to the cell in the bottom right corner and let go of the mouse button.

With the mouse pointer over the highlighted area, right-click to access the shortcut menu. Click Clear Contents. This will restore blank cells to the data array in preparation for your new data.

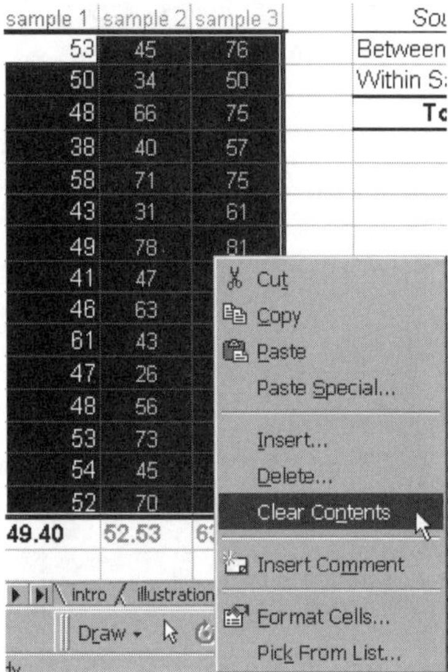
sample 1
sample 2
sample 3
Between
Within S
53 45 76
50 34 50
48 66 75
38 40 57
58 71 75
43 31 61
49 78 81
41 47
46 63
61 43
47 26
48 56
53 73
54 45
52 70
49.40 52.53
Cut
Copy
Paste
Paste Special...
Insert...
Delete...
Clear Contents
Insert Comment
Format Cells...
Pick From List...
intro
illustration
Draw

Worksheet: interactive demo 1 (continued)

This Input Range directs Excel to draw the sample data from the population in column N. Change the Input range to O3:O502 or P3:P502 to select data from the other two populations.

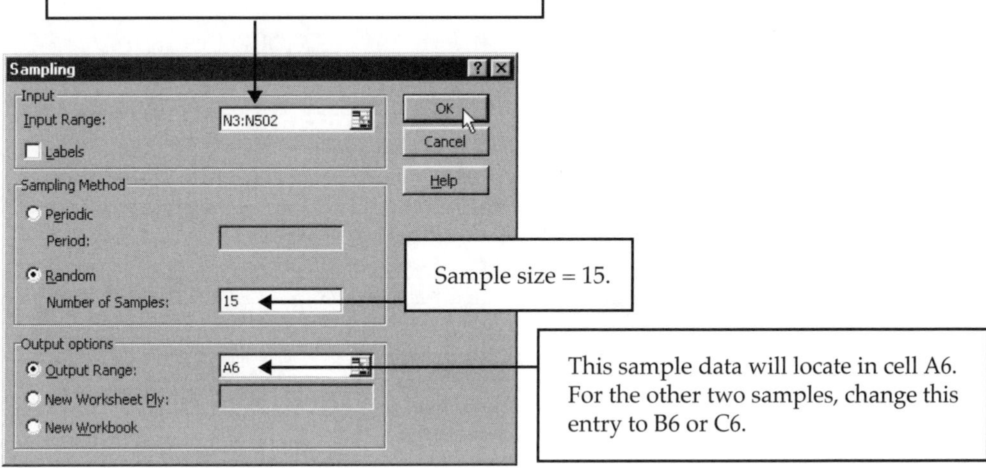
Sampling
Input
Input Range:
N3:N502
Labels
OK
Cancel
Help
Sampling Method
Periodic
Period:
Random
Number of Samples:
15
Sample size = 15.
Output options
Output Range:
A6
New Worksheet Ply:
New Workbook
This sample data will locate in cell A6. For the other two samples, change this entry to B6 or C6.

Folder: 08 Single-Factor ANOVA
Workbook: The ANOVA Model.xls
Worksheet: interactive demo 2

In this demo it is OK to type over the sample data. Each change you make will be instantly reflected in the statistical output. Follow the instructions in the text box (lower right corner of the display) for making systematic changes to effect size and within-sample variability.

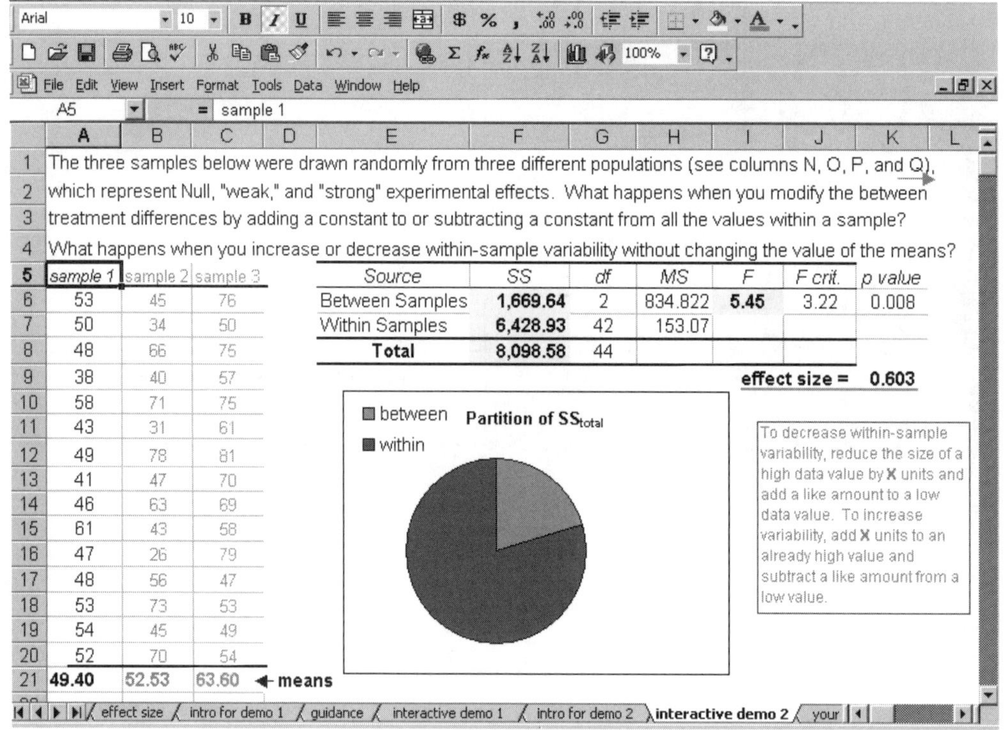
The three samples below were drawn randomly from three different populations (see columns N, O, P, and Q), which represent Null, "weak," and "strong" experimental effects. What happens when you modify the between treatment differences by adding a constant to or subtracting a constant from all the values within a sample?
What happens when you increase or decrease within-sample variability without changing the value of the means?
sample 1 | sample 2 | sample 3
53 45 76
50 34 50
48 66 75
38 40 57
58 71 75
43 31 61
49 78 81
41 47 70
46 63 69
61 43 58
47 26 79
48 56 47
53 73 53
54 45 49
52 70 54
49.40 52.53 63.60 means
Source | SS | df | MS | F | F crit. | p value
Between Samples 1,669.64 2 834.822 5.45 3.22 0.008
Within Samples 6,428.93 42 153.07
Total 8,098.58 44
effect size = 0.603
between
within
Partition of SStotal
To decrease within-sample variability, reduce the size of a high data value by X units and add a like amount to a low data value. To increase variability, add X units to an already high value and subtract a like amount from a low value.
effect size
intro for demo 1
guidance
interactive demo 1
intro for demo 2
interactive demo 2
your

Folder: 08 Single-Factor ANOVA
Workbook: The ANOVA Model.xls
Worksheet: effect size and variability

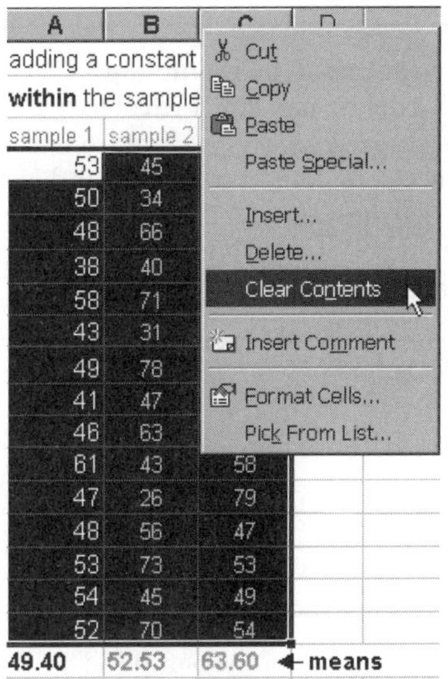
A
B
adding a constant
within the sample
sample 1
sample 2
Cut
Copy
Paste
Paste Special...
Insert...
Delete...
Clear Contents
Insert Comment
Format Cells...
Pick From List...
49.40
52.53
63.60
means

You may type over existing data values, but if you wish to draw new sample data from the populations, start off by clearing the existing data. Highlight the data with a left-click and drag operation. Then, with your mouse pointer over the highlighted area, right-click and select clear contents from the shortcut menu. Ignore error messages on the display. They will disappear once all the new data are in place.

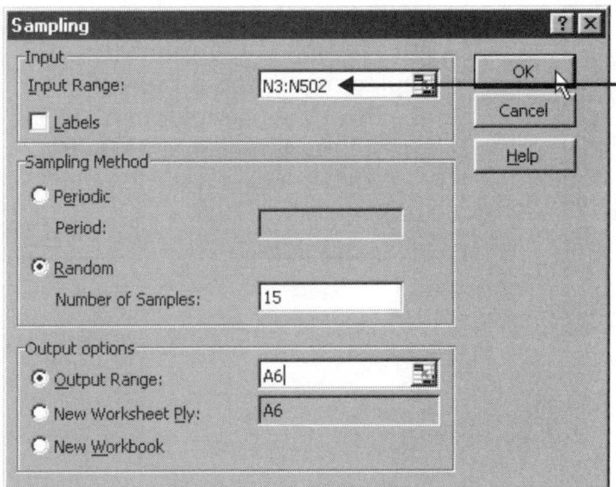
Sampling
Input
Input Range:
N3:N502
Labels
OK
Cancel
Help
Sampling Method
Periodic
Period:
Random
Number of Samples:
15
Output options
Output Range:
A6
New Worksheet Ply:
A6
New Workbook

There are three populations from which to draw data. They are located in worksheet columns N, O, and P. The entry in the Input range field tells Excel the range of the population from which to draw the sample. Here, the box is set up to draw a sample of **15** values from the population in column N and put the data in cell **A6**.

Worksheet: effect size and variability (continued)

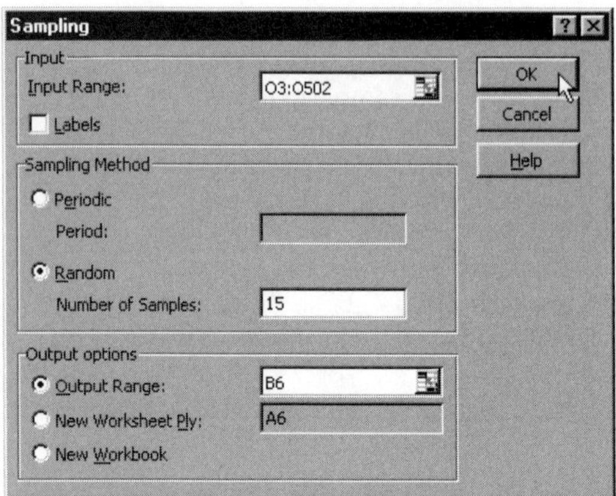
Sampling
Input
Input Range:
O3:O502
Labels
Sampling Method
Periodic
Period:
Random
Number of Samples:
15
Output options
Output Range:
B6
New Worksheet Ply:
A6
New Workbook
OK
Cancel
Help

The entries in this Sampling tool dialog box direct Excel to select 15 values at random from the population in column O and place the data in cell B6. As shown, leave the Number of Samples at 15.

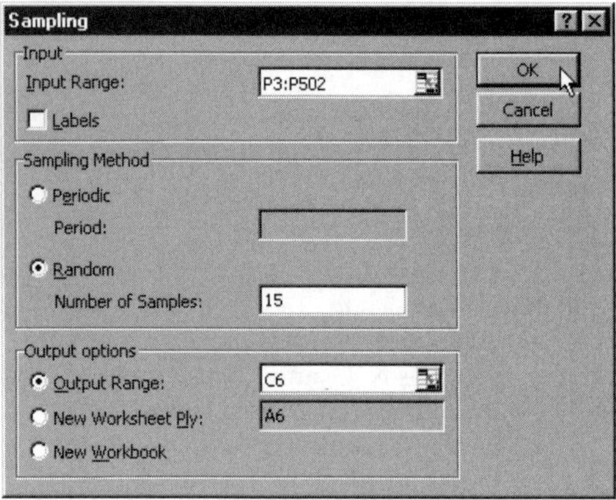
Sampling
Input
Input Range:
P3:P502
Labels
Sampling Method
Periodic
Period:
Random
Number of Samples:
15
Output options
Output Range:
C6
New Worksheet Ply:
A6
New Workbook
OK
Cancel
Help

The final run of the Sampling tool draws the new data from the population in column P and places the data in cell C6, thus completing the data replacement procedure. With the three new samples in place, the ANOVA, means, and chart will show the analysis of the new data.

Folder: 08 Single-Factor ANOVA
Workbook: The ANOVA Model.xls
Worksheet: your sample size

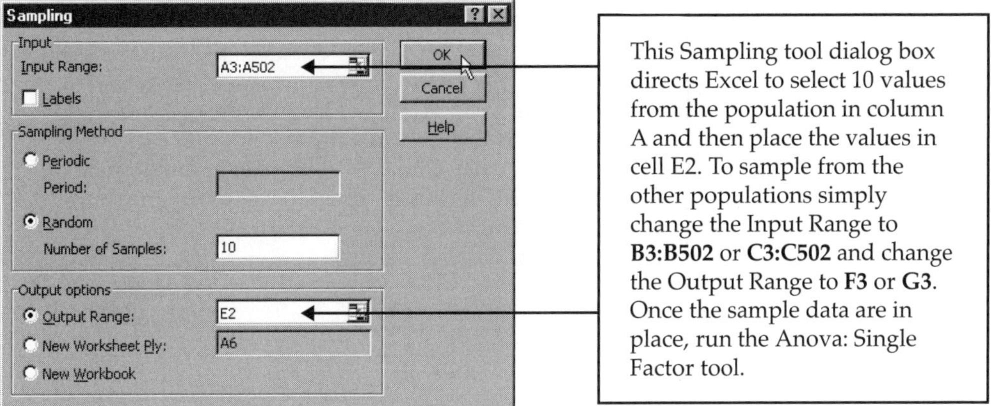
Sampling
Input
Input Range:
A3:A502
Labels
OK
Cancel
Help
Sampling Method
Periodic
Period:
Random
Number of Samples:
10
Output options
Output Range:
E2
New Worksheet Ply:
A6
New Workbook
This Sampling tool dialog box directs Excel to select 10 values from the population in column A and then place the values in cell E2. To sample from the other populations simply change the Input Range to **B3:B502** or **C3:C502** and change the Output Range to **F3** or **G3**. Once the sample data are in place, run the Anova: Single Factor tool.

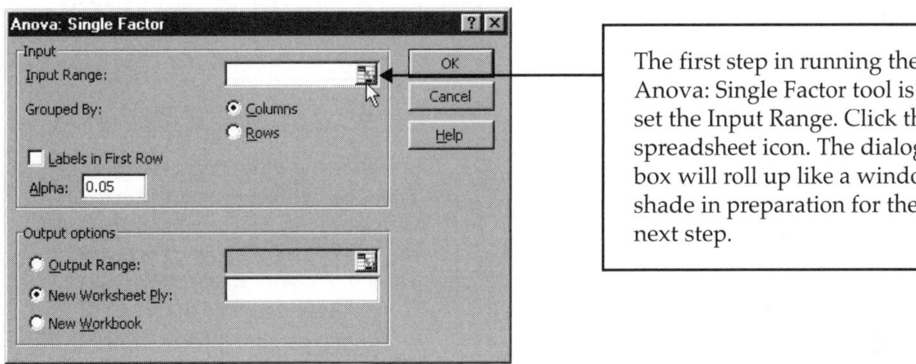
Anova: Single Factor
Input
Input Range:
Grouped By:
Columns
Rows
Labels in First Row
Alpha:
0.05
OK
Cancel
Help
Output options
Output Range:
New Worksheet Ply:
New Workbook
The first step in running the Anova: Single Factor tool is to set the Input Range. Click the spreadsheet icon. The dialog box will roll up like a window shade in preparation for the next step.

Worksheet: your sample size (continued)

E	F	G
sample 1	sample 2	sample 3
42	53	61
48	62	46
47	49	72
70	58	69
53	47	51
56	80	69
33	48	60
58	76	46
47	82	48
51	50	61

The next step is to point to the top left cell in the data array, hold down the left mouse button, drag ("fill") to the cell in the lower right of the array, and let go of the mouse button. A dotted marquee will surround the data as shown here. Cell E2 will always be the first in the Input Range, but the end of the Input Range (the lower right cell) will change as your sample size changes.

Anova: Single Factor
$E$2:$G$11

The Input Range (the cells within the dotted marquee) will show in the Anova: Single Factor dialog box. Click the spreadsheet icon again and the dialog box will unroll to its full size.

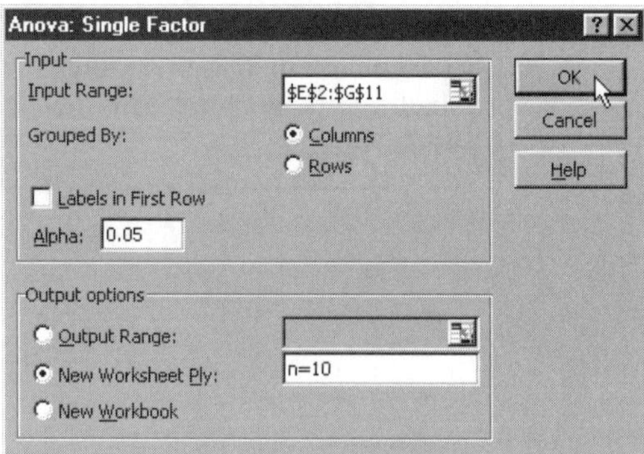
Anova: Single Factor
Input
Input Range:
$E$2:$G$11
Grouped By:
Columns
Rows
Labels in First Row
Alpha:
0.05
OK
Cancel
Help
Output options
Output Range:
New Worksheet Ply:
n=10
New Workbook

It is best to put the ANOVA results on a new worksheet with a name that indicates your choice of sample size. Here, because this illustration uses *n*=10, the new worksheet is named "n=10." When you click OK, Excel will create the new "n=10" worksheet, place the output on that worksheet, and display the worksheet on your screen. As usual, you will have to widen columns to view the full contents of the ANOVA table.

CHAPTER 9

Two-Factor ANOVA

Folder: 09 Two-Factor ANOVA
Workbook: Interpreting Results.xls
Worksheet: your sample data

This entry stays the same for all sample selections.

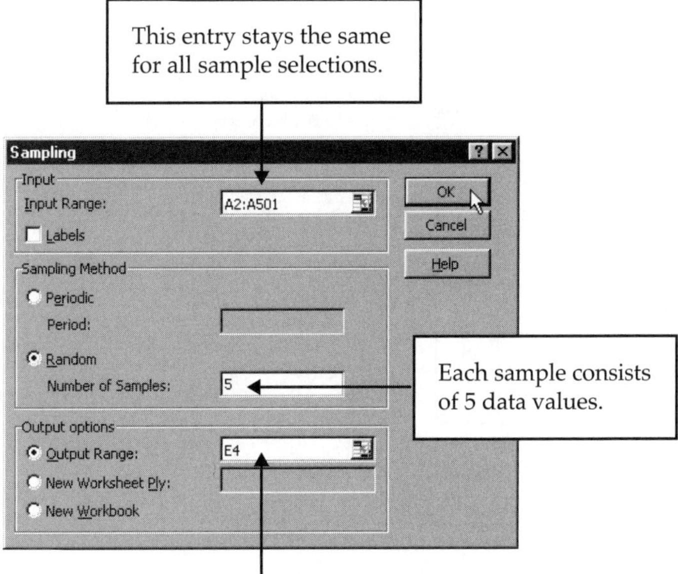

Sampling
Input
Input Range:
A2:A501
Labels
OK
Cancel
Help
Sampling Method
Periodic
Period:
Random
Number of Samples:
5
Output options
Output Range:
E4
New Worksheet Ply:
New Workbook

Each sample consists of 5 data values.

The Output Range will take one of eight values, depending on which cell in the data matrix is designated to hold the new data. Moving in the top section of the 2 x 4 matrix (One-on-one Therapy) from left to right, the entries are E4 (shown here), F4, G4, and H4. To replace the data in the cells of the lower section (Group Therapy), use the entries E9, F9, G9, or H9.

Folder: 09 Two-Factor ANOVA
Workbook: Creating Patterns.xls
Worksheet: quick change

Here you are invited to change the values in each cell by a constant. Just enter values in the yellow-highlighted cells. You may either use some of the values listed off to the right of the worksheet (scroll right to see them) or make up your own. As with some of the earlier worksheets of this type, do not change the data directly by typing over values in the data table (columns B-E).

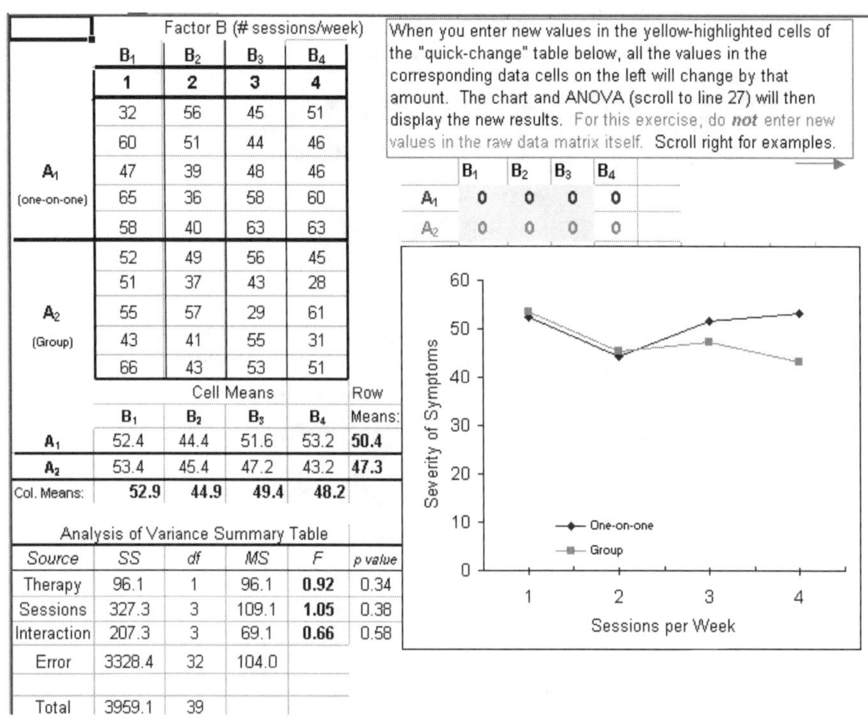

	Factor B (# sessions/week)			
	B_1	B_2	B_3	B_4
	1	2	3	4
	32	56	45	51
	60	51	44	46
A_1	47	39	48	46
(one-on-one)	65	36	58	60
	58	40	63	63
	52	49	56	45
	51	37	43	28
A_2	55	57	29	61
(Group)	43	41	55	31
	66	43	53	51

	Cell Means				Row
	B_1	B_2	B_3	B_4	Means:
A_1	52.4	44.4	51.6	53.2	**50.4**
A_2	53.4	45.4	47.2	43.2	**47.3**
Col. Means:	**52.9**	**44.9**	**49.4**	**48.2**	

Analysis of Variance Summary Table

Source	*SS*	*df*	*MS*	*F*	*p value*
Therapy	96.1	1	96.1	**0.92**	0.34
Sessions	327.3	3	109.1	**1.05**	0.38
Interaction	207.3	3	69.1	**0.66**	0.58
Error	3328.4	32	104.0		
Total	3959.1	39			

When you enter new values in the yellow-highlighted cells of the "quick-change" table below, all the values in the corresponding data cells on the left will change by that amount. The chart and ANOVA (scroll to line 27) will then display the new results. For this exercise, do ***not*** enter new values in the raw data matrix itself. Scroll right for examples.

	B_1	B_2	B_3	B_4
A_1	0	0	0	0
A_2	0	0	0	0

Severity of Symptoms
0
10
20
30
40
50
60
Sessions per Week
1
2
3
4
One-on-one
Group

Folder: 09 Two-Factor ANOVA
Workbook: Computational Method.xls
Worksheet: demo data set

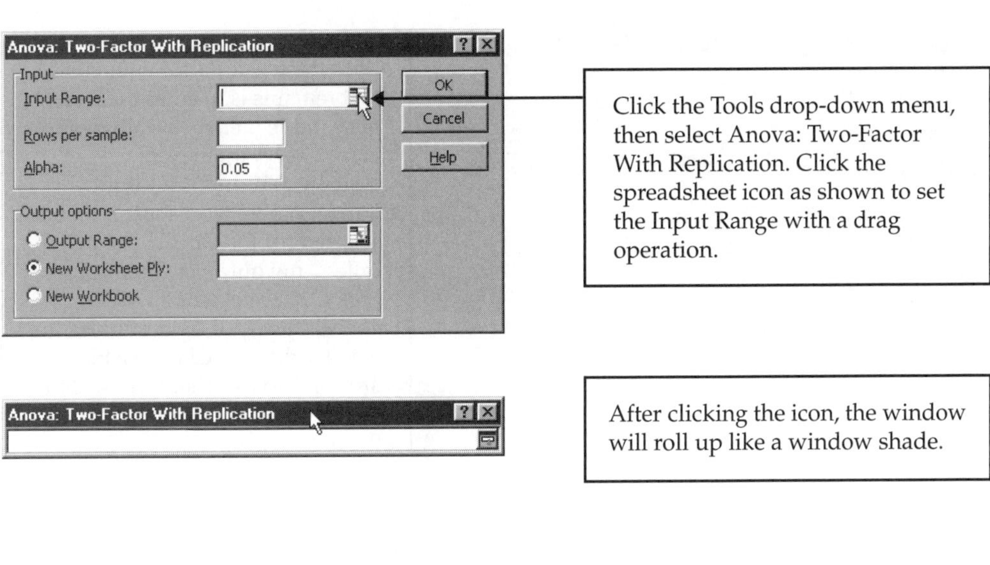
Anova: Two-Factor With Replication
Input
Input Range:
Rows per sample:
Alpha:
0.05
OK
Cancel
Help
Output options
Output Range:
New Worksheet Ply:
New Workbook
Click the Tools drop-down menu, then select Anova: Two-Factor With Replication. Click the spreadsheet icon as shown to set the Input Range with a drag operation.
Anova: Two-Factor With Replication
After clicking the icon, the window will roll up like a window shade.

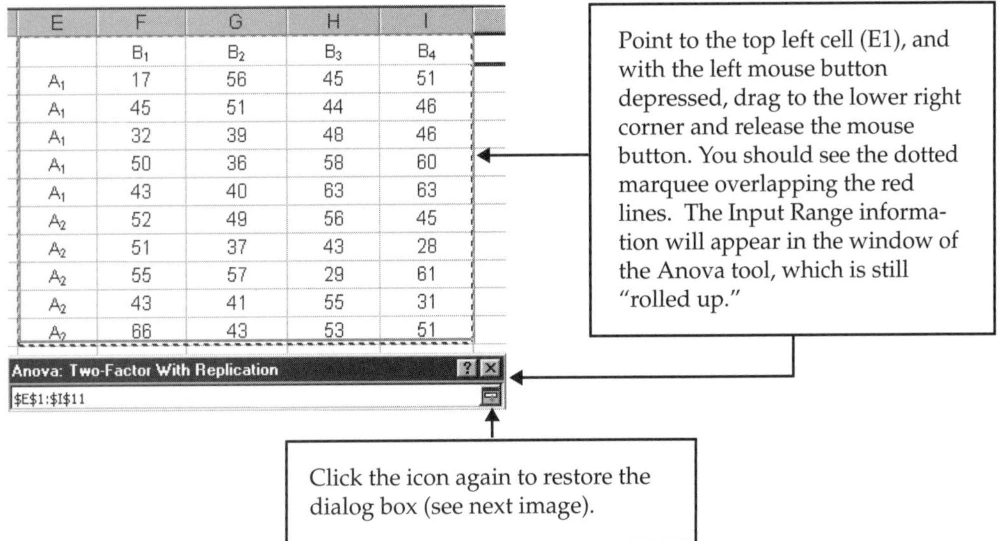

E	F	G	H	I
	B_1	B_2	B_3	B_4
A_1	17	56	45	51
A_1	45	51	44	46
A_1	32	39	48	46
A_1	50	36	58	60
A_1	43	40	63	63
A_2	52	49	56	45
A_2	51	37	43	28
A_2	55	57	29	61
A_2	43	41	55	31
A_2	66	43	53	51

Anova: Two-Factor With Replication
$E$1:$I$11
Point to the top left cell (E1), and with the left mouse button depressed, drag to the lower right corner and release the mouse button. You should see the dotted marquee overlapping the red lines. The Input Range information will appear in the window of the Anova tool, which is still "rolled up."

Click the icon again to restore the dialog box (see next image).

Worksheet: demo data set (continued)

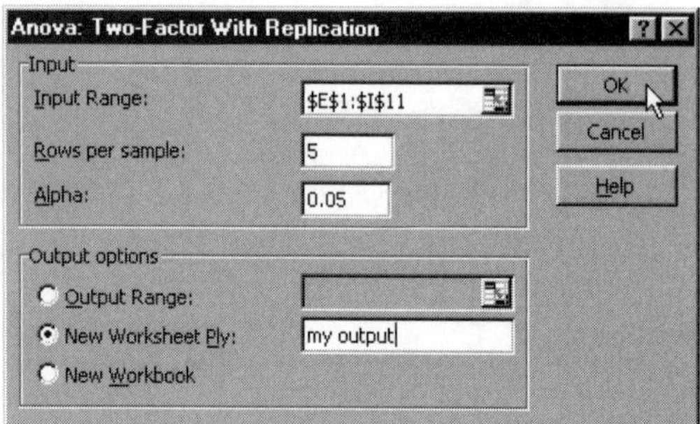
Anova: Two-Factor With Replication
Input
Input Range:
$E$1:$I$11
Rows per sample:
5
Alpha:
0.05
Output options
Output Range:
New Worksheet Ply:
my output
New Workbook
OK
Cancel
Help

With the Input Range entered all that remains is to enter the Rows per sample (i.e., the number of values per cell), the alpha level (usually .05), and an Output Range. A new worksheet has been selected for the Output Range called "my output." Once you click **OK**, Excel will do the analysis and put the results on the new worksheet. Click in a blank area of the worksheet and widen the columns as necessary to view the output properly.

CHAPTER 10

Nonparametric Statistics

Folder: 10 Nonparametric Statistics
Workbook: Chi-Sq Goodness-of-Fit.xls
Worksheet: change data

How different do the frequencies have to be before reaching the criterion for statistical significance? This worksheet permits the user to explore that question with three frequencies. Be careful to change the contents ONLY of the tinted cells in row 8. The other cells are dynamically linked to the tinted cells and will update following user inputs.

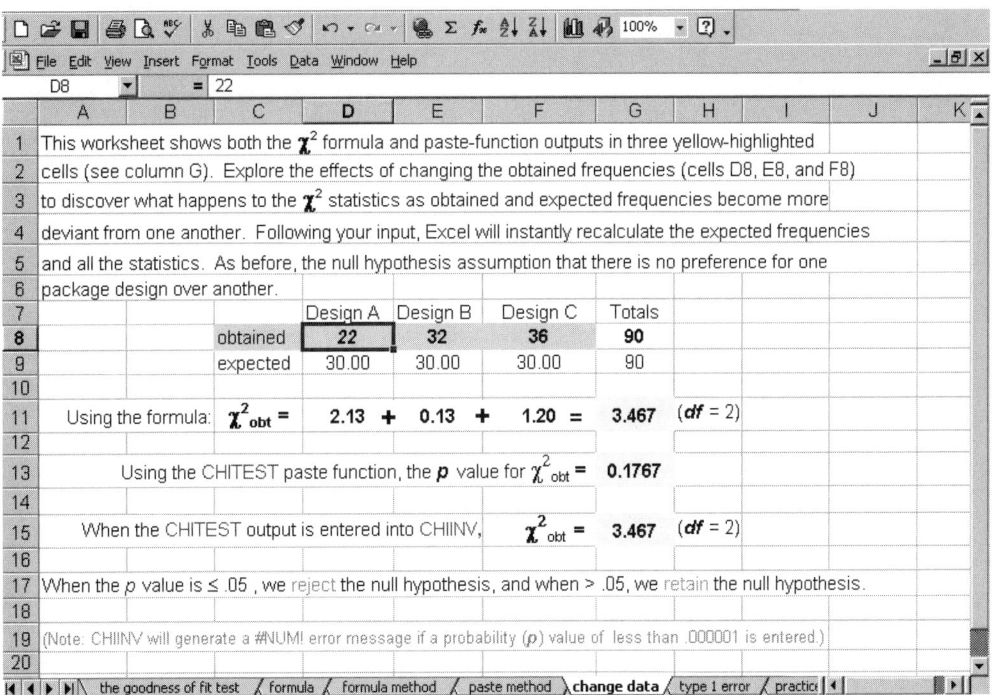
File Edit View Insert Format Tools Data Window Help
D8 = 22
This worksheet shows both the χ² formula and paste-function outputs in three yellow-highlighted cells (see column G). Explore the effects of changing the obtained frequencies (cells D8, E8, and F8) to discover what happens to the χ² statistics as obtained and expected frequencies become more deviant from one another. Following your input, Excel will instantly recalculate the expected frequencies and all the statistics. As before, the null hypothesis assumption that there is no preference for one package design over another.
Design A Design B Design C Totals
obtained 22 32 36 90
expected 30.00 30.00 30.00 90
Using the formula: χ²obt = 2.13 + 0.13 + 1.20 = 3.467 (df = 2)
Using the CHITEST paste function, the p value for χ²obt = 0.1767
When the CHITEST output is entered into CHIINV, χ²obt = 3.467 (df = 2)
When the p value is ≤ .05 , we reject the null hypothesis, and when > .05, we retain the null hypothesis.
(Note: CHIINV will generate a #NUM! error message if a probability (p) value of less than .000001 is entered.)
the goodness of fit test formula formula method paste method change data type 1 error practice

Folder: 10 Nonparametric Statistics
Workbook: Chi-Sq Goodness-of-Fit.xls.xls
Worksheet: type 1 error

As with any statistical comparison, the decision of statistical significance when using the chi-square goodness-of-fit test is subject to error. The screen below shows one such error. The probability of an event as extreme as the one shown (frequencies of 2, 15, and 7) when the frequencies should be equal (8, 8, and 8) equals .005. Type the <**delete**> key in an empty cell for new data. In 100 experiments, the theoretical prediction is that you will obtain 5 instances of statistical significance even though chance alone is governing the values of the frequencies.

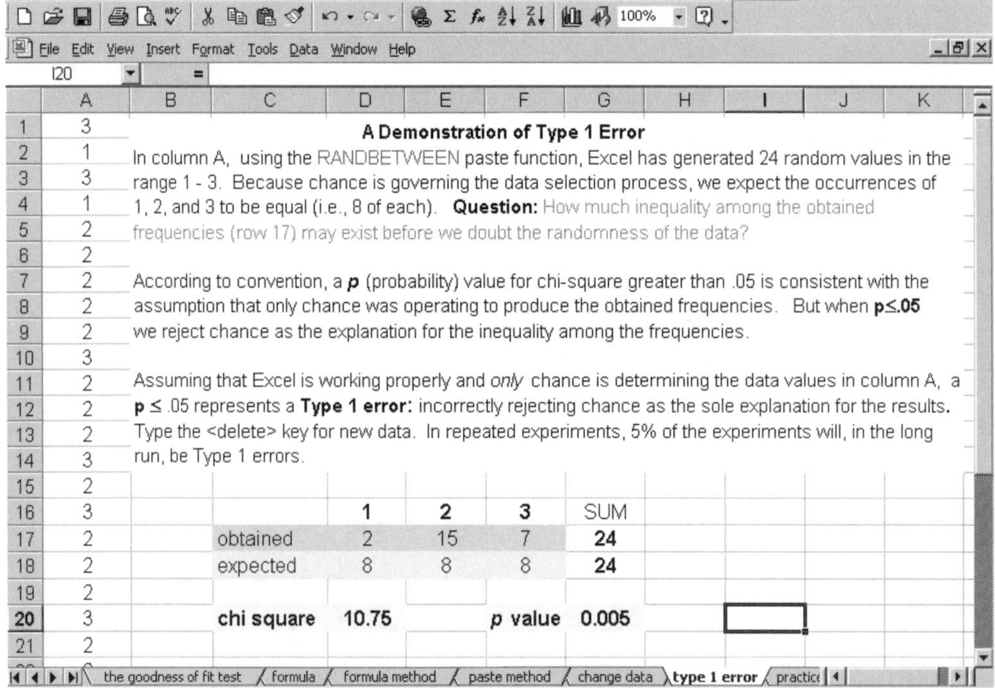
File Edit View Insert Format Tools Data Window Help
I20
A Demonstration of Type 1 Error
In column A, using the RANDBETWEEN paste function, Excel has generated 24 random values in the range 1 - 3. Because chance is governing the data selection process, we expect the occurrences of 1, 2, and 3 to be equal (i.e., 8 of each). Question: How much inequality among the obtained frequencies (row 17) may exist before we doubt the randomness of the data?
According to convention, a p (probability) value for chi-square greater than .05 is consistent with the assumption that only chance was operating to produce the obtained frequencies. But when p≤.05 we reject chance as the explanation for the inequality among the frequencies.
Assuming that Excel is working properly and only chance is determining the data values in column A, a p ≤ .05 represents a Type 1 error: incorrectly rejecting chance as the sole explanation for the results. Type the <delete> key for new data. In repeated experiments, 5% of the experiments will, in the long run, be Type 1 errors.
3 1 3 1 2 2 2 2 2 3 2 2 2 3 2 3 2 2 2 3 2
1 2 3 SUM
obtained 2 15 7 24
expected 8 8 8 24
chi square 10.75 p value 0.005
the goodness of fit test / formula / formula method / paste method / change data / type 1 error / practic

Folder: 10 Nonparametric Statistics
Workbook: Chi-Sq Independence.xls
Worksheet: your data

The concept of contingency between variables is akin to the concept of association that was covered in Folder 3 (Correlation and Regression). In the context of the chi-square statistic, a conclusion of independence between variables is the same as retaining the null hypothesis – no contingency between the variables. When we reject the null hypothesis, the data support the conclusion of *de*pendence, and we describe the variables as contingent. In this worksheet the user is invited to enter different values for the data and thereby become familiar with patterns of cell frequencies that express contingency and those that do not.

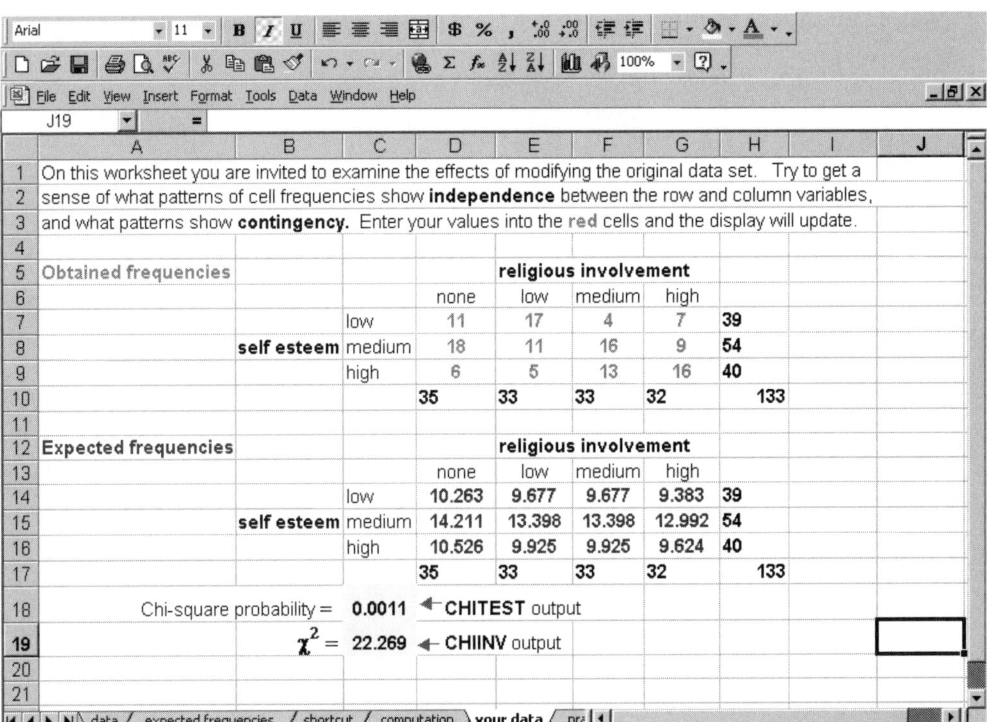

On this worksheet you are invited to examine the effects of modifying the original data set. Try to get a sense of what patterns of cell frequencies show **independence** between the row and column variables, and what patterns show **contingency.** Enter your values into the red cells and the display will update.

Obtained frequencies			religious involvement				
			none	low	medium	high	
		low	11	17	4	7	**39**
	self esteem	medium	18	11	16	9	**54**
		high	6	5	13	16	**40**
			35	**33**	**33**	**32**	**133**

Expected frequencies			religious involvement				
			none	low	medium	high	
		low	10.263	9.677	9.677	9.383	**39**
	self esteem	medium	14.211	13.398	13.398	12.992	**54**
		high	10.526	9.925	9.925	9.624	**40**
			35	**33**	**33**	**32**	**133**

Chi-square probability = **0.0011** ← **CHITEST** output

χ^2 = **22.269** ← **CHIINV** output

Folder: 10 Nonparametric Statistics
Workbook: Mann-Whitney.xls
Worksheet: calculation

The workbook develops the logic that underlies the Mann-Whitney ***U*** statistic in terms of the degree to which two ranked sets differ. This worksheet links the computation of the ***U*** statistic to the data, which allows the user to explore the sensitivity of ***U*** to the meshing (or lack thereof) between two sets of ranks.

File Edit View Insert Format Tools Data Window Help

C1 =

	A	B	C	D	E	F	G	H
1	Here is the formula for the U statistic.			**control**	**rank**		**experimental**	**rank**
2				30	6		37	9
3	$U = n_1 n_2 + \frac{n_1(n_1+1)}{2} - R_1$ =	89.00		24	3		25	4
4				17	1		46	13
5	Alternatively,			44	12		33	8
6				32	7		54	18
7	$U = n_1 n_2 + \frac{n_2(n_2+1)}{2} - R_2$ =	21.00		39	11		49	15
8				59	19		52	17
9	where R_1 is the sum of the ranks for Group 1			19	2		48	14
10	and R_2 is the sum of the ranks for Group 2.			29	5		61	20
11	U is the lower value, and U' is the higher value.			38	10		50	16
12							63	21
13	With n_1= 10 and n_2=11, the published			R_1 =	76		R_2 =	155
14	table of the Mann-Whitney U statistic (α =.05)							
15	reports a range of 26 to 84. When U is							
16	significant, both U and U' will be <u>outside</u> that							
17	range (either ≤ 26 or ≥ 84).							

Change some values in columns **D** and G and see what happens to the ranks and the Mann-Whitney U statistic. You will notice that the more uniformly high or low the ranks are within the respective groups, the more likely U is to be significant.

intro / two extremes / sorts / sample problem / **calculation** / z transforr

Folder: 10 Nonparametric Statistics
Workbook: Wilcoxon.xls
Worksheet: your data

The Wilcoxon Signed-Ranks Test is presented in the workbook as an enhanced version of its relatively weak cousin – the Sign Test. The image below shows the "your data" worksheet in which the user is invited to explore the relative power of the Wilcoxon and Sign tests as well as the features of data that are consistent with significance and insignificance of the two statistical tests.

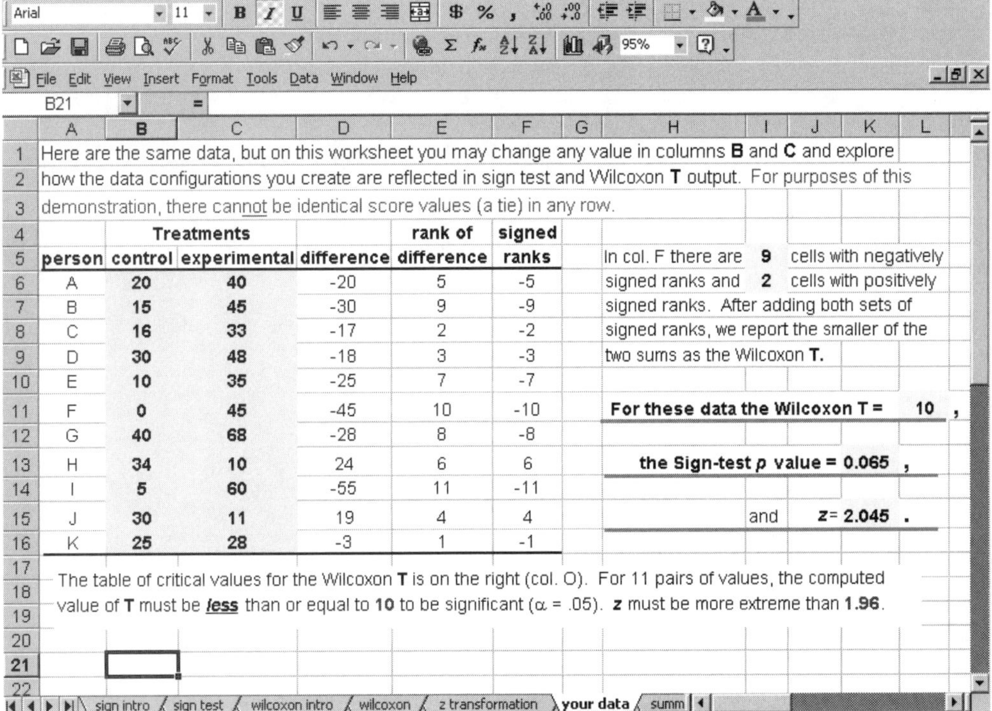

Here are the same data, but on this worksheet you may change any value in columns **B** and **C** and explore how the data configurations you create are reflected in sign test and Wilcoxon **T** output. For purposes of this demonstration, there can<u>not</u> be identical score values (a tie) in any row.

	Treatments			rank of	signed
person	**control**	**experimental**	**difference**	**difference**	**ranks**
A	**20**	**40**	-20	5	-5
B	**15**	**45**	-30	9	-9
C	**16**	**33**	-17	2	-2
D	**30**	**48**	-18	3	-3
E	**10**	**35**	-25	7	-7
F	**0**	**45**	-45	10	-10
G	**40**	**68**	-28	8	-8
H	**34**	**10**	24	6	6
I	**5**	**60**	-55	11	-11
J	**30**	**11**	19	4	4
K	**25**	**28**	-3	1	-1

In col. F there are **9** cells with negatively signed ranks and **2** cells with positively signed ranks. After adding both sets of signed ranks, we report the smaller of the two sums as the Wilcoxon **T.**

For these data the Wilcoxon T = 10 ,

the Sign-test *p* value = 0.065 ,

and ***z*= 2.045 .**

The table of critical values for the Wilcoxon **T** is on the right (col. O). For 11 pairs of values, the computed value of **T** must be ***less*** than or equal to **10** to be significant (α = .05). ***z*** must be more extreme than **1.96**.

CHAPTER 11

Capstone

Folder: 11 Capstone
Workbook: Test Selection.xls
Worksheets: part I and part II

The Test Selection workbook contains two data sets. Between them, they can serve as data for every type of data analysis covered in *The Excel Statistics Companion*. All the solutions for parts 1 and 2 of this program are linked to their respective data sets and will update following any changes to either set. The user must be careful to enter new data <u>only</u> in the yellow-highlighted data cells so as not to disturb the functions and formulae that run the displays.

Data for Part I

These are the data for the first group of problems. Excel will instantly forward any changes you enter on this worksheet to the data and solutions that follow. But for your first run through the workbook, it's fine to use the original data. Select the statistical analysis that is appropriate for the data and the research question, use Excel to do the analysis, and scroll right to see the solution. No peeking! Try the problem first on your own before looking at the solution. (Make all data changes here, NOT on the problem worksheets.)

Row		
9	8	2
10	4	1
11	7	3
12	9	6
13	13	10
14	14	16
15	19	18
16	17	15
17	20	5
18	12	11

Data for Part II

In Part II, the data array expands from 2 columns to 4. As for Part I, select and run the correct statistical analysis, then scroll right to column O and beyond for the solution. To practice computational skills with new data, enter one or more new values below. (Make all changes to data here, *not* on the problem worksheets.)

Row				
9	53	44	40	52
10	54	59	61	63
11	42	47	55	59
12	47	41	48	57
13	49	50	53	49
14	47	42	56	55
15	57	50	43	53
16	40	39	55	54
17	42	39	45	40
18	46	38	52	54

Folder: 11 Capstone
Workbook: Test Selection.xls
Worksheet: problem 1-4

Here is an example of a problem and a solution in part I of the workbook. The values in the solution are dynamically linked to the data.

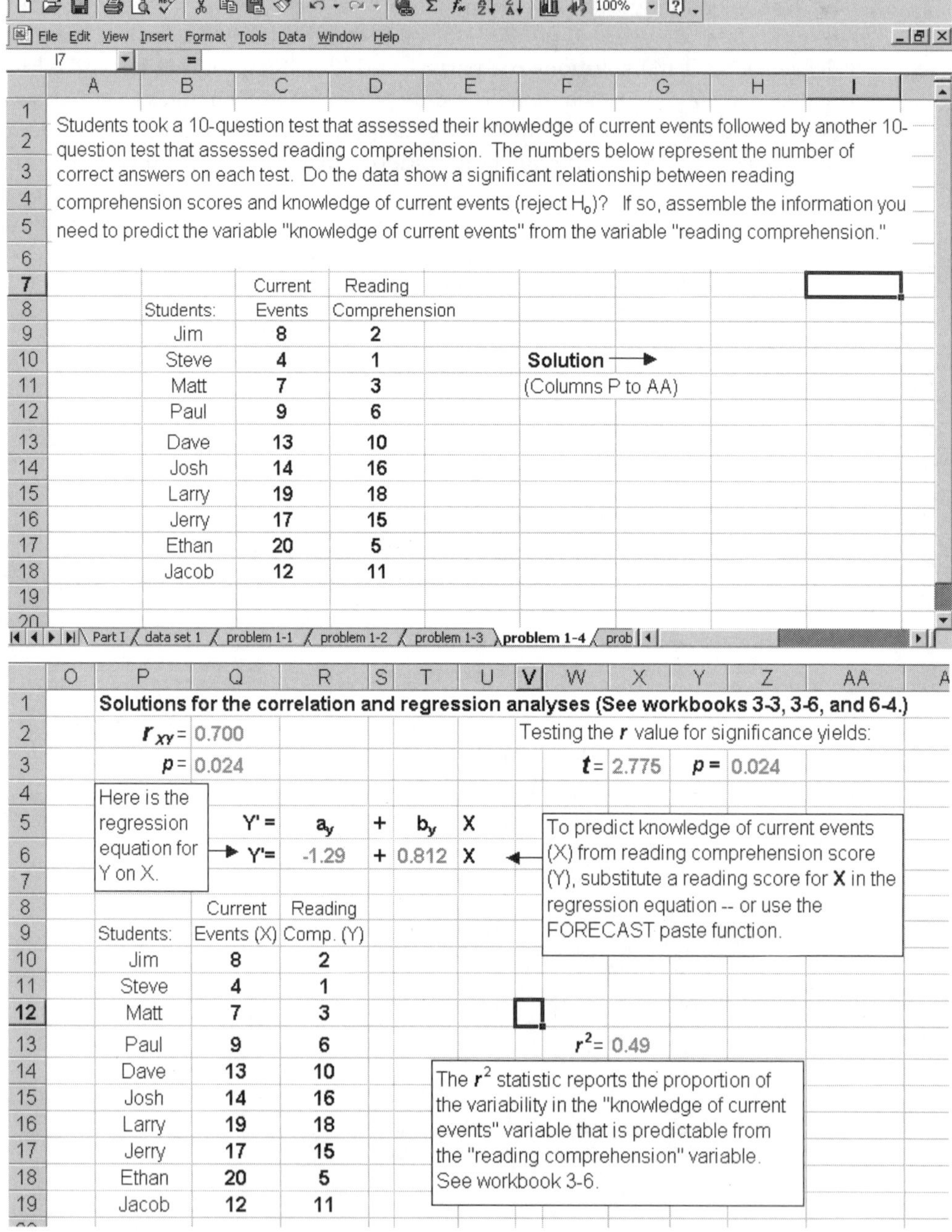
Students took a 10-question test that assessed their knowledge of current events followed by another 10-question test that assessed reading comprehension. The numbers below represent the number of correct answers on each test. Do the data show a significant relationship between reading comprehension scores and knowledge of current events (reject H₀)? If so, assemble the information you need to predict the variable "knowledge of current events" from the variable "reading comprehension."
Students: | Current Events | Reading Comprehension
Jim 8 2
Steve 4 1
Matt 7 3
Paul 9 6
Dave 13 10
Josh 14 16
Larry 19 18
Jerry 17 15
Ethan 20 5
Jacob 12 11
Solution
(Columns P to AA)
Solutions for the correlation and regression analyses (See workbooks 3-3, 3-6, and 6-4.)
r xy = 0.700
p = 0.024
Testing the r value for significance yields:
t = 2.775 p = 0.024
Here is the regression equation for Y on X.
Y' = a y + b y X
Y' = -1.29 + 0.812 X
To predict knowledge of current events (X) from reading comprehension score (Y), substitute a reading score for X in the regression equation -- or use the FORECAST paste function.
Students: | Current Events (X) | Reading Comp. (Y)
Jim 8 2
Steve 4 1
Matt 7 3
Paul 9 6
Dave 13 10
Josh 14 16
Larry 19 18
Jerry 17 15
Ethan 20 5
Jacob 12 11
r2 = 0.49
The r2 statistic reports the proportion of the variability in the "knowledge of current events" variable that is predictable from the "reading comprehension" variable. See workbook 3-6.
Part I | data set 1 | problem 1-1 | problem 1-2 | problem 1-3 | problem 1-4 | prob